John H. Braccio, Ph.D.

Three Dramas

1.

"The Football Coach and The University President
or
Power Play at State University of America"

2.

"A Man Through the Ages
or
A Man Who Walked With Caesar and Byron"

3.

"Marital Betrayal
or
The Mental Health Effects of a
Husband Philandering on the Professional Woman
from a Traditional Home Background"

Illustrations by John Leatherman

Library of Congress Cataloging in Publication Data
Braccio, John, 1943-
      Outrageous & Scandalous Satire.
     Contents: "The Football Coach and the University President" or "Power
              Play at the State University of America."

              "A Man Through the Ages" or "A Man Who Walked with Caesar
              & Byron

              "Marital Betrayal" or "The Mental Health Effects of a Husband
              Philandering on the Professional Woman from a Traditional
              Background."

1993   93-93559
ISBN 0-9637854-0-0

All inquires will be addressed to:
John H. Braccio, Ph.D.
Director, Regional Psychological Services
1401 East Lansing Drive, Suite #111
East Lansing, MI 48823
Ph. (517) 332-0153
FAX (517) 332-2960

General Contents

Drama 1

The Football Coach and the University President
or
Power Play at State University of America

Drama 2

A Man Through the Ages
or
A Man Who Walked with Caesar and Byron

Drama 3

Marital Betrayal
or
The Mental Health Effects of a Husband Philandering
on the Professional Woman from a Traditional Home Background

General Preface

This general preface will be relatively brief because prefaces have been written for each of the three dramas within this volume: 1. *"The Football Coach and the University President* or *Power Play at State University of America"*. 2. *"A Man Through the Ages* or *A Man Who Walked with Caesar and Byron"*. 3. *"Marital Betrayal* or *The Mental Health Effects of a Husband Philandering on the Professional Woman from a Traditional Home Background"*.

While I have for years used personally developed and produced tapes, articles and pamphlets as part of my work as a practicing psychologist, it was actually a May 1, 1990 article by Charlie Vincent ("MSU is tarnished by Perles-DiBiaggio feud") in the *Detroit Free Press* that inspired me to write an OUTRAGEOUS AND SCANDALOUS FICTIONAL SATIRE to be distributed outside of as well as within my normal workspace. The result was <u>"THE FOOTBALL COACH AND THE UNIVERSITY PRESIDENT or POWER PLAY AT STATE UNIVERSITY OF AMERICA"</u>. It is a fictional drama relating to the horrible self-inflicted destructiveness that was occurring at Michigan State University during the 1990-1992 period. While the public issue was one of sports versus academics, the real issues to many were ego and power needs on a colossal level. Blind raging emotion ruled and the indecisive Hamlet like Governing Board of Trustees, like a senile and tottering Nero fiddling in Ancient Rome while it burned, would not work as a unified group or even address the issue of whether its -- at no additional cost to the university -- majority decision to have the football coach also be athletic director could be given a fair chance to succeed in an environment that included public battling among Board members with the resulting negative media coverage as well as the continuous, eloquent, spectacularly effective and strident public dissent of the decision from its employee, the president. The following May 1, 1990 quote from Charlie Vincent gives some background information for his point of view as well as a most logical solution to the crisis which the Board would not implement: "<u>DiBiaggio received almost unanimous media support in his attempt to block Perles from being named athletic director as well as head football coach. I joined in that support, not because I think it is immoral to hold both positions, but because I thought it was important that the president's authority not be undermined. DiBiaggio lost; Perles won. It's over. Life goes on. It is time for the president's office and the athletic department to mend fences and move</u>

on together in unison, in a fashion that would benefit the school, the athletic program and the young men and women student-athletes. That is the reasonable thing to do. The proper thing. The civilized thing. But it is not the way business is conducted at Michigan State these days. DiBiaggio's pride has been hurt. He has lost the game, and now he has taken his ball and gone home. And he's not talking to the guy who beat him -- his football coach and soon-to-be athletic director...The board of trustees proved its strength when it overrode DiBiaggio's desires and named Perles athletic director. Now the trustees can reaffirm that strength and do something beneficial for the school. It should demand DiBiaggio and Perles meet with them, shake hands, join forces and move on to the future instead of holding grudges over the past. Michigan State University deserves that." As stated above, the Board never demanded the DiBiaggio/Perles aspect of the problem be resolved in a professional manner. (The Vincent article in its entirety is in Appendix B after *"The Football Coach and the University President* or *Power Play at State University of America"*. I state the fictional drama reflects my ideas and does not knowingly reflect those of Charlie Vincent.)

As is the case in civil wars, the lines at Michigan State University were drawn and reasonable people of good will totally disagreed on who was right or wrong. In such an environment, the lack of decisive action to end the crisis by the Board when the president would not try to pull everyone together, was disastrous to the prestige of the university and all those who cared for it. Some even confused the president's public fighting with Board members as a normal battle between the elected executive branch of government (president) versus the elected legislative branch (Board). These persons did not realize the president, like a public school superintendent, is a Board appointed employee of a regularly changing board of elected members. Writing about this in the relative calm of mid 1993 makes it hard to believe what a colossal emotional issue it was made to be in 1990-1992. For an interesting comparison, when a similar situation occurred at The University of Michigan prior to the 1989 football season, the football coach was told he must choose between being the football coach or athletic director. He balked and the Governing Board of Regents made him both; and the president, acknowledging he worked for the Board, did his best to have it work. The show of unity and total lack of public dissension after the decision was made by all concerned, allowed the coach/athletic director to do both jobs and even unilaterally choose his most successful successor with no other selection process. The reputations of the two universities have fared comparably to the football programs. The wide disparity of success between the two football programs over the past two years can arguably be attributed to how differently the two universities addressed similar situations and how powerful and concerned forces of the state interpreted their respective actions. Prior to the problems at Michigan State University really beginning, the football programs at the two schools were arguably at parity in the football seasons of 1989 and 1990. (U of M won 10-7 in 1989 and MSU 28-27 in 1990.)

I chose to use OUTRAGEOUS AND SCANDALOUS FICTIONAL SATIRE along with tragedy and even humor to show the absurdity of what heavily destroyed the reputation of a major world class university for at least a two year period; and the residual effects can be expected to last for years. While I wrote this in 1990-1991, I chose to wait until the crisis had ended so it could be read by most people without projection and passion. The other two dramas were leisurely written as I waited for the appropriate time to distribute the first one.

"A MAN THROUGH THE AGES or A MAN WHO WALKED WITH CAESAR AND BYRON" was written out of pure enjoyment and a psychologist's curiosity as to how a person would psychologically develop who did not age and had lived for over two thousand years. It was great fun to think and write about. Unlike the other two dramas, I really had no basis in reality to use to develop character or determine how events might develop. I did it as I went along after determining the person who did not age would always be thirty-five years old, well educated, calm, sensitive and a survivor. While to some persons the first scene may be slower reading than the others, the goal was to set the tone for the rest of the drama by showing the person who did not age had great personal knowledge of one period of time over a century after the last living person of that period would have died. I also happen to greatly enjoy the literary personalities and literature of the English Romantic period.

"MARITAL BETRAYAL or THE MENTAL HEALTH EFFECTS OF A HUSBAND PHILANDERING ON THE PROFESSIONAL WOMAN FROM A TRADITIONAL HOME BACKGROUND" was written primarily for therapeutic use in my psychological practice with persons in similar situations. I also desired to try to present the total emotional agony a professional and traditional woman, fully committed to a marriage, experiences when a husband philanders and she catches him. I believe what I have written is sadly very accurate for countless nameless persons.

7

When you read the three dramas, you will not find exact living characters. Even if sometimes based upon certain facts and influenced by some public figures, all characters are fictional and my creations in relation to motive and the thinking process. For the person who reads these dramas, I believe the effort will result in useful psychological insights into people as well as getting to know some very interesting characters.

I chose to use the drama format rather than that of the novel because it seemed like a more natural medium for me to present concepts and characters; and it requires readers to come to their own conclusions about what was written. In that I do not know theater, the dramas were written to be read. Only "<u>MARITAL BETRAYAL or THE MENTAL HEALTH EFFECTS OF A HUSBAND PHILANDERING ON THE PROFESSIONAL WOMAN FROM A TRADITIONAL HOME BACKGROUND</u>" was written in current conversational language.

Much appreciation is given to the most talented John Leatherman for his superb illustrations. They surely add a different dimension to the dialogue. John has a degree in computer engineering from Southern Methodist University. While John is a software engineer, he also devotes much time to his artistic career. He regularly illustrates children's books and has a monthly cartoon in Odyssey Magazine.

My long time secretary and office manager, Linda Townsend, was typically efficient and patient in the tedious preparation of this document.

While all the ideas are mine, the following persons were most helpful to me in reading one or more of the dramas and giving me invaluable insights: Sue Allen, Julie Benvenuto, Nena Braccio (my wife), Norma Brink, Gay Cowels, Andre Friedlis, Greg Geibig, Dr. Lee Lemon, Dr. Tim McKenna, Dr. Pat Scheetz, Lou Twardzik.

The Football Coach and the University President
or
Power Play at State University of America

A satire-tragedy with some comic elements

Written By:
John H. Braccio, Ph.D.

Copyright © 1993 by John H. Braccio, Ph.D.
East Lansing, Michigan

Table of Contents

A Preface To
"The Football Coach and the University President
or
Power Play at State University of America"

While I began writing this drama in the spring of 1990, it was primarily written in the spring, summer and early fall of 1991. It was actually a May 1, 1990 article written by Charlie Vincent in the Detroit Free Press "MSU is tarnished by Perles-DiBiaggio feud" (see appendix B) -- that somehow inspired me to put in writing a document to satirically, tragically and somewhat humorously address with fictional characters some basic management and psychological principles at play in the wholly destructive and bizarre situation then occurring at Michigan State University. Vincent's article also was used as the basis for a solution oriented memo I wrote to the Board of Trustees on May 11, 1990. (see appendix C). I chose not to make this drama available until mid-1993 because the intent was not to be perceived as adding more divisiveness to the conflagration that was tragically consuming Michigan State University to its very foundations. The employee of the Governing Board of Trustees, the president, was at war with it when it voted five to three to make the football coach also the athletic director over his objections. Much has happened since that fateful early 1990 Board decision was made and would include the following: 1. Strong advocates on the Board on both sides of the issue have been defeated at the election booth. (This has again validated Winston Churchill's view that as inefficient as democracy is, it is far better than government by nonelected tyrants.) 2. The football coach added the duties of the athletic director for nearly two successful and uneventful years. 3. Opposing football coaches gleefully used the civil war like turmoil and the possibility the coach might leave, due to attacks on him, to most effectively take away recruits and thus seriously wound and erode the power and focus of the football program. 4. A recently retired long time university administrator of impeccable academic, administrative, and personal credentials was elected to the Governing Board of Trustees and has magnificently done his job. 5. An apparently competent new athletic director was controversially chosen over an onstaff eminently qualified and totally loyal long tern university person. 6. The president has gone with around a third of a million dollars and has a job in a new university. 7. Like Cincinnatus in Ancient Rome, a long term loyal university person has been temporarily drafted, from retirement, by the Board to be president. With a winning personality and drawing upon decades of experience, he has eliminated most problems and controversy by working with and educating each publicly elected board member as well as pulling all involved and interested persons together as a team. Wisely, the Board made a fine choice in finding a total team player that was nurtured and grown within the very land grant institution he now heads. History says the Board will, as if under some negative ancient Greek Oracle, not comprehend this fact when it chooses a president in the near future. Hopefully that will not be true and Michigan State University will be analogously like Oedipus at Colonus as opposed to his tragic role in Oedipus Rex.

All of the above is mentioned because much of the seventeen page preface I previously wrote when the drama was originally written, now appears irrelevant in the current environment of persons apparently working hard together to make Michigan State University come closer to reaching its tremendous potential as a maturing institution.

The major purpose of this drama is to use OUTRAGEOUS AND SCANDALOUS SATIRE to hopefully teach some lessons that may be helpful in the future in such a situation as occurred at Michigan State University; however, the dynamics could occur anywhere there is a publicly elected board and a CEO employee of that board. To me, satire is using exaggeration of an extreme variety to shock persons into seeing the distorted images presented are in fact themselves or someone or something they have strongly liked and supported. In a situation with few heros, as is the case at Michigan State University, the goal is to bring about personal and group change through a reformation of thought brought about by such a realization. While satire would have been a most proper vehicle to show how many of the public officials and personalities that were involved in the tragic civil war at Michigan State University behaved, my intent was to create fictional characters to work out my views. Finding an exact duplicate in reality in this drama is indeed impossible in that that is not what I did or intended. I also do not know the major protagonists at Michigan State University that were involved in what occurred there beyond a say hello level. Good and evil were put in stark contrast to make the satire more biting. As a minimum, I believe the reader of this drama will find some interesting psychological characters and better understand the allurement of the charismatic leader as well as the effective techniques of the clever sociopathic personality. Agreement is not sought but rather that something be learned for the future.

List of Characters in Order of Appearance

Charles - Janitorial student employee at State University of America

Emilio Gomez - Janitorial employee at State University of America

Mrs. Krumm - Personal secretary to President Assassino

Dr. Colosso Michelangelo Assassino - President of State University of America

William Hill - Photographer of President Assassino

Tuffy Norkas - Football Coach and Athletic Director at State University of America

Dr. William Percival - Provost at State University of America

Dr. Michael Wimpston - Assistant to President Assassino

Harry Boylen - Board of Trustees Member at State University of America

Carla Barglor - Board of Trustees Member at State University of America

Karen Wood - Board of Trustees Member at State University of America

Students 1 - 5

Dr. Larry Christianson - Vice President for Financial Affairs at State University of America

Terry Moore - Board of Trustees Chairperson at State University of America

Dr. Guido Bucciferri - Professor Emeritus of Ancient Roman History at State University of America

Norma Norkas - Wife of Tuffy Norkas

Fred Johnson - Board of Trustees Member at State University of America

Dr. Judy McIntire - Private Practice Psychologist

Mrs. Willingham - University Mansion Manager to President Assassino

Skip Goon - Sports Editor of the University Town Journal

Bob - Editor of Big Town News

Joe - Editor of Big Town Free Press

Chuck - Editor of Middle Town Press

Harriet - Secretary to Tuffy Norkas

Jim German - Sports Director of University Town TV Station

Scene 1

(Emilio and Charles are cleaning up President Assassino's spacious and splendidly furnished university office. Things are to be perfect when he enters on a given day at any time.)

Charles: *(With excitement in his voice.)* Emilio, it is so exciting to be able to work in the office of the President of State University of America! What an experience to be near such a great leader! You must love it.

Emilio: *(With a touch of sarcasm.)* You are young and it is something you can get used to. You are studying political science, are you not? Learn your lessons well here and you can be a leader for positive change in the future.

Charles: You do not really seem to be that excited here. I have noticed this during the time I have been working with you and wonder why?

Emilio: Charles, you are young and you will learn a "Great Prince" is really not what is needed at State University or really not any other place that one desires freedom. I thought I left such things behind me when I escaped from Cuba.

Charles: You seem very confused today. You are no longer in Cuba and we are in America! We also have probably the greatest president of any university in the world with President Assassino. The name alone generates a sense of supreme excellence. His presence, words, actions and deeds create excitement and a great desire to follow his direction. You really seem to not be comfortable with him or maybe even more so to be indifferent.

Emilio: Indifferent I am not. I spent many years following and working with probably the greatest tyrant of the past thirty or forty years and I know the methods and really tire of "The Great Prince" and his destruction of democratic processes. The premeditated and mindless destruction of the reputation of his greatest supporters, who may only

15

cross him once, is hard to believe. Maybe the murder of such persons by the Dictator Prince is more humane than the shame and destruction to one's name that happens in a democracy.

Charles: Emilio, who and what can you possibly be talking about?

Emilio: Charles, you are a good young man and have much to share with the world. But in America you never really see so much of the ugliness that penetrates the earth in the form of abhorrent ideology as well as evil and wicked men and women. I am from Cuba and I was in the Sierra with Fidel Castro and fought against Batista. I saw so many good people die in the war and in often the most horrible ways. But I thought it was worth it for the general good. I then celebrated in the great victory march to Havana on January 1, 1959. I then spent many years helping to make Fidel Castro look like a combination of God and Superman. Tragically, it was a long time before my blindness left me, and then I gradually began to see it first hand what a monster he was. Here with Colosso, I am able to see on a tiny level the same type of personality at work. It is the naivete and general goodness of the American people that allows a "mierda" demagog like Colosso to appear so heroic and magnificent. He uses the people to solidify himself and his power needs. Many of them are even foolish Board members who gave him his position and who have a responsibility to set policy and evaluate his performance. However, he now never mentions them and claims to work for "the people" as he claims to be the deliverer of their dreams. In South America, he would be a Castro or a Caudillo, as the prince is called in Spanish.

Charles: Emilio, you have not talked to me at all about this in the time we have worked together.

Emilio: Charles, it is really best that we not talk about these things and best you enjoy your youth and not worry about such things as power, "The Great Prince" and how such monsters misuse the world and everyone in it. Seek love, passion, excitement, friendship and learning with the great gusto that only youth can unleash. Give free rein to your loins and your mind, as this is the time you create wonderful memories for you to remember as you enter the enjoyable but hard work of living a productive and responsible life. My days at the University of Havana, with Fidel and all the others, were heady and exciting days. But be less blind in your political outlook and never lose contact with the democratic form of government we are blessed with in America. Tragically, only those of us who know brutal dictators first hand thank God for democratic governments.

Charles: Emilio, I really must know more about this and hope you will give me the opportunity to discuss it more with you. However, you must be confused as President Assassino is a great man and an even greater leader. He is loved on this campus and throughout the State.

Emilio: *(With sarcasm.)* We shall talk later and now let us get things ready as the great President Assassino is due back and we must have this place cleaned up for his meeting.

(Mrs. Krumm enters the room.)

Mrs. Krumm: Emilio, do you have everything set up here so that our President is able to come in and meet in a room that is perfectly clean and ready for somebody of his stature.

Emilio: *(With subtlety)* Mrs. Krumm, everything will be perfect and consistent with what President Assassino desires and demands. We, of course, are here to meet his needs. As you have told me many times, he is the great benevolent force that makes State University what it is and can be.

Mrs. Krumm: Very good attitude Emilio. Of course, this is why the President has not had to complain about the work you are doing as he has with so many other persons. They just did not recognize our whole purpose is to allow him to be able to work in an environment that allows the important things to be done that only he can do for State University of America!

Emilio: I promise you I fully understand everything you say.

(Enter President Assassino with William Hill, photographer.)

Mrs. Krumm: Mr. President, you are back.

President: Yes, I am and I want no one to disturb me at this time! I expect Tuffy to be coming to meet with me shortly as he has been trying the past few days and he can just wait until I am ready to speak with him. *(Snapping his fingers.)* You two out! *(Exit Emilio and Charles.)* Now let us look over the pictures you have taken of me. Remember, I only wanted you to bring me those that really captured my personality as the President of State University of America.

William: Mr. President, we work very hard for your business and see it as a great opportunity to present you in picture form the way that you so magnificently present in real life. *(With great devotion.)* You can never imagine the feelings of pride I have to be able to help you due to my love for State and what only you can do to make it so great! With you in command, State's potential is limitless.

President: Well, let's see how you have done this time!

William: *(William puts the folder with the photographs on President Assassino's desk.)* Have you been satisfied in the past Mr. President?

President: I have not said anything like that. I simply am looking for improvement. Now, let me take a look. *(Looking through the photographs on his desk.)* Hum, this looks fairly good. It kind of captures my personality in Presidential form and I can use it when I present my State of the University speech to the media and the State family. Hum, this one here kind of captures me in a more relaxed state and I think I will use this when I am modeling the casual atmosphere of the university. Ha, and in this here I look like when I must take on the role of the President in dealing with things that are not always pleasant but must be done. This picture from last year, and you must always be trying to improve on it, is the one I still must use when I am personifying the embodiment of what is State University of America. Try to make an even better one on this concept. Do you understand me?

William: I will try sir.

President: It must be regal, mellow, authoritative, serious and completely persuasive to adequately reflect my essential role as President of State University of America.

William: You will note Mr. President that this set is only made up of a very select eighty pictures of the 5000 that we have recently taken to try to capture the essence in picture form of what you present in person.

President: *(In an irritated tone.)* Well you certainly must know you cannot capture me in picture form; but it is the best representation you

18

have of me in that format to present the overwhelmingly important work I am doing. You can now be off until the next picture setting when you take pictures of me at the Presidential Gala Ball. This is one of my most important functions. Be there at least an hour early and be ready to work at my command.

William: Yes sir, Mr. President. Would you like me also to take some pictures with you and the Governing Board of Trustees at the Presidential Gala Ball?

President: *(Icily.)* No. Did I tell you I wanted you to take pictures of me with that dull gang of boring farmers and meddlesome boobs? If you have other persons in the pictures, try to do it in a way that they kind of have a fuzzy gloss to them next to my crystal clear image. This is the Presidential Gala Ball and the emphasis is on the President; and you had better not forget it! Now, off with you so important things can be done.

William: I am sorry Mr. President, I certainly did not mean to offend you.

President: You simply showed your stupidity and a total lack of respect to me and my position. I did not like it! Now, again, be off and do not do anything until you talk to your supervisor, Howard Smith. *(In comes Mrs. Krumm after being buzzed on the intercom.)*

William: Please forgive me. *(Silence and an icy stare to William from the President as he leaves.)*

Mrs. Krumm: Mr. President, the football coach has arrived and seems very anxious to meet with you.

President: I am entirely too busy to talk to him at this time; but shortly I will give him a very brief audience to put him in his tiny place. He is really a dangerous man. He wants my power and if he had it, he would badly misuse it against me and my work.

Mrs. Krumm: He has indicated, and I only report this to you sir, that he has been here four days in a row waiting to meet with you.

President: *(With a tone of authority and annoyance.)* Mrs. Krumm, you can tell him I am the President of this university and if he has any desire of meeting with me at all, he had better wait for me. If he is not willing, then I do not want to speak with him and want him not to do anything unrelated to his approved functions. Is that clear?

Mrs. Krumm: Yes sir, very clear.

President: Tuffy can wait again for a while and then he will be even more appreciative to see me. Get Howard Smith on the phone immediately.

(Mrs. Krumm leaves, makes the phone call and she gets Howard on the phone. She calls the President on the intercom.)

Mrs. Krumm: *(On the intercom.)* Mr. Smith is on the phone, Mr. President.

President: *(He picks up the phone and begins speaking.)* Howard, your photographer, William Hill, who has done work for me for years, just left here and I found him disrespectful. You can talk to him about it. I never want him here again and I want a new photographer as good or better at the Presidential Gala Ball. If he is not as good, then that will be the end of your business at my university. He must be very respectful. Is that clear? Good. *(The President hangs up.)*

President: *(Speaking on his intercom)* Mrs. Krumm, come in here immediately! *(She comes in.)* Mrs. Krumm, tell the football coach I am not in a good mood today and my important activities have me very busy. Tell him I want him to come in and sit on that chair in the corner *(pointing)* and say nothing until I speak to him. If he says anything to disrupt me, then I will immediately send him away.

Mrs. Krumm: Yes sir, Mr. President. *(She leaves.)*

(Head Football Coach Tuffy Norkas comes in and sits down in the appropriate chair and waits while President Assassino slowly looks through his pictures. Various facial expressions are shown by him as he looks at the pictures. Without looking up, he then snaps his fingers and points for Tuffy to come and sit in the chair next to his desk. Tuffy gets up, moves over to the chair and sits down.)

President: *(With a look and tone of condemnation.)* Tuffy you wanted to see me and here I am. I am very busy, so very quickly tell me what you want.

Tuffy: *(Firmly and politely.)* I am the football coach and...

President: I know that Tuffy. Tell me something I do not know.

Tuffy: ....I want the opportunity to be both the football coach and the athletic director. I want to make sure we talk and try to work something out together. I have another opportunity to go to the pros for millions and....

President: Then go to the pros and good riddance. You know this is silly conversation. I have declared this will not happen at State and it will not. I have had it with sports having so much power in my institution! I am the President and I do not want this to be and it will not be. I promise you that.

Tuffy: I certainly have the right to try to do both if I can.

President: *(With anger in his tone.)* You have no rights other than what I give you! I am State University of America and I am getting annoyed at your impudent statements. Just do as I say and you will get what you need and everyone will be happy. Just do as I say or leave to the pros. I will gleefully let you out of your contract.

Tuffy: You are not aware of it, but you work for the Board of Trustees and so do I. You behave like you are the God damn Pope and the Board merely the subservient College of Cardinals that voted you into total power.

President: What the hell are you talking about? What nonsense you coaches speak.

Tuffy: The Board and not you has constitutional authority over employees like you and me and it has taken the responsibility to appoint the Athletic Director. It is not part of your every day general management responsibilities. Even if it were and the Board changed it, the Board rules as in any school system and can override you on anything it desires. In that we disagree on the Coach/AD matter, the Board will resolve it and make a decision. You recommend things to the Board, but it makes the decisions. It is your job to convince the Board to go along with you and not the reverse. This will be decided one way or the other at the Board meeting tomorrow if we cannot come to some agreement. I want you to go along with this so we do not again look disunited and stupid around the state and nation. Colosso, I believe I have the votes.

President: *(With rage in his voice and a clenched fist waving in the air.)* I work for the people and that is who I report to! If you try any power play tomorrow with that bunch of boobs and goons that worship you, then the people and I will gleefully oversee your complete and pathetic demise. I am State University of America and you are nothing more than an overweight fellow who bullies people around because he knows how to have a football move from one part of the field to another! If you fight me on this, I will personally destroy you, your cronies and your career!

Tuffy: *(Firmly and with great determination.)* I have the right to try to be both football coach and athletic director. It happens at a number of fine universities. Men such as Joe Paterno, Bear Bryant and Bo

Schembechler, to name a few, showed one person can effectively be football coach and athletic director. I am going to fight you on this and I certainly have support from some important people who see you for what you are: A duplistic and manipulative bastard.

President: I heard that Tuffy and will not forget it! You do not mean that little wimp the Governor; or that pompous Senator in charge of the Senate Appropriations Committee; or the intolerable representative in charge of the House Appropriations Committee? They want to control State and I will not let them. I do not even return calls to them unless I desire. The people need representation and I give it to them. They have dreams and I fulfill them. You did not answer me. Are you talking about them?

Tuffy: Maybe I am. Certainly the persons you named are men of integrity; one and all.

President: I could give a hoot about those power hungry people. They do not want to help me and continuously give more support to the University of America. I only report to the people and if the people want me to be in control and do what must be done for their good, then I will do it at State University. There is already too much power given to athletics and I have had it. You will note, I am Chairperson of the GOD Committee of Presidents who are reviewing intercollegiate athletics. I will squash you like a bug, if need be, because the people will demand it. The weasels on the Board will also be destroyed by me as will any persons if they side with you. Now get out of this office and do not let me ever see your face around here unless I call; and then come quickly. You also will find the editors of the major newspapers in this state agree with me on this and all issues. They recognize I represent the people, in that I am State University of America, and what will be done here is what I demand. Now, get out!

Tuffy: We will see. You also should return calls to your Board Chairperson and other members who want to talk to you about this matter. As I said, I am going to the Board on this and it will decide this at the meeting tomorrow. Of course, they can say no and I will leave; but then asshole, you know that will not happen. We will see who oversees the demise of whom.

President: Out! Out! Out! Out!

Tuffy: I am leaving Colosso. *(With great sarcasm.)* Oh yes, even though you are from Big Town, in our section, we took the lunch money from wimps like you and dressed them in their mother's underwear. Ha! Ha!

President: *(With great anger.)* Get out! Get out! Get out! Get out!

(Tuffy leaves in a determined but unrushed manner, glaring at Colosso as he leaves. Colosso ignores him and does not look at him.)

President: *(With rage in his tone and look.)* I hate him, that no good bastard. He and his clones are planning to destroy me. I must destroy him first and now must plan a war of annihilation against him and his cronies. Greatness is often challenged by inferiors and I am up to the challenge! Finely honed greatness with purposeful action will crush inferiors that are foolish enough to enter battles they cannot win. The people will demand I act decisively and with a vengeance. *(With glee as he rubs his hands together.)* They will not be disappointed. *(Still looking very agitated but pulling himself together emotionally. He presses down on the intercom.)* Mrs. Krumm, come in now.

(Mrs. Krumm enters.)

Mrs. Krumm: Mr. President, what happened? Tuffy left here with a very strange look and color?

President: I am sure it was hatred. His flaw is that he loves State University but does not recognize I am State University of America. I will destroy him, all he stands for as well as all his pathetic macho buddies! We are about education here and there will be no compromise! Better that State be razed to the ground than come into the crazed hands of Tuffy and his gang of thugs.

Mrs. Krumm: I do not understand all this but he is a very bad person if he does not do what you want.

President: *(Rubbing his hands together with glee.)* Indeed he is and he will suffer deliciously and horribly. I will see to that personally.

Mrs. Krumm: Trustees Moore and Johnson continue calling and say it is essential you return their calls.

President: Tell them I am about my important work and will call them when I can. Those insolent bastards!

Mrs. Krumm: Very well sir. Provost William Percival and Assistant to the President Michael Wimpston are here to see you.

President: Send them in.

(Mrs. Krumm leaves. Provost Percival and Assistant to the President Wimpston enter.)

President: Gentlemen, good to see you.

Provost & Assistant: Same here.

Provost: What happened? Tuffy looked pretty mad when he left here and you certainly look every bit as mad.

President: That man is dangerous. He wants to destroy me and this university. Sheer brutal power motivates him and I plan to destroy him! Oh, do I plan to destroy him!

Provost: What has he done?

President: He wants to be both football coach and athletic director! He is planning a power play at tomorrow's Board meeting to make him both. I wish he would go to the pros and get the hell out of here. Can you even imagine that gall? Tuffy knows I will not allow that and still he seeks it. He hopes to get disloyal Board members to vote for him and against their President! I have hated him since I first saw his disgusting macho face. He is dangerous to me and he always will be dangerous to me. Tuffy cannot stand persons greater than himself. I am, he knows it and he seethes with hatred and limitless jealousy of my superior nature. Oh, how I hate him. Oh, how the reputation of Tuffy and his cronies will be dissolved in a very painful and slow process.

Assistant: Lesser men always try to rise by attempting to destroy greatness. You are great and it is bothering him to total distraction. Until he destroys you with his big sweaty body, he will not be happy. Of course Colosso, that is not possible.

Provost: The man is not a fool. Sometimes approximations of greatness and even greatness are hidden in coarse men like Tuffy. Let no one

24

underestimate him or he indeed will destroy that person. Colosso, Tuffy even now may have the votes to complete his act of insubordination to you at tomorrow's Board meeting.

Assistant: You speak in riddles. Are you challenging the authority of the President? Are you suggesting Tuffy is greater than Colosso?

Provost: I am not. However, history is loaded with examples of greater persons being destroyed by far less distinguished persons through better preparation, confidence, tenacity, a thorough understanding of the enemy, more realistically using their resources, picking the right moment for action or some combination of the above. You are State University of America Colosso, but Tuffy is an able strategist and not an enemy to be taken lightly. Hidden beneath his coarse exterior and limited cliche ridden speech are the earthy perceptions of a wise peasant. He also has many powerful friends who hate and fear you. Tuffy may join them in some powerful alliance against you. A successful Board vote tomorrow could very likely occur. The new Board members have not proven their total loyalty and obedience to you. The environment is very perilous.

Assistant: You seem to praise Tuffy too much. *(Sarcastically.)* He seems so powerful in your mind. Maybe he is the eighth wonder of the world. Why not just give him whatever he wants?

Provost: That is not what I am saying and you know it! To not adequately assess strengths in an adversary, regardless of how much one hates that person, is indeed very foolhardy. I simply state the man is very clever, heavy handed, has many powerful friends and will use all resources at his command to win. Such a man is dangerous and a most able and efficient adversary.

President: What do you believe motivates him?

Provost: Colosso, in his own way, Tuffy loves State and the tradition before you came here. His great and fatal limitation is that he will not acknowledge your supremacy. Tuffy sees you as a carpetbagger out to make State your own island and kingdom for international recognition and glory. Of course, this is absurd; is it not?

President: Bill, you have made some points to think about. Like you and Mike, I see Tuffy as a negative force trying to destroy me and State University. We cannot allow that. Indeed Tuffy is a dangerous man. I wish him the worst and plan to bring it to him in spades. Being right is good; but getting even is divine indeed. If the opportunity arises Bill, I will use you as an honorable sheep to give him a most cruel, fatal and unexpected cut. The opportunity will definitely occur if that bunch of clowns on the Board makes Tuffy both coach and A.D. I will then put Tuffy under your administrative control and his destruction will be subtlety planned. Oh, how he will be destroyed. Even the buzzards will have nothing left to pick at.

Provost: Of course, I am at your disposal Colosso. He is dangerous, very capable and he may have the Board votes to do what he damn well pleases. The fact I am seen as honorable works to your advantage; and of course doing what you desire is the honorable thing. Thus, as the opportunity arises, I will do as you ask. Tuffy actually trusts me and that is foolhardy indeed in these circumstances. To save you and State is what we are about and success shall be yours.

Assistant: Bill, you now sound more reasonable and yes honorable. The way Colosso will destroy Tuffy will be something to see and then to study. He will get the worst, Colosso; and yes, it will be in spades. Colosso, you have a way with words and your actions and results always pale them in comparison.

President: You are very perceptive Mike.

Provost: Colosso, what do you expect Tuffy to do?

President: He will try to enlist traitorous Board members to go along with his insubordination to me. I know who they are all too well. They are led by the equally powerful and foolish Terry Moore. His fatal flaw in this battle will be his indecisive personality. He does not know or is incapable of going for the kill. He and the rest are goons or political clowns who can be pressured by powerful persons who only want to hurt me personally and destroy State University of America. Indeed, a dark pall is ominously hanging over me and my great institution. Audacious action and punishing force are the only ways to counter such a man and the evil forces of insurrection he can muster against me and all those who love State University of America; but first, I must lose this vote in order to open my all out blitzkrieg. I could not have picked a better issue and how I will turn defeat into complete and glorious personal victory. However, my heart is heavy with such treason; but, oh am I ready for decisive victorious action. After they take their Judas vote of betrayal, I will muster such a media blitz against Tuffy and these sports clowns that they will never again dare defy me at a Board meeting. War has been declared and I am in it 100% and will not fail! I plan to turn this Board vote against me into a holy war of academics against sports. I actually have been looking for an issue to destroy this group of bullying morons

26

who hate my obvious and overwhelming superiority in comparison to their insignificant selves.

Assistant: Colosso, I will do anything you desire to help you to a glorious and victorious end. Ask and it will be done! The definition of questioning will be non-existent as you give commands.

President: Thank you and any final words from you Bill?

Provost: To appropriately defend your honor and promote your programs is my job. It will be done as best I can. If given the opportunity, I will help you destroy Tuffy in a way that will be perceived as honorable. Tuffy trusts me; I will plunge the knife deep and true at the right moment. It will be at the most vulnerable time for him; when he thinks he has my support. He will be weakened by my honorable treachery and destroyed by your great strength and unquenchable thirst for justice and the destruction of evil. If the opportunity arises, I will not fail you and will be a great support to you. Colosso, I might add the situation appears to be perfect to allow you to use your unique genius to score a total victory from an apparent defeat: the sports/academics issue will be a splendid holy-like punishing tool for you to use without respite to destroy your enemies.

President: Well said Bill. Thank you gentlemen. I knew I could count on you two. You are honorable indeed; and yes, to the very core of your hearts and souls. We are going to war and are taking no prisoners. Total victory will be mine as the valid representation of State University of America and all that is good in education. I will be dramatic and play my role magnificently tomorrow evening. Oh how I will play it.

Provost: Colosso, assuming you lose the Board vote tomorrow, what will you do then?

President: An excellent question and I have an excellent response. The day after what my enemies will perceive as a defeat, I will give a speech to the people that will send Tuffy and his hated macho clones into hiding. I promise you the people will be very, very angry and will support me 100%.

Assistant: Oh Colosso, to know you and watch you in action makes my life so meaningful, and yes, even exciting. You are State University of America and let no one forget that. We are with you all the way. Please call me day or night if you believe I can be of any help; even at the tiniest of levels. Oh God, do I want to help you reign supreme at State.

Provost: May justice prevail at State. May your victory be as great as your spirit. I await your direction.

President: *(Colosso gives an all knowing and approving look.)* I have confidence you will make a difference. I expect you to be pivotal in the victory and I am greatly comforted knowing you two are so loyal to me and the truth.

(They leave. Colosso walks around the office feeling and looking very positive about his meeting with key employees. Mrs. Krumm rings Colosso.)

President: Come in Mrs. Krumm.

Mrs. Krumm: Mr. President, Trustees Barglor, Boylen and Wood are here to see you and they say they must see you immediately. They really seem out of control emotionally.

President: This day is going crazy; even the little people are out to see me. Some people hate lawyers; others hate doctors; still others hate journalists; and others yet hate psychologists. I hate dumb football coaches and defiant Board members. For my tastes, I particularly like dull witted but appreciative and obedient to my vision Board members. Their personal insignificance can lead to their eternal glory through my actions. *(With a smile.)* I greatly enjoy the flushed look on their faces when I invite them to my major events within my university. But enough of this ruminating. *(With boredom.)* Send in Trustees Barglor, Boylen and Wood.

(Mrs. Krumm leaves and Trustees Barglor, Boylen and Wood enter in earnest. They look very nervous and agitated.)

Harry: Colosso, we must talk to you.

Carla: Please give us some of your most valuable time.

Karen: Thank God we can talk to you now!

President: *(With a look of great sincerity.)* Harry, Carla, Karen, please settle down. What is going on?

Harry: Tuffy has the other five Board members to vote him to be both Athletic Director and Coach at the Board meeting tomorrow. It is an evil and done deed.

Carla: They are out to destroy you and the greatness you bring to State.

Harry: I hate them all! What can we do to put you back in total power to save State? This is like the earth without the sun. What will become of us?

28

Carla: Oh, please give us direction, we are lost.

President: *(With a calm and reassuring voice tone.)* Keep yourselves under control my good and loyal friends. Like you, I am touched with true inextinguishable rage.

Harry: I am so upset; your life and soul are merged with State. You cannot be humiliated like this without State being grievously wounded. Oh, how cruel is fate today! The votes are there and nothing on this earth can change what will occur because of those damn Board members who do whatever Tuffy demands. Oh, woe is me and those of us who love State by giving total support to you.

President: Keep calm dear and loyal friend.

Karen: What can we do?

Carla: *(In despair.)* I am lost; we are lost.

President: *(With an earnest look of sincerity.)* Please keep calm and relax. Your integrity can help save State. What you do now will guarantee you and your families an honored place in the history of State.

Harry: Tell us what to do and we will do it. No questions will be asked. I have been accused of worshiping you as well as blindly supporting you; I say thank you and now await your command.

President: Harry, you have always been special to me for the way you do not waver from high principle and your demanding that right be put in the sunshine and thus be upheld. We need to bring in our loyal allies in the media who are as outraged as are we at Tuffy and his sports clique. They see him and his allies on the Board as the venomous creatures of the night they are. God's vengeance is thorough and most convincing; he will see us through this situation; but the test will be great and we will be greatly challenged. We will tragically lose the vote tomorrow; but victory will be ours in the long term strategy of totally vanquishing our infidel enemies. Using the media is our key tactic at present; we must use it indefatigably. When we lose the vote tomorrow, the very next morning I will give a speech on the matter that will bring passionate support to our holy cause by even those that previously never even knew there was a State University of America. Our loyal supporters will be greatly inspired to do their best to help us in our just cause.

Karen: Oh God, what a situation. I know you will be able to do that magnificently Colosso; but what can we do to get the media more involved at this critical time? I hate Tuffy and his followers so much. I would make a deal with the devil if it would defeat them.

Carla: *(With renewed heart.)* If we can defeat these bastards and raise you to the pinnacle of power you must have, I would give up all the profits on the farm this year as well as much of the inheritance I have planned for my children.

President: Your total commitment greatly touches me. The victorious battle to put me back in legitimate control will be hard and will begin in earnest after the vote tomorrow. The media will begin the war immediately and you will be part of this as you support me and your dreams.

Carla: To see them hurt your glorious name and undermine your rightful role as governing President just hurts me and enrages me simultaneously. I will not be silent to this damn bloody purge attempt against you. Colosso, you are State University of America! I will publicly fight for you. Tell me what to say and do; I beg you.

President: Dear loyal friends, we are in a crisis, but our brave and morally correct hearts and souls will merge into a vengeful punishing instrument to vanquish Tuffy and his thugs. Each of you will have a critical role in the battle. We will not take survivors and total glory will be ours in the name of State University of America.

All three: What is the plan and what do we do? *(They look at each other and nervously laugh as they all had the same thoughts and words at the same time.)*

President: To begin with, be available to all calls from the media. I promise you they will come fast and furious. I know God will guide your tongues. Remember and never forget, to be tested by God is to be a chosen person; to answer the call will lead to unimaginable rewards here and in the next life.

Harry: What can we say? Inspire us so we do not fail you.

President: *(With passion.)* Tell them the truth and nothing more. Tell them what you told me and yourselves today. Be angry and vengeful at Tuffy and his macho cronies. Say how enraged you are at your fellow Board members for breaking the sacred public trust they were elected to protect as they choose to succumb to the pandering demands of Tuffy and the other pimps of his sports clique. Make your words into trumpet like war tools to relentlessly attack and ultimately decapitate this damnable Tuffy and his lackies. Vengeance is our holy purpose in that forgiveness necessitates pure and true contrition and apology for one's sinful acts. Tuffy and his cronies are like the bad thief on the cross; their fate will be the same: hell on earth and eternal damnation.

Harry: Their pride is so great they will not acknowledge their grievous sins or your moral and personal superiority. We must attack them publicly for they are trying to destroy you.

Karen: That is crucial, we must do that.

Carla: As you demanded Colosso, we must defend you above all in the media. Tell us what to do and it will be done without question. Loyalty demands perfect obedience and you will have it.

President: *(Softly and firmly.)* Friends, again I ask you to just tell the truth . If you feel compelled to tell the media how angry you are about my being humiliated and treated worse than the most brutalized prisoner in a Nazi concentration camp, then trumpet your feelings on the highest! The state and nation will watch my public humiliation tomorrow night when the SS like thugs attempt to destroy me and thus the present and future of our beloved State University of America. I will survive to fight another day; you can be sure of that. Do what you must to destroy these creatures of the evil night who want to destroy light and truth at State. Your loyalty to me makes me indebted to you for the rest of my days. Only you can save State's future by helping me be your own champion by strong, truthful and vigorous communication with the media. They will call. Please be available and speak with the eloquence that can only come from trying to right unimaginable wrongs like we have received full flush in the soul here at State. The present and future of State are in your hands and I know you will not fail in your sacred mission!

Harry: Oh, God, we will not let you down. I will call all media persons I know and talk to those that call. I am with you 100%. With no offense to the others, I know I am the most obedient to you.

Karen: That is probably true Harry, but we are all of the same 100% commitment to our President and moral leader. I will do the same and hang with all the people I know in the media. Colosso, we desperately need you; for ourselves and for our beloved State.

Carla: I am so damn pissed. Tuffy and those bastards are as full of shit as is long a summer day. Colosso, war is on. I am not eloquent, but I know how to fight as dirty as need be to get the job done. You are State and we must save you to save ourselves and what we love.

President: *(With great sincerity.)* Even on this bleakest of days, your loyalty to me moves me nearly to tears. Your glory will be your knowledge you saved State and that your actions today will be remembered, played out and emotionally discussed as long as human beings respect education and desire it for themselves and those they love. Go forward and do what you must. May the vengeance of a fair and angered God be at your side!

Harry: We are with you and victory will be yours completely. Light will conquer darkness!

Carla & Karen: Right on!

All Three: *(With great emotion and voices cracking with emotion.)* We are off to do what must be done.

President: Just a moment my dear friends in crisis. Your loyalty and comradeship are as overwhelming to me emotionally in a positive way as are the wretched and traitorous acts of Tuffy and his clique of thugs in a negative way. I know a benevolent and righteous God is with us and we cannot fail! Go forward!

(They leave Colosso's office with strength and vigor infused into them by the positive support of their great charismatic leader. They will relentlessly do what Colosso has directed them to do.)

End of Scene

Scene 2

(The setting is Colosso's office. Colosso is going to speak to the media, the citizens of the State and some sympathetic students that were invited into the President's spacious office the morning after the Board vote that made Tuffy both Football Coach and Athletic Director over Colosso's vigorous, histrionic and indefatigable objections. Colosso promised Board President Terry Moore before the vote yesterday he would quit if the Board decided to override him on this matter; but Colosso's buddies in the media and his obedient Board supporters have not let him down and he can now dramatically back off from his promise. There has been an overwhelming and unified media support for Colosso. His Board supporters, obediently following his desires, are blasting Tuffy and the Board members who voted in opposition to their President in support of Tuffy being both football coach and athletic director. Derision and anger have been the response to Tuffy and the State University of America Board of Trustees that voted for him. The general belief is that Colosso will now quit due to the humiliation to him as well as his inability to now work with the governing Board of Trustees. Of course, he has himself generated this belief in the media so "the people" will demand he stay. Terry Moore and Board members who support Tuffy are counting on him leaving and are nervously waiting for Colosso to state this publicly. However, they do not really know for sure what the crafty and devious Colosso will actually do and they must wait like everyone else for what he has to say. His speech is being carried live across the state and beyond on radio and television. Colosso is not in the room yet, but some of the invited students are speaking about what has happened.)

Student 1: Do you know how President Assassino feels after the Board ran over him last night and made Tuffy both football coach and athletic director?

Student 2: We will know shortly.

Student 3: Do you think he will leave?

Student 2: It will be tragic for State, but I think he must in order to salvage his dignity.

Student 3: I hope he stays and fights Tuffy and this disgraceful Board.

Student 4: I feel so bad I could just sit down and cry. Why would anyone want to destroy our great President?

Student 1: I hear the light was on in the President's bedroom all night. How he must have suffered.

Student 2: Think of his mental agony. He must decide whether to leave for his own sanity or to stay and fight for us and State.

Student 5: I would surely leave. It would be a statement. Also, he surely cannot work with this Board.

Student 1: He must be happy with the protests on campus and around the state on his behalf as well as the tremendous media support.

Student 2: That is true, but I feel he must leave for himself. We cannot ask him to stay and be humiliated even more.

(Enter Provost Percival)

Provost Percival: I ask all of you to please sit down. *(They sit down.)* Our President will be here shortly to give an important speech. He is so proud of how the students have supported him in this most difficult period for him and our beloved State University of America. The President invited you to represent our great student body. Applaud before and after his speech only. Look serious and pay attention to everything our President is saying. He will enter in a moment. When he does and the cameras are on, please stand, cheer and applaud your President with strong support. He needs it today.

Student 1: What is President Assassino going to do?

Provost: That is for him to say and us to hear.

(Provost Percival leaves and enters again with Colosso. The cameras are going and the applause and cheers come strongly from the small group of invited students as well as the students in the hallway. Colosso has a look of determination and hurt on his face. He slowly walks to the podium, takes a nitro pill and begins to speak.)

President: Hello, I am not even really sure of what words I can use to express the feelings of sadness I have today. I have had but one goal since coming to State University of America and that has been to academically

make it the greatest institution in the world. My goal has not changed. *(He wipes some tears from his eyes.)* Please be patient with me as my emotions have a mind of their own today; and let me digress and give a little of my personal history. I am not prone to this in that all of my thinking time is geared to doing what is academically right for this great university. I believe my six and a half years as your President have been good for the institution and the countless thousands of students, alumni and State followers throughout the world. My background is one of great modesty. I am the son of poor Italian immigrants who came to America for the opportunity to succeed. Working long hours, being called names like Dago and Wop and maybe never getting as far ahead as the English surname Anglo-Saxons were considered part of the price an Italian paid to come to this great country. I remember as a young dark curly haired youngster hearing that only in America can one really get ahead; however, the price is heavy and one must be willing to work hard. First, we Italians were abused by the upper classes of Italy and then here in America by the previously persecuted Irish Catholics. I saw this with my father and I understood it. The psychological wounds on his soul were clearly visible up until the day he died; but he never gave up his goals for me or his great pride in being a U.S. citizen. He was modestly successful and inspired in me the goals to do my best. Dad told me to never forget an Italian discovered America and we were coming back! I remember him telling me if I worked in the gypsum mines like Uncle Tony did, to do it the best that is possible. If I could ever become a teacher, to educate persons and give them the greatest possible education was to be my goal. If I were to pick up trash like Uncle Frank, then do a great job and make the world a cleaner place. But, we never talked about my being the President of State University of America! Oh no, that was way beyond me even at a dreaming level. I remember growing up in Bigtown, USA and often thinking of this spectacular multi-thousand area oasis of academia and farm production that was like a magical kingdom; and I never even imagined being here other than if I were astonishingly lucky enough to be here as a student. To imagine me in the enormous shoes of the late and always great John Vandenburg was unthinkable; but, I was chosen by you past the half century mark of my life to be your President. Miracles still occur here in America and you made one occur for me when you made me your President of our beloved State. I am even now embarrassed to admit how many tears of joy I have shed since you chose me for what I feel is the most important job on this earth. Dad has passed on, but I know his honorable spirit is here today cheering me on to do my best and what is right and ethical. My mother even now cannot believe I am the President of State University of America and simply tells old true and humble friends that I am an educator or a teacher; and of course, that is true! I am so proud of the titles of educator or teacher that words cannot explain it. As your President, I have been able to implement your dreams, which of course are my dreams and previously were those of my father and mother for me. The dreams now are being transferred to your children and my children and then on to their children. I again ask you to please have patience with me today as my voice wavers and my mind wanders to my humble past. *(With tears in his eyes that he tries to clean up by working his hands over them.)* Oh God, how my feelings punish me today! Please do not think unkindly of me. I love you all from the depths of my heart and soul. I have found over the years that emotion and tears come more quickly at times of great emotion; both positive and negative. I thought to myself many times over my happy years here that if ever my authority to manage this university for you were undermined by powerful ruthless political forces, then I would have to step aside; to just give up. However, I really am not sure if I can ever do that to you; you that I love as one in communion with me. Today, more than any other day in my life, I am not feeling strong physically and emotionally; however, I love this sacred to me university and the prospect of turning it over to a power hungry sports clique that would run it for its own glorification really is a situation I cannot even fathom. Do you wish me to be a figurehead President presiding for you over a modern day Sodom and Gomorrah? Today, I slipped back through the years to those early days in my life when I was called demeaning names because I was an Italian Roman Catholic. The burning tears came back to my eyes and all the old wounds

36

on my soul were reopened; it was like the scabs were torn open and branding irons were put on them to intensify my pain and memory. While I know now that the kids who called me those names and beat me up did not really know any better, we all know that is not true for what is being done to me now. I feel I am being crucified and the bad thief is chuckling and mocking my dreams for you and those you love. Tuffy and his bully crowd of personality and institution assassins know better and are out to destroy me as your leader as well as State University of America as a great and becoming greater university for their own sinister glory. Such self-glorification at your expense; at the expense of the dreams of our children; and at the expense of academics at our beloved State University of America is just too much for me and my life history to bear. Oh, I know you might think I am being too harsh and maybe even showing some meanness for having lost academic power to the football coach and the powerful jock supporters who just want to keep him here and destroy State's academic integrity as a world class institution on the road to becoming the greatest university in the world. I honestly and firmly believe that is really not true and that we have a crisis to overcome that is of cosmic proportions. Even though I am not with you personally today, except for the few students that have been able to come into this room, my heart is with each and every one of you. You show me how detestable are the acts of Tuffy and his negative clique by your huge and unified support of me. We all love State University of America; we all want our children to have the best education possible; we all want all students, including athletes, to have the best opportunities in life that are possible; I want this and you want this. Let there be no doubt your trust was undermined yesterday and our mythical keys of the University were given to the football coach by those who idolize sports and detest academics. These forces of darkness are clearly in control at this time. History is sadly full of such examples: Hitler in Germany, Stalin in Russia, Castro in Cuba and Hussein in Iraq. Obviously a few people cannot control all of us all of the time, but the levers of power were in their hands yesterday and I was overrided as your President by the football coach. I was more or less blind sided and grievously injured on our field of integrity and honor in a very dirty and unfair manner. And do hear this, the football coach at one of the great institutions of America, was in effect told he can do whatever damn well he wants to do! I said there was a conflict of interest in having one person being his own boss. I was told it did not matter and to go back and just read some books and be a figurehead President. Well, I am not the type who is just going to disappear and be shoved into the corner by a clique of persons that worship jocks as opposed to higher education. I was thinking of leaving, but that would be an insult to my father, my mother, my children, my good friends, my students here at State University of America and most importantly, you the citizens of this great State. I am not leaving until I know I cannot manage what has to be done at State. You brought me here to do a job and I will do the best I can to finish it; in spite of being squeezed into the corner and my integrity as your leader trampled upon like a piece of sand in a fierce Texas windstorm. The first thing I am doing and I am doing it as of this moment, is to take the football coach and new athletic director and place him under the direct responsibility of Provost Percival; who will supervise his evaluation. We all know him to be an eminently fair and most honorable human being. Tuffy will no longer report to the Vice-President for Financial Affairs, who has been in charge of sports. We are going to have the athletic director report to an academic person just as the other deans do within the university. This is something I should have done before. I humbly apologize to you because it is probably part of the reason that the current situation has occurred and why the independent and fair media writers in this state have all come out in outrage at what is appropriately perceived as sports ruling this institution as opposed to academics coming first. I am simply relating what has happened to our image. While I am feeling horrible sorrow and sadness over the current perceived lack of stature of State University of America, it probably is of no value for me to again present the many complaints against Tuffy and his followers being stated most vigorously in the media and discussed informally by the enormous numbers of enraged citizens that believe this institution is here for academics and not just to make the football coach and his clique of macho sports types happy. As I may not have dreamed for anything other than an opportunity to do my best as a young dark haired Italian-American boy in Big Town USA, my goal now is to fight to continue to do the type of job I have tried to do: to have State University of America become the greatest university in the world and to have academics rule and not sports. Remember, we are not in a game where you win or lose and then you play another game next Saturday. We are in the type of tremendous competitiveness at the university level that when you destroy your reputation, it is so hard to get it back and it can take years and yes even decades. With your full support, this total destruction of State's reputation will never occur. Can I count on you in this grave hour of decision? I believe I can. I now want to begin the end of my talk here by stating yes, I am here to stay; yes, I am going to try to do the best I can for the citizens of this great state;

yes, I am committed to education over sports; and yes, I hope with your support, I will be able to keep doing the job I am doing, knowing this fiendish nightmare we are all living through can end and we can again all rush forward into the sunshine of academic glory where I believe we were headed. While we have horribly descended for now, like the Phoenix, we will rise again to greater academic glory with your support. I humbly and sincerely pray to our God in front of you that you will give me the opportunity to continue doing what I believe is the most important job in the world: serving you as your President at State University of America and making it the world's greatest university. Please do what you feel you must and know I am here at your command and greatly love and trust you all. *(With great emotion and choking back the tears.)* If you decide you want me to leave, I will do it immediately and will thank you for the opportunity you gave me to be your President. These have been the great heady days of my life and I hope they will continue. I say this in spite of the shame and havoc thrust upon me and you by the forces of darkness that hate academics at this school and what I am trying to do for you, your children and their children. Talk to your neighbors; talk to your friends; talk to strangers you meet; talk to legislature members; talk to media persons; and tell them all how you feel and what you desire me to do for you, your family and all our dreams. May the God we place our faith in, bless you all and give peace and love to each of you personally and all persons you know and care about.

(The invited students jump to their feet and burst into applause and cheers as the scene ends and cheering can also be heard coming from the hallway.)

End of Scene

Scene 3

(Emilio and Charles are cleaning up the room after President Assassino's talk explaining where he stood after he had lost the crucial Board of Trustees vote and Tuffy Norkas was made Athletic Director in addition to being the Football Coach.)

Charles: Emilio, I have been looking so forward to seeing you to talk about what a tragedy has occurred. I am angry and have even been crying. Oh, I am so mad!

Emilio: I told you this was going to be a great learning experience for someone trying to learn about politics and power. However, you must clearly analyze what has occurred without bias and preconceived beliefs.

Charles: I just feel horrible about how President Assassino has been humiliated and treated like a mere scoundrel by the damn football coach. *(With sarcasm.)* His clique of political friends and Board members have catapulted him to such power within the university that maybe we should call this school Tuffy Norkas State Football University. Did you hear the President's talk?

Emilio: Oh yes, I heard his talk and thousands like it during my years in Cuba.

Charles: You are not going to try to compare President Assassino to Fidel Castro are you? The President is so damn sincere.

Emilio: For as wise of a young man you are, you really do not understand the principle under which the prince or caudillo functions. Once you understand how he thinks and what he represents, it is quite simple to understand his motives from his actions. One must not confuse words with output. Americans are naive and really very good; however, periodically they seek out the great prince like all humans. It sadly is a tragic human flaw that has led to so much of the world's historical misery. This particularly absurd outlook has had many Americans perceive left wing dictatorships as liberal in the American sense and good for the people. In effect, such dictatorships control all private and governmental sectors and thus have total power. What happened in Eastern Europe shows the validity of my concerns and the moral bankruptcy of such dictatorships.

Charles: You are hard to understand. What do you believe happened here? Is President Assassino like a communist dictator?

Emilio: Nothing has happened here other than a person who works for a constitutionally governing board has gone to war in the media over an unimportant but populist matter to destroy its credibility at a general level and to destroy individual members who voted against him one time at a specific level. From Colosso's point of view, Tuffy's enormous flaw is his unwillingness to obey him blindly. Any supporters of Tuffy are silenced by the pressure of the great Caudillo using the masses to destroy all opposition to him. How important is it Charles, that this football coach be given some additional athletic activities at no additional cost to the university? Is not the football program the overwhelmingly largest program in the sporting field? Is not this a situation that occurs in other schools throughout the country without incidence?

Charles: The whole issue is academics versus sports. Which will rule this university is the question?

Emilio: Oh Charles, are you so blind that you cannot see that the issue is power? It has nothing to do with academics and sports. There has generally been a successful football program here over the years and an overall effective sports system. It is the only one in the conference that made a profit this year. It would be good if the academic component could stand to the same level of national prominence as does the sports program. What you have here is the great charismatic nonelected field commander versus a crude, heavy handed but basically democratic football coach. Assassino is out for power and is more than willing to destroy this university to make himself look good nationally and meet his own perverted needs. The fact the governing board of elected public officials is so confused about its role and function is really the key problem. Colosso is an employee who works for the Board. Some Board members do not know this in that Colosso overwhelms their senses. The role of the media has been disgraceful. They support the demagog and not the right of the governing Board to make this dual appointment of Tuffy; even if unpopular. Remember Board members can be voted out of office and such is not true with their employee Colosso.

Charles: None of that can possibly be true. The President is a great and caring man. He must be allowed to manage the university without interference from Tuffy and meddling Board members. You speak of the President but do not understand him at all.

Emilio: Coño[1]! Charles, use your brain and ask yourself who has been the only person who has been gaining good publicity during this whole crazy thing? Has it been the students?; Has it been the graduates of the university?; Has it been future students of the university?; Has it been faculty at the university?; Has it been the Governing Board of Trustees?; Has it been Tuffy?; no, it has only been El Gran Caudillo-President Colosso Michelangelo Assassino. He is playing the masses the way I saw Fidel Castro do so effectively for so many years. Like Fidel, his speeches are very verbose. He just overwhelms you with words and more words that come from a man of powerful and convincing charisma. Americans are very good but foolish. They do not understand that the prince who comes along to save the people, seeks to solidify his own power by magnificently raising and lowering their passions as he promises everything and makes everything and everyone against him look horrible and evil. He then will allow them to take part in the exorcism of the evil. What is impeccable virtue in him, he turns into unspeakable evil when done by those who oppose him. There is no question that Tuffy could have handled this whole thing differently and that the Board could have functioned differently. They believed the concept of an open debate on the matter was good and that once a decision was made, everyone pulls together. But here you have an employee who sees himself as working for the people and the people are his to do with as he feels. He becomes brazenly drunk with his power and destroys his enemies in great orgasmic like bursts of destructive frenzy. This is indeed a very dangerous type of a man. Certainly no one who is needed in this university. I do have horrible pain and sorrow in my heart as I watch this tragic situation occurring due to the activities of this power hungry prince. The memories of Cuba came back to me at night in images that are overwhelming me with their intensity. I have been trying to bury them for years, but now they are again let loose to torment me in a way that I hope you never know or even comprehend.

Charles: Emilio, you seem to really be suffering by all of this. Why would a Cuban working as a janitor and getting ready for retirement get so involved emotionally in something so foreign and distant from him?

---

[1] Coño! Damm it!

I really do not understand this and wish I could help you. I actually care for you a lot.

Emilio: Your feelings for me are very appreciated and treasured. I feel very bad Charles; for in my great moment of opportunity to bring about changes in Cuba, I failed. I say this to you with the hope that it may help you sometime in the future. Oh, how the conscience tortures and burns one's spirit when it was made dormant inappropriately in one's life for so many years. I knew Fidel Castro from the early days of my life. Our families owned and lived on large plantations near each other in the province of Oriente. Like Fidel, my mother was Cuban and my father was from the Spanish Province of Galicia. I was in the mountains with Fidel. I took part in the Great Victorious March to Havana and all the glorious activities that were part of the victory. Even the great Caesar at the height of his powers could have felt no more satisfied than Fidel and the rest of us at that moment in history. We were young, had won against an enemy hated by nearly all Cubans and were heroes to a growing new order in the world. Each of us thought we could populate a colony. For so long I was blind to Fidel and his ruthless behaviors to meet his own gargantuan princely needs. I very slowly but surely began to see him over the years for what he was. One day I had the opportunity to kill him while he slept. All the evil, the lies, the pain, the destruction of impeccable reputations, the countless political killings he had committed, and the horrible things he had done to my beloved Cuba came before my eyes in graphic visual and emotional fashion. I knew I was going to kill him; but at that moment of opportunity, I failed. I pointed the gun to his head and knew he would die. My finger was on the trigger and my finger froze. I had killed so many men without even thinking about it twice; but now with the great prince helpless and in my sights, I inexplicably could not kill him. I hate myself for this worse than any man has ever hated himself. When Fidel woke up and saw me, he seemed to know what had happened and gave me an all knowing look of contempt for my weakness; he must have seen it in my eyes. Fidel then turned over and went back to sleep. I felt humiliated and felt I had not done what had to be done. It was one life for a nation and I was not willing to do it. Purposeful fate has determined I will now live with it daily. The worst penalty is that I am now working for an insignificant prince on the world stage, but still a very evil person who will destroy this university so he can win total control. No price is too great for him.

Charles: Emilio, I do not pretend to tell you I understand all of this but I certainly know you are a good man and your intent is to see the truth and not do wrong. Sometimes we all must let the past go and maybe that is what you need to do now.

Emilio: You are a good young friend Charles and I appreciate that in my loneliness. I can let it go to some extent, but the burden of being a human being who failed his countrymen is hard to overcome. The misery that continues is due to my failure to have acted decisively and it weighs on me heavily. Such moments of great opportunity rarely come in a man's life. How sad when they come and one fails miserably as I did. This is particularly true when the destructive impact is on countless human beings as in my case. The end result is the constant and throbbing hurt I always have in my heart. I have tried to bury the past in an anonymous lifespace and a job where I need not use my mind or interact with people on political matters. Things were going fairly well until this sad war began at State to make the present seem so much like the past.

Charles: Emilio, I am young but I have learned some things in my life. You really do not know what would have occurred if you had killed Fidel. For sure, I would not have known you and that would have been a great loss for me. *(They embrace.)*

End of Scene

Scene 4

(The setting is the large spacious office of Tuffy Norkas. On the wall as you enter to the left is bold print writing that says "Hall of Champions"; and underneath it are various pictures of "All Americans" during the ten year coaching career of Tuffy at State University of America. Behind the huge desk of Tuffy is a very large portrait of him in his football coaching outfit. Around the room are plush chairs and a meeting table. The meeting is called in the afternoon of the day after Tuffy was made athletic director by the Board of Trustees, on a 5 - 3 vote, over the vehement opposition of President Assassino. The media, led by the giant and powerful newspapers in Big Town, unleashed an unprecedented flurry of editorials and articles attacking Tuffy and the Board members who allowed him to be both coach and athletic director. The meeting is to plan strategy to deal with the fierce opposition to Tuffy in the dual role. The level of opposition was not anticipated. Vice President Larry Christianson has brought in a psychologist and professor emeritus of ancient Roman history to help plan a strategy against Colosso. Colosso's influence with the media was grossly underestimated and a horrible price is now being paid.)

Tuffy: Well I am glad you were all able to meet here with me today. I can guarantee there will be more as we appear to be in a God damn long term quagmire. The attacks on me and those that support me have been overwhelming in their hypocrisy today. I hate those damn editors and all the bullshit they spread. The one by Coe particularly incensed me; that pompous bastard. I have been attacked by many people over the years, but nothing like this. Now, as far as today is concerned, while I certainly have no control over what any of you say, I certainly hope what we discuss here is simply among us. *(General nodding of heads and statements of agreement.)* But before I go any further, Larry has two persons he would like to talk to us. Who are they Larry and why do you think it would be useful at this time? We will probably only have time today to listen to them and ask questions.

Larry: Tuffy, that is probably good. Our feelings are such that to react to someone else is better than to let loose with our anger and frustration. We need to better know who we are dealing with and get some ideas on what to do at this time. I think these two persons can give us some interesting insight into Colosso from their particular areas of expertise and some strategies to use to take control of the situation. I know most of you are really not interested in academic, historical or psychological type constructs in relation to dealing with people and problems; however, I believe that Guido can certainly give some good information on Colosso from his particular historical outlook pertaining to Ancient Rome. Judy, who is a practicing psychologist, can certainly give some insights into his personality. I have known both of these persons for many years and they are really of impeccable integrity and certainly team members as far as we would be concerned. In this dark hour when reputations are being destroyed as easily as a field mouse by an eagle, information from fair and extremely perceptive persons of integrity can be useful.

Tuffy: Well, let each come in and give us their input and we can see what we think. I will try to be courteous even though you know my approach to a scoundrel like Colosso is not from an academic point of view. Reconstructing his pretty sissy face would be more to my liking. Particularly when I am getting roasted across the state by every media thug that is able to put something in writing. I am really enraged but ready to listen.

Terry: Tuffy, I certainly know what you mean and let us face it, we are all getting roasted today for making a decision we really thought was best for State. However, Colosso has gone to war with us and we can certainly use any insight we can get. The man is a media magician with the scruples of a drunk snake.

Tuffy: Good example and I agree! We will call in one at a time. *(On intercom.)* Please send in Professor Bucciferri.

(In comes Professor Bucciferri.)

Guido: It is certainly a pleasure to meet you Tuffy as well as the rest of you.

Tuffy: Do you know the other people here Guido?

Guido: If not personally, certainly by reputation.

Tuffy: Well let me make it easy by doing introductions. Terry Moore-Board President, Fred Johnson-Board Member, Judy Norkas-my wonderful wife. You certainly know Larry and I am obviously the same Tuffy The Barbarian that you have been reading and hearing about today.

Guido: Thank you Tuffy and now let me begin talking; which I warn is very easy for me. I am sure to a group of effective take control of the here and now type people such as yourselves, that meeting with an expert on Ancient Rome is certainly not what you would see as useful. I hope you are wrong and I will try to explain why I am here. I have had various talks with Larry about Colosso over the years and how he really perfectly fits the definition of the prince as defined by Machiavelli and lived out by men such as Caesar and Hitler; to name a few. The example of him declaring war on his governing board in the media is a perfect example of this. Colosso sees himself as one thousand feet tall, bullet proof and with a huge 24 carat gold crown on his noble head. He is above the rules and regulations of other people and in effect is the rule giver and enforcer of "the people". He is them: one and indivisible. Due to extreme charisma, clever ability to understand the needs of the masses, and no sense of right and wrong, he is able to take otherwise reasonable people under his spell to the point that they will do whatever he wants. We have seen it historically in the greatest example of them all: Julius Caesar. He destroyed the republican form of government in Rome and brought on the empire. We have seen it in more current days with the likes of a Douglas MacArthur, who was ready to discard the constitution in his battle with his Commander and Chief, Harry Truman. The best current example of course is Fidel Castro; who is the prototypic prince of the generation. All of these men have many things in common. All had extreme egos, all were charismatic, and all offered something to the people they wanted. Caesar offered land to the peasants and greater fairness than they were receiving; MacArthur offered the glory of the American Eagle in Korea to the masses and Fidel Castro offers the Cuban people dignity and respect in the form of himself against the Yankees or any other particular adversary that might come up. And now to the point: Colosso is cut out of the same block of wood. Look at the rage written in the newspapers today and the talk shows throughout the state. He is being lionized as the greatest defender of education on earth while you are pitted against him as brutal destroyers of academia and worshipers of football. He has with adroit manipulation of the media, infected the minds of the citizens with rage and has you and all your

49

supporters presented as jock sniffers out to destroy education for the edification of your sports engine and empire. Please excuse the analogies, but I read them today in the papers.

Tuffy: *(With a gruff chuckle in his voice.)* Guido, such examples are pretty damn tame compared to what we use around this place.

Guido: Of course, the issue is simply power and has nothing to do with sports and academics. As you know Mr. Moore, Colosso has been angry with you and the new board members that are actually trying to hold him accountable for his outrageous traveling, his coddling of the media against the Board, his outrageous expenses, and his absentee management of the university. He has cleverly picked an issue of great national interest and is trying to present himself as the great defender of education against a wild destructive sports empire out to gobble up the integrity of the people, their dreams, their university, and, of course, the great and always loyal to the people - Colosso Assassino. He is presenting himself as the one person who represents the views of the masses. In his talk this morning, he made himself one with them and whipped them up into a frenzy. His responsibility is obviously to defend his governing board, educate it, acknowledge that it exists and do everything he can to pull its members together; but the great prince does not do such things. He is State University of America. Any one who challenges that is to be destroyed by the masses. Because the masses identify with him and his demands completely, they do whatever he desires. Colosso of course does the destroying in their name. Never underestimate Colosso's magnificent charisma and ability to bring the people with him. Amazingly, Terry and the rest of the Board gave him the power he is now using to flog hatred of your very existence into the minds of the masses. Incredibly, your only employee, the Secretary to the Board, actually reports to him. All the organs of communication at the university are in his morally corrupt hands. The results of abdicating the control of all communication to your employee is evident today. Stalin would love it and Hitler's burn scarred bones are warm and vibrant today.

Tuffy: Guido, a bit dramatic but you make your point.

Guido: From a practical point of view, this Coach/AD situation was the wrong issue to have been brought up at this time. It played into Colosso's devious hands and he will not let it go easily. However, that is a moot point at this time and the governing board must make decisions it feels are appropriate.

Tuffy, the offer to you of millions of dollars from the pros came at a bad time.

Tuffy: One need not be Sherlock Holmes to figure that out. I certainly did not plan it. Be that as it may, why does the bastard feel he has to be so God damn superior?

Guido: It is the nature of the beast you confront; but let me tell you what I see now. I see tremendous problems for all of you in the immediate future if you go by state and nationwide publicity and what it is saying. There is no question that Colosso has been allowed to pick the highest ground with his constant catering to the media editors. He has gloriously wrapped himself within a Caesar like shroud of indignation and is going to certainly try to flog every dissenter into the ground as he makes himself omniscient and omnipotent at State. In his perverted mind, he is the light of higher education in the world and beyond. *(With a chuckle.)* His only redeeming quality is that he loves the golden voice of Mario Lanza.

Tuffy: Guido, while I cannot lie and tell you I really fully understand what you are saying or accept solutions of professor types in cases such as this, what do you think ought to be done?

Guido: I unequivocally am convinced he needs to be fired immediately and a person brought in who can pull things together. Bold and decisive action will be required if you hope to carry the day.

Terry: I really do not think we can do that with the current public outcry. I am hoping he will settle down once he realizes he lost the vote and that really nothing that dramatic has changed except for the giving of a few additional duties to the football coach at no additional cost to the university.

Guido: With all due respect sir, you do not understand the charismatic prince personality. He was waiting for an issue to go to war against a Board trying to control him. Colosso does not even have a job description under which he is evaluated. He is deliriously feasting on the current turmoil as do starving sharks on the flesh of shipwrecked sailors. He will gleefully chew up and destroy all of you for his own self gratification and it is with great relish that he watches your agony as your reputations are destroyed and his soars. Colosso is a dangerous man and has no sense of right or wrong. It is only what the great prince desires that matters. And now, he smells blood and will go for the jugular with limitless zeal.

Tuffy: I am beginning to like your examples. Again questioning but not belittling any of your views, what are his weaknesses?

Guido: He cannot stand dissension. It is essential he somehow be exposed for what he is and then he will self-destruct as many princes have done in their moment of crisis. If exposed and thus humiliated publicly, Colosso will either look weak and silly or overbearing and shrill. Either will destroy his ego and he will be relegated to a tiny infamous footnote in the history of State University of America. Even the newspaper editors who now champion him as a hero will note his basic character flaws and in effect will write his obituary.

Tuffy: Do you see this as probable or something easy to be done?

Guido: Unfortunately, it is not probable or easy to do. He has enormous power and prestige with the media and they now are very sensitive to him and his cause. The public is enraged and sees him as the great educator that has been destroyed by the football coach and his clique of jock lovers and jock sniffers.

Tuffy: That is a damn lie and you know it!

Guido: I am simply reporting what I know of princes, of human nature and what I see happening at this particular time or might happen in the near future.

Tuffy: You are right, Guido. I am so damn mad at this silly faggot that if I run into him, I am not sure what I will not do to him. I know his prissy face and body would be spread all over this campus and would be a sorry sight.

Guido: *(With a chuckle.)* It would then match in looks his perverted soul and psyche.

Tuffy: I do understand that statement and I like it! If you have nothing more to say, we need to move on to talk to Judy.

Guido: I have essentially said what I planned. I appreciate the opportunity you allowed me to come in here. I do implore you to not underestimate the adversary you are dealing with. The greatest problem Colosso has is that we are in a democracy and ultimately demagogues wear very poorly. However, it will probably be a long time until this occurs due to the passionate rage and fury he has spectacularly channeled into the very psyche of the man on the street against you. Even great supporters of Tuffy and the Board are very intimidated by the fact they simply will be presented as football lovers and academic haters if they go against the splendid Colosso and support you folks.

Larry: Well thank you for coming Guido and I really think you have shared a lot of valuable information with us. Perspective can save persons from doing rash and foolish things.

(Everyone says thank you and stands up to shake his hand and say goodbye.)

Tuffy: *(Shaking his hand, holding his shoulder and looking intently into his eyes, Tuffy speaks.)* I do appreciate your coming in and I really have listened. Your ways may not be my way to approach the problem, but I thank you very much and I know many of these thoughts will keep coming back to me. They may help me from letting anger overcome reason. I sometimes know I am not just a dumb football coach.

Guido: *(With great sincerity.)* That you definitely are not.

(Guido leaves the office.)

Tuffy: Larry, you were right; the man has some good ideas. I wish we could attack by having Terry and the majority on the Board just fire the bastard.

Terry: I would like that too, but the timing is just impossible for that. I still hope as things settle down, Colosso will become a team player.

Norma: Terry, you just do not get it. The no good asshole will not change.

Fred: Terry, old Norma may be right on this one. Sometimes that crazy Dutch and Lithuanian concoction says damn smart things.

Norma: Letting the "old" go, you occasionally see the truth in a tough old broad like me.

Tuffy: Okay, everybody cut it for now. Let us turn this back to Larry and get on with this meeting.

(Everyone sits down and Larry stands up to speak.)

Larry: I would now like to bring in Judy to give us some insights into Colosso from her unique position as a long term private practice psychologist as well as one who has long studied the unique characteristics of the sociopathic person with power who also has tremendous charisma.

Tuffy: With all the turmoil and hell breaking out in this state right now, you really think we need to hear from a psychologist? I know what a bastard Colosso is and how he would destroy all of us. So why waste our time with this stuff?

Norma: God damn it Tuffy, you complained about Guido and then you thought he was helpful. Just give her a chance.

Terry: Tuffy, I have met Judy before and she may help us some. Colosso has gained tremendous moral leverage with his most effective misinterpretation of our vote to the public. His total command of the media has me actually in awe and somewhat even in fear to tell you the truth. I really believe any advice we can get would be helpful.

Fred: The bastard is good; better than I ever would have imagined.

Tuffy: There is no question the man is a media hog and that the Big Town media people are just loving to attack us in an effort to destroy us and of course help The University of America. I am not ready to budge an inch on this situation. He lost in a fair and honest debate. Anger and the will to fight express how I feel as opposed to fear.

Fred: I feel the same way; there is no compromise with Colosso.

Terry: I still think compromise is the only good solution to really resolve this mess.

Fred: That is stupid Terry; you gotta destroy the son of a bitch.

Tuffy: I sure as hell will put an amen on that. Terry, wake up to reality and put your balls back on.

Larry: Gentleman, the last thing we need to be doing now is arguing among ourselves. Colosso has obviously made himself a hundred feet tall, bulletproof and he feels like a fire breathing dragon ready to destroy us emotionally. Of course, he really does not have the power at a legal level and I think rather than being motivated by anger and fear, we need to make decisions based on a valid understanding of our adversary. I still believe that trying to understand what Guido has said and what Judy will tell us will be helpful in our overall strategy of dealing with this huge problematic mess. Let us not let our feelings overwhelm us and give Colosso a victory just because we cannot work together. The Prince is always able to gain power over people that play by rules, have high moral standards and are not able to agree among themselves as to what is the appropriate course of action to stop his destructive behavior. Let us join together and work as a team. However, if letting Judy come in here is going to cause us to have problems among ourselves, then I will tell her there is no need for her to come in. I say this even though I believe it is important she come in.

Tuffy: Larry, like always you are reasonable and able to deal with feelings in a way to have people take a cooler outlook. Let us bring Judy in and let her try to help us. Terry, let us try to come up with some strategies here that will be strategies of strength and not of fear and awe. I still like the way boxers settle their disagreements.

Terry: You know I am a competitor and a person who understands politics. Maybe fear was the wrong word to use. I have certainly been in awe of the way he has been able to orchestrate the media and to spectacularly present his views in a way to make those of us who really love State University of America look petty, destructive, overbearing and ready to destroy academics for the sake of sports.

Tuffy: On that note, I am going to ask that Judy come in to see us. *(Tuffy calls his secretary on the intercom.)* Please have Judy come in to see us at this time.

(Judy enters.)

Larry: *(In a casual and light hearted voice tone.)* Judy, good to see you. I think you will find a receptive audience even if not excited.

Tuffy: Judy, that is not true. You must know by now that I am a man of action and not one who has a lot of faith in psychologists and preachers. I determine who plays football and that has been enough to motivate people to do their best.

Judy: In all respect to you Tuffy, you are certainly not dealing with a football player and I hope you will at least listen to some insights I have into a tremendously effective and yes dangerous adversary. Colosso's charismatic presence and ability to control minds in this situation is really impressive as well as just plain mind boggling. I am just flat out impressed to hell with him. However, he is really scary at a character level. Now, I have a more or less prepared talk on Colosso's personality, but please interrupt me for questions or clarification.

Tuffy: Fair enough. I am ready to hear what you have to say.

Norma: *(With a tone of true annoyance.)* I personally am getting tired of hearing all this nonsense about this idiot. I have a good mind to pull his pants down and show the frilly panties that one of his many boyfriends has given him. I would then give him a blistering until his damn pride was gone and he was begging me to let him leave State

55

University of America. I would let him but it would be a world class blistering he would never forget.

Judy: Believe it or not Norma, that may be one of the few ways to really unmask and eliminate the threat of Colosso to all of you as well as to the legitimate future and present needs of State University of America.

Terry: I am just afraid we are not able to use such tactics with Colosso at this time.

Norma: That is why he is on top at this moment and you are now looking pretty foolish and horrible.

Judy: This only shows the great advantage Colosso has is that he has no sense of right or wrong and he will not play by any rules but his. Colosso and his life run an exact parallel with the identity of State University of America; to him they are one.

Tuffy: *(In a jovial tone.)* I thought you were going to come in and tell us something new about Colosso and now you tell us he is State University of America.

Judy: I did not say that Tuffy. I said this is what he believes and his actions are motivated by his beliefs. I judge not by what a person says but by what he does. A basic and simple principle; but most people do not understand it; do not use it in their daily dealings with people, and thus we psychologists in effect have a full employment act. Most people just do not realize a person's actions in effect state his belief structure. If Colosso is out to destroy you and those he sees against him, it would be helpful for you to at least understand he does this under the belief he is State University of America; thus any time, even if in the tiniest way you attack his authority, you are attacking the university and him personally; because they are one and the same. Adolph Hitler and Germany would be a comparable example.

Tuffy: Well let us get on with this Judy and see what happens.

Norma: I still think I have the best strategy. If you guys have any sense, you would let me implement it. I would certainly not fail like you folks have done and continue to do; *(with sarcasm)* but then I am only a woman!

Tuffy: Norma, leave this alone and let us get on with some strategies that we can do.

Norma: I again state I could solve this problem but you folks have no strategies other than to try to play within the rules with a scoundrel that will only play by his scheming and dishonest rules. It would be fun to watch that fragile, effeminate boy with woman like features turn into a blubbering child while I gave him a good blistering.

Judy: Norma, while I support your concept, it is evident these men are motivated by law and rules and not by a solution that Colosso would implement immediately if it were to suit his purposes and he had the power. His conscience is a putrid wasteland where fairness and justice are squashed like an egg under a tank. Let me state that in my opinion, Colosso has a definite character disorder. He is a sociopathic personality and his conscience is nothing like the conscience of any of us in this room.

Tuffy: Talk to me in English. What the hell is a sociopathic personality?

Judy: A sociopath, or person with a sociopathic personality disorder, has no sense of right or wrong and is only motivated by what he or she perceives as right from his or her particular needs at that moment or in a long term plan devoid of conscience. In the case of Colosso, he learned quite early in life that using charm and flattery in attempting to deal with the needs of people is a better way to get them to do what he wants rather than to act out anger and destructive behaviors with people. As a result, Colosso has developed a manner and way about himself that people really welcome him and his company. You will note he sees himself way above the world we live in and rarely spends a lot of time with persons at social settings in that he really has no desire for people to get to know him. He is really not at all concerned with all the mundane normal activities of the university and is the university hero that only the image he creates is known. He flatters, builds up and entices people that can help him by appearing to be sincere, honest and having their needs at heart. Colosso can ferret out what is important to a person and convince him or her that it is also very important to him and he will try to resolve it if it is a problem. When he is devious or plotting with persons, it is with people he has completely sized up and he knows will do what de desires without question. Many are foolish persons who blindly follow him. He makes their little lives seem important. Skip Goon is the most pathetic of them all. Colosso's fierce anger and rage with Harold Burns, his long time assistant who was picked up in the compromising sexual situation with a young man, was not over what he did but rather that he got caught and how it then negatively reflected on the image of Colosso. While showing some level of support publicly, you will note Harold disappeared into history in much the same way as persons did who displeased Stalin or Fidel Castro. Because Colosso has such a great ability to make other persons feel so good, he does not really have to resort to the more drastic measures that sociopaths do who do not have his particular personality skills in such splendid abundance.

Norma: Is the fairy a freak that would kill people if he had the chance?

Judy: He does not seem to have the homicidal tendencies or compulsions of a sociopath like Ted Bundy; who in effect used his horrible sociopathic skills to entice young women and then kill them.

Larry: Judy, what does Colosso want and how does he get it in your opinion?

Judy: What Colosso wants is total power and control of State University of America. He is the great "Prince" of the masses. He used them to get what he wants. A good example to look at would be that of Fidel Castro, who has been able to use "the masses" the same way Colosso is able to use the citizens of this state in a way to help him in any desire he has. You will note his talk today is really to enlist them to rise up and destroy those of you in this room specifically and at a general level any person who would disagree with him at all in the future. Just look at the anger he is directing at the Board members who only this time disagreed with him. He was also able to indirectly enlist the enormously powerful supporters of The University of America, and directly the media princes in Big Town and throughout this state to add their shrill voice against anyone who goes against him. You will also note he did training at The University of America and has maintained many of those powerful ties and is using them now with devastatingly great effect. Back to the situation of the long time assistant who he ignored and let go through the form of putting him into an insignificant position and eventually having him leave the university. Due to Harold's indiscreet sexual encounter that made Colosso look bad due to their close association, Colosso never showed any support or compassion for his totally dedicated long time loyal assistant. In person, be berated him with great anger and passion. Harold said this to some close friends that I know; he is still devastated. Colosso did this because other humans are really objects for a combination of exploitation and manipulation. In no way would he feel any responsibility to a loyal lieutenant who was with him for many years if he failed him in any way. You will see he will not support Board members who for years have supported him 100% but this one time have voted against him. As you can see today, his only goal is to destroy them completely; forgiveness and understanding of differences of opinion do not exist in his egomaniacal mind: You are blindly obedient to him or an enemy. For emphasis, this pure sociopath's attempt to destroy otherwise loyal Board members is being done because one time they voted against him on a really unimportant matter as far as the academics of the university is concerned.

Norma: Okay Judy, I see an inconsistency in the bastard. He seems to love his dog Chamberlain. Is he faking it or does he love him? If he does, how come?

Judy: His affection for his dog Chamberlain is not inconsistent in that many sociopaths have shown great love for animals while they show great hatred and resentment for human beings. Hermann Goering loved dogs as he had his Luffwaffee kill thousands of innocent civilians all over Europe.

Norma: Inconsistent, but I understand it.

Fred: I still see the bastard as a bastard because of how he treats people.

Judy: No argument from me Fred. An important concept for us to understand is that unlike Colosso, we in this room all have a conscience and it limits behaviors and stops us from doing certain wrong things. A conscience punishes and puts the raw human passions under control. There is no conscience in Colosso and thus what is occurring is even predictable.

Terry: How would you describe his conscience?

Judy: His conscience is really like a morally decadent wasteland with no sense of right or wrong.

Terry: How did he get this way?

Judy: He either picked this up from his parents, from those around him when he was growing up or somehow learned these behaviors are appropriate for him to further advance himself. While Norma's idea of blistering Colosso in those female panties in front of a nationwide television audience seems like a graphic and absurd concept, he of course would orchestrate such a situation with one of you if he could. He would present it in such a way as if he were trying to help the person and save State as he destroyed him emotionally and professionally. Colosso does believe he is State University of America and that everything within it really represents him. Everything Colosso does is done with the goal of furthering himself, his goals and his future. The very fact he went into the role of a university president is very enlightening about him. In what other position in America can one be treated like a true king in a kingdom? Colosso is able to spectacularly masquerade in the robes of academia as he does everything he can to further his own grotesque needs. The reason he is more than willing to use persons in the media or any other persons and institutions to support him in his declared war on his governing board is that he has no sense of working for a board and only will report to himself. You will note in his talk today he spoke of "the people" as who he reports to and he then told "the people" what they think and what they believe. This is the demagog at his best. The remarkable thing to a psychologist like myself is that many of the most brilliant, perceptive and sensitive of persons, who can spot a demagog in any other situation, are so easily misled and used when one comes into their lives and is ready to meet their needs and desires over and above what really is reasonable in our earthly environment. Colosso is the best I have seen and thank God he is only at a university level and not in the role of a man like Hitler, Stalin, Castro or Hussein. I mention this so you can realize you are dealing with a man with no values and who will really do anything he can to meet his own needs.

Norma: The pathetic shit really seems to believe he is the greatest bastard that ever lived; what an asshole.

Judy: Colosso actually sees the greatest of human beings that have lived as merely having prepared the way for his superior greatness; they at best were approximations of the superior nature and ability he sees himself to encompass. They needed to exist to have comparisons to his obvious superiority.

Tuffy: *(With a laugh.)* You make sense to me Judy; even though my old Italian buddies in Big Town would say things in a more down to earth manner. In fact, their talking would not be with their mouths.

Judy: I get the point Tuffy; also thank you for the complement.

Larry: Judy, are you sure he is not homicidal?

Judy: I am not sure if he is homicidal, but it appears he is able to meet his needs through the power of words and influence and not murder. Homicide would really be destructive to him and not helpful. But remember from a personality point of view, homicide is something he is very capable of doing without remorse in that dark immoral mind of his; and his not committing homicide is only based on the needs of the situation and the political system in which he lives.

Fred: *(With sarcasm.)* I could not imagine that fucking fag trying to kill anybody; he might make a mistake and hurt his satin smooth hands. His weapon is his tongue; I would like to cut it out and pin it on his nose.

Tuffy: Ha! Ha! You sound pissed off Fred.

Fred: You are god damn right I am mad.

Tuffy: Judy, you actually make sense to me. Assuming this is all true, is it better to kill a man physically or to destroy him and his reputation to the point he is really a mere shell of what he was previously?

Judy: A philosopher is with us. I believe most people if given such a choice, would vote for ending a life as opposed to being totally humiliated and destroyed in life. Tuffy, while you often belittle your intelligence, I do believe that is a very interesting and perceptive question you raised.

Tuffy: *(With a smile.)* Hey, I am just the football coach.

Judy: It just so happens that Colosso is in a situation where he can totally destroy a person's reputation as opposed to killing the person. This is due to circumstances and the fact we live in the United States of America and not in a place such as Castro's Cuba. As a result, the methods of the sociopath in a democracy are more at a level to destroy one's reputation as opposed to killing the person. The sociopath in a democracy must be very clever, intelligent and often charismatic in gaining and keeping his position of great power and authority. It is also interesting that Colosso came to a university with the historical fact of previously having a legendary president who built State from a tiny little farm school into a great university. While he may have tiny shoes in comparison to those of President John Vandenberg, there is no question much of his authority and prestige comes from the remarkable work that great man did over many years at State University of America. Colosso loves to invoke the name of President Vandenberg to enhance his own role as president. Again, one can see the great sociopath at work as he uses everything at his disposal to enhance his own prestige and really belittle everything around him. A dead legend is no threat to a living sociopath who can use him to his advantage. Castro did it with Che Guevara and Colosso does it with John. You will note only he can gain from the great turmoil that is coming about in this civil war he in effect has declared with his governing board. The students lose, the alumni lose, the faculty lose, the governing board loses, Tuffy and the athletic program lose but Colosso gains as the great representation of academia; and he gets more and more control of his powerful empire.

Terry: What would happen to Colosso without this crisis of his own making?

Judy: He would lose power if there were not this great turmoil. The new Board members were slowly but surely closing in on Colosso and were going to make him accountable to the Board. He knew this and believes destiny made this situation for him to be more powerful than ever. His being on the God Committee of College Presidents to look at collegiate athletics at this particular time could only cement this view of destiny choosing him for further greatness and glory. Colosso really needed a crisis to solidify his total power and he got it. The very crisis he created with your help gentlemen, leads to the situation where he is needed as the hero of the people to destroy you in the name of State University of America. Without the crisis, he is just another run of the mill university president with a great personality on the verge of being fired or finding another job.

Terry: No doubt about it. But what are we to do to slow him down and stop him? Sadly, you are right in that we did help create this mess.

Judy: There really are not any easy solutions to such a situation. I again say and you have to remember that Colosso has no sense of right or wrong as all of you do in this room. I have followed him for years and it is obvious he is a callous and very emotionally immature person with great prince like qualities. One solution would be to try to control his being able to travel about at will and in effect do whatever he wants to do. His world traveling is done somewhat out of boredom as well as a desire to be highly visible throughout the world and also to not have anybody close in on him back at State. Some very foolish, limited and naive board members, under his spell so to speak, do not even want to check out his itineraries and expense accounts. If there is any way to control his movement and make him personally manage the university, then he will probably move on to somewhere else. Unfortunately, this is something the Board might have done over a period of time rather than having picked this particular battle to fight; but then, we only have the present and future to deal with as the past is gone.

Terry: Colosso said he would leave the university if he were outvoted by the Board of Trustees on this matter. This was part of the reason why we carried through with the vote. It appeared we would be able to do the right thing for the university, keep Tuffy here and also have Colosso leave. We then would have been able to bring in a President who really would implement the goals of the governing board and who would do what was best for State University of America. The person would have pulled everyone together. The bastard lied and I am shocked and do not know what to do.

Judy: I could have guaranteed you that Colosso was not going to leave under the circumstances unless you had him publicly state this before the vote and had voted him out after the Coach/AD vote was taken. You will note he was able to totally control the media up to and now after the vote. He had no intention of leaving unless he was not able to manage the environment. Colosso has been able to control the media power forces in Big Town and the rest of the state. Most pathetically, he even has a really insignificant little boot licking worm, in the form of the sports editor of the University Town State Journal, doing what he desires to the total disgrace of the human race.

Terry: What should we do as the Board of Trustees?

Judy: I believe you need to call the Board back together and call Colosso in and tell him you expect him to defend the Board and to pull everyone together as a team. He will not do this and thus you will have every reason to fire him. Do it quickly and declare your own media war. Initially, he will kill you but you will win. You also must have a planned successor to immediately replace Colosso who will pull everyone together. Someone with credibility with the media is essential as well as with the various power forces affiliated with State and those that share your vision of its future.

Terry: I do not think we can do that at this time in that he is controlling the media and really the minds of university persons and the men and women on the street. I must admit that bastard Colosso is devastatingly effective.

Judy: That is true, but he is only able to do this through audacious and calculated action. Why not try a similar approach? It would appear if you were to try the same strategy that he has, you could undercut him and force him to expose himself as the egomaniacal, nonelected charismatic field commander media hog sociopath that he is and hopefully can force him out even without a vote. A powerful unified attack by you and your colleagues against the boob Board members to demand unity might at least make them flinch at the decisive moment of decision. To not do this is to invite total strategic defeat rather than only a major tactical defeat.

Terry: I am just not sure we can do that. It would appear the best thing to do is to let this situation simmer down and hopefully Colosso will try to work within the confines of his role with the Board.

Judy: With all respect to you Terry, it is rather clear you have no understanding of Colosso and his personality. We are dealing with a sociopath and not somebody who lives by the finer rules of a constitutional environment. He will try to win at all costs and reputations of good persons are irrelevant to him. He is State University of America in his confused thinking and he has magnificently been able to trumpet this outlook to the point that certainly the media and the majority of the citizens in this university and throughout the state believe it to be true. The man is a charismatic genius and media magician who has been able to master this situation in a way that probably no one else could within the country. The man is as remarkable as he is evil.

Tuffy: Are you not giving him a little too much credit?

Norma: Here you are questioning the person who is explaining to you what in effect has occurred. You have all been made humble; been made fools out of; are in a situation where everybody is damn mad at you; and here you are challenging somebody who is giving you good advice. You did the same damn thing with Guido. I may not be a psychologist or a historian, but it is rather clear that Colosso is a combination of sociopath as Judy has told you and "the great prince" as Guido has told you. I still think my idea of exposing him in his fancy panties and giving him a blistering in front of a huge television audience would be the best solution to humbling this bastard and exposing him for the fairy he is and getting him the hell out of here.

Judy: Norma, it appears that these guys, as tough as they are, are very concerned about living by the rules. They are just not able to see what a devious and tremendously effective and ruthless adversary they are dealing with at this time.

Tuffy: You gals are probably right, but we must try to live by the rules as best we can. I still do not believe two wrongs can make a right.

Fred: I am not quite sure what is going on here but I am aware Colosso has been able to take a relatively unimportant matter and really make all of us look horrible. I am really somewhat fearful to walk around this campus at this time with the level of hatred and anger that has been leveled against us for the one vote we took against Colosso. I, like Tuffy, would just like to kick his ass. I would go after him in the ways I learned how to fight many years ago in this very community when a Black had to fight for everything he got.

Judy: I am sure that is true, but your rules of the playground had a certain level of legitimacy to them and Colosso does not adhere to them at all. As I said before, Colosso obviously grew up in a way that he learned to effectively cheat, lie, charm, manipulate and use any other person or strategy to get him what he wanted. He learned long ago he could get much further ahead by charming rather than being a toughy. The problem with you and Tuffy is that you learned to resolve problems with your fists or by being just overall a tougher character than your adversaries. The rest of you learned how to resolve things through the use of bureaucracy or the law. Amazingly, it would appear Norma best understands Colosso and would really attack him at his most vulnerable point-his pride; that is his fatal flaw and weak point. However, giving him a blistering in his lacy panties would probably not be reasonable. If there is a way to undercut him at an authority and integrity level, then some success can be had. This particular vote makes this most difficult because Colosso turned it into the sports versus academics issue at a time that the whole nation is upset about collegiate athletics. He is able to splendidly present himself as light against darkness and the champion of academics against the evil sports empire headed up by Tuffy and his supporters. On top of that, he has the media trumpeting his view powerfully and this will probably occur for a long period. The enemies of Tuffy and the friends of Colosso are without leash and are foaming at the mouth and racing to destroy and kill their adversaries. The time really is bleak and would appear to be so for the future unless you take some decisive, swift and effective action immediately.

Tuffy: I am not ready to give up on this damn thing and I promise Colosso is in for a war if he thinks he can ruin me.

Judy: Good. That is the attitude you will need; but you must be as smart as you are strong. The Board also needs to be as decisive as was Truman with MacArthur; remember Colosso works for the Board and not vice versa.

Norma: *(With a laugh in her voice.)* As the saying goes, I wish I could buy that stupid bastard for what he is worth with a penny and then sell him for what he thinks he is worth. I could then give every person in the world two billion dollars, buy the universe and still have more wealth than all the gold on earth. What an asshole!

Judy: *(With a laugh in her voice.)* You are too much; but very smart and perceptive. I like that statement and will use it myself sometime.

Larry: I told Judy she would have been out of here by now and I suggest we let her go now. You have been very helpful. Tough old Tuffy might not admit it, but I know that is true.

Tuffy: *(In a jovial tone.)* Larry, speak for yourself. For myself and really for all of us, you have been helpful. Your insights are really very good. I admit to have been blinded by rage.

Terry: I thank you also and will try to see if I can implement some of your ideas. The timing seems bad for too dramatic of an action.

Judy: Well thank you fellows. Good luck! I am glad to not be a part of this battle. *(Looking intently at Terry.)* Terry, have more confidence in yourself; you and the Board only have the power if you have the will to use it.

Terry: Well.....

Larry: Again, thank you.

(Everyone stands and says goodbye as Judy leaves.)

Fred: Damn! As a man of action, I am so pissed about all this bullshit. In the private sector, even if screwed, you respect someone who beats you for a deal.

Norma: But Colosso is the manipulative bastard Judy and Guido described for you. You need to attack him front up and not have fear of him. He is only a God damn pile of shit as far as I am concerned.

Fred: You are right.

Norma: *(With a laugh.)* A red letter day; Fred admitted I was right.

Tuffy: *(With a jovial tone.)* As always Norma, you are right my dear.

Norma: What a husband! Even though you two are bullshitting, I love the words!

Tuffy: Well folks, things are tough. I am glad you all came today and I admit that Guido and Judy are very good. We all need perspective to keep our heads above water. Colosso is at war and the bastard is top gun for today; but in time we will knock that little fairy out of the air.

Norma: Tuffy, how corny.

Tuffy: Ha! Ha! You prefer bottom gun to top gun? Get it?

Norma: *(With exasperation.)* Oh God Tuffy!

Tuffy: I accept that name. Hey, a little lightness is good.

Norma: You fat shit; how would you know?

Tuffy: *(With a chuckle.)* You know what I mean. But one thing is for damn sure, we will try hard and give that sorry son of a bitch a good run for his money and kick his ass as best we can.

Everyone: We are with you on this.

Tuffy: Thank you for all coming here today. I especially thank Larry for bringing in Guido and Judy.

Larry: I was glad to do it. In reality, I thought we needed outside perspective to keep our passions under control.

Tuffy: I agree. I think we needed some other views today as we are all so God damn mad that we would probably have accomplished nothing. Let's keep in touch as needed. I will call our next meeting in the very near future. For now, let's see what happens today. For sure, Fred and Terry need to decide what the Board will do. I think tough within the law action is needed and I will be available for consultation. *(In a jovial tone.)* For sure, you will seek it and I will give it; but it is up to you guys to do what must be done to put Colosso in the freezer forever.

Terry: We will be in touch daily. Damn, this situation is tough and I still hope he will be a team player and do what is best for State.

Norma: You just do not get it at all yet.

Fred: I just want to get the bastard in my hands.

(Everyone gets up and leaves.)

End of Scene

Scene 5

(The scene takes place in the large study of Colosso in his university mansion. Colosso is sitting behind his magnificent desk and in comes his home manager, Mrs. Willingham. She speaks with a crisp English accent.)

Mrs. Willingham: President Assassino, Mr. Skip Goon is here to meet with you. He has such a frenzied look of appreciation on his face because you are allowing him to see you today; his feelings for you are true adulation. He has promised me he will not take too much of your time and thus tire you after such a difficult day as you must be having. He actually had tears in his eyes and a look of wild rage when he first came in and said some wonderfully appropriate if crude descriptive adjectives about Tuffy Norkas and what he has done to you. His puny childlike hand trembled and was in a pathetic fist as he waved it in the air throughout his talking to me. In the past, I have honestly thought of him as the most spineless, revolting, annoying and pathetic creature God ever created. However, his wise total support for you at least gives me one thing positive to see in something that is otherwise totally wretched and disgusting. Mr. Goon truly worships you and everything about you. Such abject loyalty is hard to find in this day and age, regardless of the person's station in life.

President: Very true, but that fellow really does have a last name that fits his personality. I really cannot stand him at all but his three articles today were superbly accurate. There really is no point in outwardly showing contentious disdain for someone's pathetically weak character and lack of insight in most areas when that person is helpful to you. If possible, I actually believe his character is even more pathetic than those of Trustees Bargler, Boylen and Wood. I will be nice to him as long as he continues to see things at State University in an accurate and fair manner. You can show him in Mrs. Willingham.

Mrs. Willingham: I believe Mr. Goon will always see you for what you are sir. *(Mrs. Willingham opens the door.)* Mr. Goon, you can come in and see the President. *(Mr. Goon enters and Mrs. Willingham leaves. He ignores her completely and rushes to shake the President's hand. The President has a most sincere and solemn look and manner about him. Skip's hair and clothes appear in total disarray. His eyes are red and he is in great emotional turmoil.)*

Mr. Goon: Mr. President, it is with heavy heart that I come to see you here today. What Tuffy, the bad Board members and Tuffy's clique of sports lovers have done to you ranks as one of the worst injustices in history and a horrible example of total disrespect for such a great person as yourself. I just feel horrible. I am ecstatic you have been willing to meet with me so I could express my views and unequivocally show my support for you. I know I represent the view of the vast majority of our students and citizens. Some students are even wearing black arm bands in support of you.

President: Skip, I appreciate your sensitivity to me and your decisive accuracy in analyzing the total situation. Such men of loyalty and intelligence are rare on this planet. My only goal at State has been to turn it into the greatest university of all time. Academics have been my focal point while Tuffy and the football clique have done everything they can to destroy me as a representative of everything that is good and positive about State University of America. Your brilliant and fair insights have been appreciated throughout this insipid war by those of us that have been fighting against these horrid sports lovers who want to destroy academics at State. Winning at any cost is their game and that is what I am fighting against. I feel much like the valiant Polish horse soldiers taking on the full might of the German Wehrmacht and Luftwaffe in 1939.

Mr. Goon: You are completely right Mr. President and I really appreciate your kind words about my insights. I really believe I am representing the only fair position that could be taken at this time. Is it even ethical to believe someone other than you can represent State University of America and its thousands of students, graduates, faculty and followers?

President: Skip, I really ask you to answer that question as I can only do what the people ask. I hear them telling me to stay, fight on and defend their honor in this horrid war to destroy State as their university.

Mr. Goon: Mr. President, I hope you noted this morning in my front page article that I did indicate you are State University of America and what you believe is what we believe.

President: Skip, I hope you will not drop the torch of truth and justice in this most critical moment in the history of State University of America. Torches burning brightly and carried by persons as yourself, who will not compromise the truth for better football tickets, is what this critical moment needs. We are on the verge of greatness; great deeds and words done decisively and without fear can carry the day. As your President, I feel it is safe to say we have been in the shadows of the University of America for a century and it is going to end. To this end and way beyond, I have tried to marshal all the positive forces against the dark forces which will destroy this university and what it stands for. Do you believe I am the person that can make State University of America the greatest academic institution on earth?

Mr. Goon: You represent everything that is good in this university, and yes, you can. We desperately need you. Please stay and fight. Your example will help education worldwide.

President: Skip, why do you believe this attack on my authority by these horrid psychopaths is occurring at this time?

Mr. Goon: The dark forces are out to destroy what you are doing and trying to end the swift ascent to greatness that State is on with your leadership. They want to meet their own needs through the glorification of sports. Winning at all costs is all that is important to Tuffy and the others. They know you are great and are hopelessly jealous of the great light of truth you represent. They want to destroy you so their flickering candles will look bright. It is their poor comparison with you that incites their rebellion. Pride must be destroyed in them or others will try the same thing in the future. Your greatness is blinding; however, those of us who recognize your obvious superiority can be part of your glory by simply joining and becoming a part of your team.

President: Skip, you have some excellent insights. What can I do, representing all of you, to turn the tide in this academic and moral crusade? My first thought was to quit; but then I knew that would not be the right thing to do. Not with all the people that love State and who so strongly want me to continue leadership for them to best realize their dreams. I could not let those countless thousands of people down as I represent their dreams for themselves and their children.

Mr. Goon: You must stay on and fight for what is right and appropriate for State. This horrid clique of sports lovers cannot destroy the academic ascent of this university. We need you and really have no other person that can take control and meet all of our desires and dreams at this time. I will do everything I can to present the truth that is presented by you.

President: Thank you Skip and I think that is really essential. You will note that Tuffy has one strong follower and he is on your staff.

Mr. Goon: That is true Mr. President; but I am putting a lot of pressure on him to make sure that his distorted views, as presented by Tuffy and his clique, do not easily come to the light of day in the newspaper.

President: That is very good Skip. While you and I believe in complete freedom of the press, it certainly would be wrong to allow Tuffy and his clique of academic destroyers to be allowed to just present lies that represent the worst form of yellow journalism that I have ever seen. Is that not true?

Mr. Goon: You are absolutely right Mr. President and I will continue to stress that there is no place for yellow journalism in the newspaper. There will definitely be a hard and arduous attempt on my part to make sure that only the truth is presented and any views that represent the forces of darkness in this matter will be closely scrutinized and there will be strong editorials against such lies and horrid views. I just pray I can do what you desire in an effective manner. Letting down my parents, my children and friends would be insignificant to my letting you down. You give me great purpose in life.

President: Skip, your work is so important to me. I want you to know I am with you in spirit and we are together doing such important work to make State University of America the best university it can be. We will continue communicating on this important matter and we will never give up. I need you and I know you will not let me down. *(The President stands, raises his arm and motions to Skip to come to him.)*

Mr. Goon: *(Skip stands up and with his body trembling with emotion, walks to hold the outstretched hands of Colosso. He speaks with total devotion and in a wavering voice.)* Mr. President, I am with you 100%; my life plan now has come into full bloom as I do as you demand.

President: Skip, I am most proud to have a man of your known character as a comrade during this most bleak hour of the war to save State against what may be called hopeless odds. Such loyalty is really impossible to find in this day and age.

Mr. Goon: I will always be absolutely loyal to you.

President: I would like you to leave by the back entrance just in case any members of Tuffy's clique are in front trying to show you are not the impartial and fair journalist that of course we know you are. Go in peace and may God guide your pen as you present fair and high minded views of State University consistent with my views; for as you know and have said, I am State University of America. Remember the biblical statement: To whom much is given, much is expected. You have been given great talent to see the truth; use it and fight those that live on lies and hypocrisy. Skip, greatness is waiting to anoint your noble spirit and pen.

Mr. Goon: *(With joy and tears.)* Thank you Mr. President. Thank you Mr. President. (With great emotion in his voice.) I will never let you down. Greatness had no meaning in a university until you came to State. God personally shed his grace on State when he sent you to us.

President: *(Skip is holding hands and looking awestruck into the eyes of the charismatic Colosso.)* Come to me and let us embrace.

(Colosso embraces him and Skip has joyous tears of emotion as they hug. Then Skip leaves sobbing emotionally and saying thank you Mr. President over and over again.)

Skip: Thank you Mr. President, etc.

President: *(A feeling of disgust comes over Colosso immediately after Skip leaves.)* That is the most repulsive of all God's creations. To see him is to question a God; to know him is to know there could not be a benevolent God. *(Colosso is looking at his jacket and taking things off it with his fingers and looking at them. He has a look of disgust on his face.)* Oh my, look at what Skip left on my jacket; it is a vile concoction of sweat, tears, snot from his nose and smelly greasy hairs. *(He then goes to his desk, opens his desk drawer and takes the bottle with nitroglycerin tablets in it and takes one. He then gets on the intercom and calls Mrs. Willingham.)*

President: Mrs. Willingham, come in now.

(Mrs. Willingham enters.)

Mrs. Willingham: Yes sir.

President: Are my three editor friends here yet?

Mrs. Willingham: They are in the sitting room.

President: Send them in immediately and let no one disturb me.

Mrs. Willingham: Yes sir.

President: I say it again: let no one disturb me!

Mrs. Willingham: Yes sir.

(Skip Goon has appropriately left through the back servants' quarters. At this moment, Colosso opens his door to the living room and is greeting the editor of the Middle Town Press and the editors of the major newspapers in Big Town: The Big Town Free Press and The Big Town News. He has dismissed the despicable Skip from his mind and now will use his great charisma to maintain the editors' friendship and total support for him. Colosso has no doubts about his charismatic sway over them. He considers them useful associates, even if of pedestrian intelligence.)

President: Bob, Joe, Chuck, good to see you gentlemen. Your superb support in the newspapers today for what I am trying to do at State is greatly appreciated. You give me hope for the future. I thought old Coe Currents particularly berated Tuffy in a most fair and blasting manner.

Bob: We are glad to see you Colosso and certainly this is a difficult day for you and a bleak day for this place. You are right about Coe but he cannot be trusted 100%. He and Tuffy are actually a lot alike and even grudgingly respect each other. But he is right on this one completely and above all, *(with a smile)* he works for me. The key thing is that you have been treated like a dog and we will not allow that.

Joe: That is really true but we believe justice is going to be served this time. We are at war with you and you can unleash us at your whim.

Chuck: No doubt about it Colosso; however, it is important you be willing to stick in there and stand up for what is right for this university.

President: Let there be no doubt to that; I am committed to defend the honor and future of State University of America.

Bob: On a lighter note, Colosso, I am sorry you were not able to be with the three of us when we were meeting with prestigious Board members and other prominent members of the alumni of The University of America last month. As a prominent graduate, you know you are always welcome and you were missed. We had a great talk and quite candidly had some real chuckling about the nonsense that goes on in this crazy place. We decided the greatest flaw at State is a delusion of adequacy when compared to The University of America. *(With scorn.)* Such stupidity really makes one hate this place.

President: Well, I am sorry I was not there. As you know, I rarely miss those meetings. It is an intellectual and social oasis away from all the backbiting and obstructive little persons that I must battle here at all times. However, you know I do care for this place and my goal is to shape it into the type of institution that I want and we deserve.

Joe: Colosso, you are loved by all people who care for this university and even more so by the citizens of this state that are demanding that this crazy sports clique get kicked out of any authority at State. You are the only alternative.

Chuck: Over and above all this nonsense, let us not forget that State has a major role in this state. In our area, State has given opportunity to many that might not have had the opportunity and we want that to continue. I am also sure that is true throughout the State.

Bob: In some ways, it really would have been better if State had not become a university and gotten into the same conference as The University of America. Its legitimate inferior complex in comparison with The University of America has led to the crazy things that are occurring at this time. The inferior quality of the students leads to a life long inferiority complex. Who in their right mind would come here if he or she could go to The University of America? A Chevette will never be a Ferrari and a Ferrari will never go to a Chevette school. The glory of the University of America and the total lack of such at State show there is some legitimate and purposeful order in this damn world.

Joe: This of course is somewhat true. Hopefully if Colosso can kick out all of the negative, destructive, paranoid and ineffective elements of the sports clique and the residual impact of the old Vanderburg infrastructure, then State can really become a great university and be worthy of being in the same state as The University of America. Colosso, the beauty is that you are a product of The University of America and will not waver in making this institution as great as it can be. If it can be fifty percent as great as the University of America, then you will have done your greatest achievement. We must admit it; having gone to The University of America just has an impact on people that allows them to distinguish themselves with great achievement.

President: My only goal is to help this school and turn it into a great institution. From what I am hearing today from the students and faculty on campus, phone calls, telegrams and the media as a whole, I am perceived at this moment as State University of America and the last chance to turn these renegade sports types on their damn rear ends. Honestly, I feel it is forth and seventy-five and I have no receivers and am alone on the football field against the top professional players in the world.

Bob: Nonsense, we are with you Colosso and there is no way you will lose this political game. We University of America graduates, as well as our supporters, must stick together to save State from itself. Too bad it is not just another branch campus governed by The University of America Board of Regents. Then reality would be given in a strong helpful dose that would set things right at this crazy place.

President: Well, this current board is made up of jock sniffing lovers of the sports clique and are not willing to see a new day and a greater future for State. I am in the horrible situation of being forced to do exactly what they want or I will be humiliated and my face pushed into a mountain of dung as long as I am here.

Chuck: Nonsense! Colosso, we are going to make sure this is not going to happen. If you thought the editorials and articles we put out today are strong, you just wait and see what we are going to do. We are at war and will bring your enemies to their knees because they are also our enemies. All the time we have spent together since you came here, lets us know the kind of man you are and that your vision for State is the valid one above all others. State is bigger than anyone, and of course, we know that.

Joe: That is true.

Chuck: Lost in all the words about this tragedy, I thought Harly Innocent of the Free Press pretty much said this. Joe, he is his own man and a wise one at that.

Joe: I agree, even though he too often sees too much on all sides of issues.

Chuck: Such men are often dangerous; but he is very much on point today; but for now, let us deal with the problems here today.

Joe: Often The Big Town News and The Big Town Free Press are at odds; but we are not at odds at all here and our goal is to destroy Tuffy and the clique that are out to destroy you and the future potential of State University. With Chuck and all the other editors in agreement, a media blitz is in place and moving forward to destroy Tuffy and his cronies. I am sad and very angry it has come to this.

President: *(With great sincerity.)* I am just overwhelmed with your commitment and really do believe you are the last line of defense to allow me to manage this crazy place and hopefully bring it into a potential period of greatness. I am not really saying I can turn it into anything like The University of America, but I can try to turn it into the greatest university that is possible for a peasant based land grant type place like State. While I may not fully agree with Bob's analogy to Chevettes and Ferraris, there is a great deal of truth in it. Staying with the analogy, my goal is to produce the best Chevettes possible.

Bob: In agreement with Joe and as I have said many times before to you gentlemen, I still think it would have been a better idea if we had turned State into another campus of The University of America. Then it could have been controlled by the Board at The University of America and none of this nonsense would be occurring. It would know its place; a distant second at best.

President: I am not sure our goal is to have State lose its identity and fall completely under the sway of mighty University of America. It would appear our goal is to have it be whatever it can be within the really more limited academic and service role of a land grant university.

Bob: That is probably a good way to put it. I quite candidly have hated this place for so many years and it was not until you came here that I could even have any respect for it. I have always felt this state really only needs one major university and a lot of other lessor ones. At another comparison level for you fellows, State is clearly a lessor university and at most would be a small and outdated destroyer with The University of America being a magnificent modern battleship aircraft carrier. Maybe this stupid attempt to destroy your authority and put the jocks in control will set up an environment whereby we can really put you completely in control and lead to State taking its legitimate second or third place in the state.

Chuck: I am not sure that State does not have a vital role in the agricultural and generally applied areas, but I do agree it does need to be put in its place at this time. We have a lot of people from the middle and western part of the state that love this place and let us not forget the great President Vanderburg came from our region.

Bob: What he did is really old news and he did that in a time when this was really a Moo U type school. He and his successors have tried to turn this into a University of America and have really tried to do it through the sports empire. They need to accept a subordinate role and just work within those limits. Poor State has the misfortune to be in a state that has

The University of America; which is a paragon of integrity and glory in both academics and sports on a world class level.

President: Gentlemen, let us try to get on point on this bleak day and help State move forward into its rightful academic and agricultural role. There is potential greatness here and I will really try to have it occur; however, I desperately need your help at this vital hour of decision.

All three persons: Colosso, you have it!

Bob: We are going to bring Tuffy and his cronies down to their knees with a big crash. Colosso, I think it is really time to say again you really are the right type of an academic task master to put this place in order; you can make sure the second class citizens of this state at least can get a good education within their limits. To see so many of them masquerading as academic types under the flag of their sports empire is humorous and disgraceful. Colosso, we really need you to stay and do what can be done for this place. Being a University of America man, you bring greatness to this gin joint. Why you would waste your time here is a tribute to you; however, foolish seems to describe what you do rather than wise.

Joe: Overstated Bob, but generally accurate. Colosso, I want to add a few words to all of this: it is really essential you not leave. I do believe State really has an important role in this state and that you are the only one that can really fully develop it.

Chuck: I actually think State is a fine institution and really has a very important role irrespective of The University of America. My concern is really the way Colosso has been blasted to smithereens by the sports empire. This has been going on for a while with the newer Board members really out to destroy Colosso and do anything they can to help the sports clique. I for one am not all that concerned about whether Tuffy is the athletic director as well as the coach. To me, the issue is who runs this place; and to me, Colosso is the one person who can really bring this place as far as it can go. Certainly it is not a University of America, but the potential is here for this to be a tremendous school in its own smaller way. But again, this school is bigger than any one person; and there are no exceptions.

Bob: I enjoy you Chuck but I think you have too high of an estimation of this joint. I also choose not to deal with the implications of your last statement.

Chuck: *(Sarcastically.)* I think I am far enough away from The University of America that I do not let its glorious shadow completely dominate my thinking and what I think of anything else; be it positive or negative. I also note you chose to ignore the ethical implications of the charge that The University of America made a prearranged deal with a high school coach to hire him if he brought in certain players.

President: Gentlemen, let us be here to break bread and come up with a common plan to save this university in a really critical hour of its existence. In spite of its many flaws, I love State and really think our goal is to make it as great as it can be. I am overwhelmed with the feeling of psychological devastation in my heart for the way I and my dreams for State have been crushed by Tuffy and his cronies. I just want you dear friends to do what you think is right and not just what I believe ought to be done.

Joe: You know we are 100% with you Colosso and we are not going to let you down.

Bob: We are going to blast these suckers out of the water. You are going to be back in control where you belong.

Chuck: I fully support you Colosso and we want to make sure you are put back into control and do what is best for State. However, I want you to know this school has a tremendous responsibility to be as great as it can be and it really has had a lot of greatness, regardless to which institution it is compared. I am a practical man and the support I am giving today is based on what I believe is best for State. There is no one without some level of blame in this matter; but clearly Tuffy and his clique are the worst.

Bob: There you go again. You seem somewhat confused and you must be related to old Vandenberg. You always defend his memory and his strange archaic visions like the stubborn old Dutchman you are. He is yesterday's news!

Chuck: Your inability to acknowledge Vandenberg's greatness is not a credit to your character. My commitment to State is a credit to me and I stand by it.

President: Again gentlemen, we are here to save State and if you believe giving me your total support is what is needed to do that, then I appreciate it and will not let you down.

Bob: Do not take us too seriously; we love to raise hell with each other.

Chuck: Our banter does not negate our unflinching support for you.

All three persons: We're with you 100%.

Bob: We will daily be putting in articles and editorials blasting your enemies and praising you.

Chuck & Joe: No doubt!

President: Let us have a toast on this with brandy I know we will enjoy from the time of Napoleon himself.

(Colosso fills the glasses himself. They lift their glasses, hit them and Colosso gives the toast.)

President: Gentlemen, we are here together as supporters of a free and vigorous press that believes State University of America deserves to be the greatest institution it can be. You have supported me as the person who can do this, if not controlled by sports empire thugs supporting the football coach; and yes, now the athletic director. Let us toast that united as one together, we can work to crush all the horrible opposition against the truth and light we represent; and that success will come to us in our important endeavor to make State University of America be as great as it can be. Salute!

(They again hit glasses and now drink their toast.)

Bob: Colosso, you do have a way with words. They translate to strong feelings. *(Looking at his watch.)* Well, I am going to have to be getting back to Big Town.

Chuck: I guess I have to go also; and I am sure Colosso has many things he is working on at this particularly difficult time for him.

Joe: I must be off also.

Bob: By the way Colosso, was that loathsome jerk Skip Goon over here today? When the three of us were walking in, someone passed by honking his horn and furiously waving his hands. He looked like a vibrating dildo in an asshole coming up for air.

Bob, Chuck, Joe and President: Ha! Ha! Ha! Ha! Ha! Ha!

President: Yes he was.

Bob: He looked like the pitiful clown he definitely is. How could a mother love him? He really is the world's prototypic asshole. Why would God waste time creating him?

Chuck: *(With a chuckle.)* Obviously an off day.

Bob, Chuck, Joe and President: Ha Ha! Ha Ha! Ha Ha!

Chuck: He really is a jerk.

President: Yes he is.

Joe: His name totally fits him; he really is a goon.

President: Gentlemen, while it is hard to argue with you about him, he has certainly been trying to be helpful in this tragic situation; and as dull witted, pathetic and bizarre as he is, at least he has gained a little stature in my mind by being able to see the truth in this matter and fight hard to present it accurately.

Bob: Only you could find something positive in him.

Chuck & Joe: Amen.

(Bob, Chuck and Joe leave in a festive manner with Colosso in an affable and collegial mood.)

End of Scene

Scene 6

(The scene takes place in the spacious office of Tuffy Norkas. Twelve months have passed since the Board vote that made him both Football Coach and Athletic Director. The media continues to blast away on an almost daily basis against him while Colosso is presented as the great hero who has been greatly damaged by Tuffy and his supporters. Overwhelming pressure is being put on Tuffy to step down from one of the two jobs and the public is greatly aroused and demonstrations are a regular occurrence at State. Little mention is made that Tuffy has effectively handled both jobs. Colosso has quietly hired a public relations firm to handle his war against Tuffy and the board members on his governing board that voted against him. The campaign has been fabulously successful. The divided and wounded Board is impotent against Colosso; and his campaign against the individual Board members who voted against him leaves them incapable of any action in their defense; let alone Trumanesque action against their employee: President Colosso Michelangelo Assassino. Tuffy is looking through various newspaper accounts of the week which show the litany like support for Colosso in the editorial and feature writers sections in the Big Town newspapers and generally throughout the state. He appears very intense and even bewildered by it all; he also knows something must happen to change the current equation. Tuffy's secretary enters.)

Harriet: Emilio is here to see you.

Tuffy: Now again, tell me who he is and why he is here to see me.

Harriet: He is the chief custodian for Colosso in both his offices in the university and in the university mansion.

Tuffy: Do you know why he is here to see me? He must have a reason. This meeting was set up some months ago.

Harriet: I have no idea but he said it is very important and he appears very intense.

Tuffy: Well, send him in. This fellow may be helpful.

(Harriet opens the door to call Emilio.)

Harriet: Emilio, Mr. Norkas can see you at this time.

(Emilio passes by Harriet and comes face to face with Tuffy and shakes his hand very firmly.)

Emilio: Mr. Norkas, I am very glad to meet you. I know you are a very busy man at this particularly difficult time.

Tuffy: Call me Tuffy, Emilio, and lets not worry about how tough things are for me. Please sit down. *(Emilio sits down.)* What can I do for you?

Emilio: I am not sure if you know what work I do but it has put me in a situation where I have information that can be helpful to you.

Tuffy: I do know what you do Emilio and I am still not quite sure why you would be coming to see me. *(With sarcasm.)* Would not mighty and holy Colosso be angry at you if he knew you dared come and talk to me?

Emilio: I could care less what that depraved monster thinks and it is actually because of him that I am here. What he has done to you in the past year since you have been coach and athletic director greatly angers me.

Tuffy: Be more specific Emilio and tell me what you want. *(With a jovial tone.)* I think I like you.

Emilio: I want us to talk with total candor and I would ask that you be willing to finish listening to what I have to say.

Tuffy: I think that is fair. Now go ahead and tell me what you want.

Emilio: I would like to begin by just making a statement that I have total revulsion for Colosso and see him as the real personification of evil in this university. He lies and projects himself into something sanctimonious in a high minded hypocritical way that is really disgusting. It also disturbs one's heart and stomach simultaneously.

Tuffy: *(With a chuckle.)* Emilio, tell me something new and what I do not know. You can certainly suspect I would not disagree with that characterization of Colosso. Again, I ask you what do you want or maybe even more, what do you have that you think could be helpful to me at this time?

Emilio: Normally, a man's private life is his business. The problem with Colosso is that he has been making tremendously negative statements and outright lies about you personally and about many publicly elected officials that just happen not to agree with him. I find that disgusting and reprehensible. As a result, I believe using information about him personally that would be very unacceptable to many people could be an appropriate method to fight this abomination of the human spirit. It would be called fighting fire with fire.

Tuffy: I am not sure I will like the information you have; but Emilio I actually like you. Certainly a fool you are not. However, I guess I am really curious what you have to share and let us get on with it. As an aside Emilio, you do not seem to be a run of the mill custodian. You appear to have rather remarkable verbal skills, personality analysis and even the experience of a man that has been through a lot. I say this as one who has been often attacked, and I believe underestimated, due to not having polish and top notch verbal skills.

Emilio: You are very kind; however, my background is not really important. What is important is that Colosso be exposed for the horrid creature he is and that you have the opportunity to be treated fairly and to continue in an area that you have already shown solid success in the past year. The dual appointment was obtained legally and after a good democratic debate. I hope I can help to expose him, help you and have justice win out.

Tuffy: Obviously the information you have to share with me is difficult for you to talk about. I am assuming the package you have clutched in your hands has something to do with this. Emilio, come out with it and just let me know what you have. *(Said with great vigor and sarcasm.)* You know I cannot stand the bastard and my wife would love to beat his frilly panty clad ass on national television in front of our sold out stadium for a football game. So, come on, let it out.

Emilio: Your wife's desires open up the discussion of what I have to share. I have been taping Colosso for a period of time on his phone. Additionally, I have been able to take some pictures of him that show him with various men in compromising gay sexual situations. The phone conversations are taken from longer tape recordings that directly relate to his amorous relationships with various men. Here, why not take a look at these.

(Tuffy opens that packet and begins looking at the pictures and at the tapes with the titles and persons involved.)

Tuffy: This is funny Emilio, but I am not really quite sure what I can do with this particular information. His pathetic body is as I would imagine it. How feminine and delicate like I have thought he is, is only proven with these nude photos. It would seem a man would have to be pretty desperate to be with this glob of putrid vomit. Emilio, I am not really interested in his sexual preferences and am not really quite sure what really can be done with this. In fact, I am not comfortable doing anything with this information. Particularly, in that a few of these men are friends of mine and have done great service for State University over the years.

Emilio: I was afraid this might happen but felt an obligation to try to do something to undermine this depraved moral monster. It seemed that even if you did not use this information, you could use it as a wedge to have him back off and at least function as a moral ethical person out of self interest.

Tuffy: As I have said to you, I hate the bastard and would love to do anything I could to undermine him. However, quite frankly, I am not willing to do something of this type. I might add, he would never be moral and would self-destruct if exposed. But I cannot do it here. I would lower myself to his level and I refuse to do that. There are times a man must risk defeat with dignity rather than have certain victory won by unethical means.

Emilio: You know he would do it to you if he could Tuffy.

Tuffy: You are right, but that is the difference between him and me. Once I would determine to use information the same way he would, then I would become as lowly and insignificant as is Colosso. I really do not want to do that. If I cannot beat him fair and square, then I am going to go on to the pros and pray a lot for State.

Emilio: But you do not want to leave State.

Tuffy: I do not want to leave State at all. I love this place and I really want to carry on the tradition of my mentors when I was here as a player and my first years as a coach. Remember, I met my wife here, my children were born here and some of the greatest years of my life were spent here. I am not going to do anything that will discredit friends and this university.

Emilio: Tuffy, do you believe that at critical times a person must do things of questionable character with the idea of destroying a far greater evil?

Tuffy: I do believe that, but I am not quite sure I am at all comfortable dealing with one's sexuality to do it. If he were defrauding the university of money in a way that could be challenged, then I would feel a lot more comfortable. If he were screwing some employees in an unethical fashion, then I would feel comfortable with that. But going after him just because he is gay is just not something I am comfortable with.

Emilio: *(With great sadness.)* Windows of opportunity to bring about great positive change come rarely and we must be prepared for audacious action; such a window is now open but will rapidly close. I was afraid this might happen and I feel very bad. I have for a second time failed to stop a prince despot from chewing up the flesh and souls of people around me that are good and deserve better.

Tuffy: *(With humor in his voice to lighten the situation.)* Settle down, you are sounding like an Italian history professor I know. Emilio, we all must try to do our duty the best we can. You have brought information to me with the idea that it might be helpful to me. It is helpful for me to know that somebody as close to Colosso as yourself supports me and shares my view of this university. Do not be so tough on yourself and just do your job and things will work out. I am a tough guy and this university can withstand the greatest of attacks on it by people like Colosso. That bastard will eventually pass like a damn gallstone. If I believed this institution needed just me, then I would approach it differently and would probably not even be comfortable in such a place. I am a tough son of a bitch and know how to defend myself. I learned that in Big Town and I certainly learned it more so over the years. I hurt and my family hurts from what Colosso is doing with his dirty underhanded tactics; but we will survive and I will do it without resorting to the type of tactics he uses. Eventually everyone will see him to be as full of shit as a summer day is long.

Emilio: I feel horrible and am afraid I have again failed in another major crisis in my life. I really want to destroy this horrid bastard before he destroys you and other people that I know are really trying to do what is best for State.

Tuffy: You have done a good job and you have to let it go. Now I have to go and I suggest you take it easy. You really ought to leave these materials and not pass them on.

Emilio: From the vantage point of your life history, you are probably right. Thank you for your time Tuffy. *(Emilio stands up to leave.)*

Tuffy: *(Tuffy gets up and walks over to Emilio. With his hand on his shoulder, he is looking into his eyes and speaking with sincere feeling.)* You are a good and loyal man and I appreciate you. I can see much good in you. At a loyalty level, we actually are a lot alike. Do not worry, everything will work out regardless of how things look now. Do not give up on yourself and in what you believe. Integrity is something you have; but take my word for it, using these types of materials against Colosso to destroy him would end up destroying you and me as persons of integrity. It would not be worth it.

(Tuffy gives Emilio a big hug and then looks at him and begins to speak once more.)

Tuffy: Emilio, please realize I appreciate what you have tried to do and I really understand your intentions. To have done this certainly shows you to be a brave and resourceful person. Remember, and I know this more than most, trying is more important than not having tried. You tried and gave it your best. In life, that is the most you can ask of yourself; be proud of what you stand for and what you are trying to do for State. Whatever you failed at in the past, your attempt here makes up for it. Life is upward and not backward. One makes up for failures in the past by learning from them and doing one's best to be successful in the present and future. Your commitment to State as well as seeking fairness for me will give me strength in this God damn battle with asshole Colosso. You can count on that.

Emilio: *(Looking down, he begins to speak with a solemn tone.)* Tuffy, I have failed in the past and feel I have failed again. I will try to see this for what you say it is; but I do not believe I really can. I always believed a man controlled his own fate. Now I am not sure; but I will not give up this thought easily. Will you please at least listen to the tapes and maybe there are things in them that may be helpful to you.

Tuffy: I will keep them, review them and do not worry. My advice to you is to do your best and really leave this alone and things will ultimately work out. As I said, this university is a lot bigger than old butthead Colosso, me or any other person or group of persons. I am sure our paths will cross again during happier days.

(Emilio walks out and Tuffy's wife Norma immediately walks in.)

Norma: Tuffy, what the hell is going on in here? You look like hell and he looks worse.

Tuffy: This man has tried to be helpful and I just feel bad for him that I cannot use his information and use the same type of tactics as Colosso would under the same circumstances.

Norma: What in God's green earth are you talking about?

Tuffy: Look at those pictures on my desk.

Norma: *(She goes to his desk and opens the package. She has a big laugh as she looks through them.)* Ha, I told you that son of a bitch is a fairy! I never knew he was a transvestite too. Ha Ha, he kind of looks pretty in this one. *(Laughing.)* He looks particularly pretty in this one in his see through panties, bra and heels; what an asshole, even if a pretty one.

Tuffy: Come on Norma, that shit is really not appropriate. We need to kick this bastard's ass but not with this kind of bullcrap.

Norma: I still think you play fair too much and I am really worried about you honey. You will lose a vote if Colosso calls it. It does not look good. Colosso is overwhelming us in the media and his aims are clear. His goal to vote you out of the dual role is nearly in place and even your friends on the Board are shell shocked.

Tuffy: I hurt and I feel bad about this. I particularly hurt deep inside for what you have to put up with, with me presented as Attila the Hun and asshole Colosso as a combination of Jesus Christ and Superman.

Norma: We are one and quit worrying about me you fat shit. We have had great years together and they will be back. In fact, we will look back on this time as a period of great victory for you and a time we grew closer together. If I wanted a dull life, I could have married a professor and heard history all night. With you, we make history all the damn time. Loosen up and let us get loose tonight.

Tuffy: Hey, you are the greatest; however, I am obviously not winning at this particular time. I have just got to fight and do things the best I can. My feeling has always been that if you do your best job and do not complain, then ultimately good things are going to happen. I am not sure of that now.

Norma: I wish that were true Tuffy, but it certainly is not happening in this case. I just want you to know that whatever you decide to do, I am with you. I will stay here or go anywhere with you if you decide you want to go back into pro football. Certainly, I will have a hell of a lot more money to spend and less bullshit in my house. But as I said, we are one regardless of what cards are dealt to us. The words I promised to God, to you and that wild old priest about forever were said with meaning! (They embrace and kiss with passion.)

Tuffy: You know I love this place. I cannot let down the memory of the guys from here that helped me be what I am today. I would feel like a failure and a terrible person by letting them down, even though they are now all dead. I am not sure why I love this place now when hate would be more reasonable for the lack of loyalty and commitment to me. It happened to Rucky, the most lovable coach that ever coached here and I guess I should not be surprised at what is happening to gruff and rough old me. I am hurt and pissed; but I love this place in spite of those who would destroy me and the memory of those who came before me; they also loved State not for themselves but for what it can do for those seeking only the opportunity to succeed.

Norma: Tuffy, you have to be practical and not be an idealist ready to lose his head and ass simultaneously. As you said, they tried to destroy Rucky and sure as hell will do it to you if they can. We may hate The University of America, but loyalty and unity are why it is great and we look like a bunch of God damn cannibals eating ourselves in a God damn eating frenzy. Maybe saying the hell with these stupid sheep and fools is what you need to do. Colosso is a son of a bitch and he has the media on his side. He also has such an incredible speaking ability and personal presence that I think he will really be tough to beat. The people wanted Castro, Stalin and Hitler and look what happened to them. Let them have Colosso if they want; he will fuck them over the same way. As I said, I will support you in whatever you decide to do.

Tuffy: I do not give a God damn what he is or what the odds are. I am committed to State and have never run away from a pansy or bully in the past and am going to play this one out. To hell with them all, I will do what is right!

Norma: Hey, I am with you coach!

(They again hug and kiss as the scene ends.)

End of Scene

90

Scene 7

(Emilio has returned from his meeting with Tuffy to the President's Mansion. He is feeling dejected and is sitting at the desk of Colosso and is rummaging through his desk drawers. He takes out a pill bottle and puts something into it. He knows no one is in the mansion at this time except for him and Colosso. Colosso opens the door to his study and meeting room and finds Emilio sitting at his desk. He is very angry at seeing him sitting at his desk.)

President: How impudent! What are you doing at my desk Emilio?

Emilio: *(With a smirk on his face.)* Are you blind? Can you not see I am sitting here and looking through your drawers?

President: Get out of there at this moment and get out! You are fired!

Emilio: *(With a smile in his face.)* Oh, you really think you can do that, huh? *(With a laugh.)* Que cabrón tu eres[1]!

President: *(With righteous anger.)* Damn right! No disrespectful spic is going to try to run this place. You will do what I want and that is to get out of here immediately. You are fired! Do not snivel and beg me to change my mind; my mind is made up and I never reverse myself. Do not put my name or my university as references in that there will be nothing said about you but bad. Now get out of here immediately! *(He snaps his finger at the end of the statement.)*

Emilio: *(With a chuckle in his voice.)* Oh poor Colosso, you really are an insignificant little worm. Maybe I ought to rearrange that pretty little feminine face of yours; but then maybe you might look manly. Neither you nor I would like that falsifying of reality, would we? Que maricón tu eres[2]!

---

[1] Que cabrón tu eres! What a bastard you are!   [2] Que maricón tu eres! What a queer (homosexual) you are!

President: *(With a startled look and sound in his voice.)* Get out and I mean at this time. I do not know what has gotten into you, but no drunk spic will be allowed to terrorize the President of State University of America! Is that clear?

Emilio: *(He walks up to Colosso and grabs him by the shirt.)* Colosso, only you and I are here at this time and I have had it with your pretty little face and your disgusting ways. This is the end of your bullshit, right now! I am intoxicated, but with the elixir of justice avenging duplicity hypocrisy.

President: *(With a look of fear on his face.)* What do you mean? Get out of here and I mean now.

Emilio: *(Slapping him on the face and pulling his face close to his and talking with a snarl.)* You do not get it, do you Colosso? You have had it and I am going to be the one to end it all and let everybody see you for what you are. I want to see great fear in your little faggot face.

President: *(With a wavering, whinny and crying voice.)* Emilio, I do not know what has happened here but let me go and I am sure we can talk about this and work it out. *(Trying to sound presidential.)* A great man reviews decisions; therefore we can discuss why you are behaving the way you are today; my mind is not closed to fair and civilized discussion.

Emilio: You still do not get it. I am not begging you for a job. I am your judge and jury today and I have made a decision.

President: We must talk Emilio.

Emilio: There is nothing to talk about. I have you right where I want you and am going to make sure you are presented for what you are. You are trying to destroy this university and a lot of good people over a stupid sporting situation that has nothing to do with sports trying to take over State University of America. You are a scoundrel and you are trying to run everything. The bad thing is not so much you want power but that you are willing to destroy the reputations of good people and this great university to get it. Effectively making yourself glorious and Godlike is just too much for me and my life history to accept.

President: That is not true. I have not done that at all. My goals are to make State University the greatest university in the world.

Emilio: *(Slapping Colosso again and pulling him again closer to his face and speaking through his teeth.)* That bullshit is for other people Colosso, not for me. I know what you are doing and you know what you

92

are doing. At least in these last moments, I suggest you try to be honest with me as well as yourself and let all the bullshit go.

President: *(With great fear in his voice.)* What do you mean in these last moments?

Emilio: Just what I said. Now, I want you to talk to me about what you are doing here at State right now. Really let it out what a scoundrel you are. I want to hear you say what you are; it will actually be good for your soul; as tiny, horrid, ghastly and sick as it is.

President: I do not know what you mean; please let me go.

Emilio: *(Grabbing him around the neck and pushing him against the desk.)* You know what I mean and I cannot wait to hear you say it. I am ready to reconstruct your whole prissy body in a way that it will be better than what it is now; but it will not work well in its broken state. Que pedazo de mierda tu eres[3]!

President: I want this to end; just tell me what to say. Whatever wrong you believe I have done, I will admit to it.

Emilio: Oh please Colosso, you know what I am talking about. You have made this irrelevant AD/Coach issue into something titanic and evil. You are now out for total power for you and to destroy this university, Tuffy and a lot of good people. You are not worthy to lick their boots clean after they have walked in a field of shit.

President: Okay, that is what I am doing; whatever you say and I mean it.

Emilio: Cut the patronizing mierda. I am really not in the mood for you to just say what I want. I want you to mean it! I want the truth; anything less will be horrid for you. Do not learn what I mean by this; it would bring terror to the core of the bravest of men.

President: *(With anguish in his voice.)* Then I just do not know what to do. Please let us talk and let me go.

Emilio: *(Pulling a gun from his pocket and putting it to Colosso's head.)* I think Colosso, that with this gun at your head that you might begin thinking a little more clearly.

President: *(Tears in his eyes and speaking in a very childish type half crying voice.)* Emilio, please let me go. I will do or say whatever you want. Please just let me go.

---

[3] Que pedazo de mierda tu eres! What a piece of shit you are!

Emilio: You know what I want to hear and begin talking. Let us begin with your having a public relations firm help you destroy your governing board.

President: I did that because they would not do what I knew was best for the university. It was important...

Emilio: *(Klug, Emilio hits Colosso slightly on his head with the butt end of the gun. More for shock value than pain. He then cuffs him a few times with the side of his hand.)* I told you to talk to me not about justifying your doing wrong but to really let out what you have in fact been doing. Your job is not to destroy a democratically elected board of good persons that love this university; even if they are not always very bright and never united. What is your job?

President: *(With fear in his eyes and a trembling voice.)* My job is to do what the Board tells me to do and not try to destroy the university.

Emilio: Do you have a responsibility to make them look good, educate them and bring them together on issues?

President: Yes, Yes. Of course I do.

Emilio: I am not sure you believe it, but I want you to say it. Progress in contrition starts with words and ends with actions. In your case, I am afraid it is really too late; even the hope of approximations of the beginning levels of human decency deserted your potential long ago; if ever it were possible.

President: Please do not do anything to me. I will change and just want this to end. Please end it not for me but for a misguided human being that now wants to make right what he has done wrong.

Emilio: You are such a scoundrel; such a despicable piece of mierda. You really have no intentions of changing at all. You now appeal to me as a human being knowing that I know you for what you are. Your only goal is to have me stop this and nothing more. You want me to let you go and then you will bring in the police. What a fool you are; how you misjudge my intelligence and your obvious stupidity.

President: That is not true; just let me go. I will do whatever you want. I will obey you completely.

Emilio: I am enjoying watching you squirm as you clearly depict the pathetic scoundrel you are. You do not even have the dignity to defend what you believe. At least, Castro is a man that would die for his principles. You would do anything you could right now just to save your life and not to get hurt. Que pocos huevos tienes tu[4]!

President: Yes, yes, just let me go and I will do whatever you want. I can promise you that that is true with total certainty.

Emilio: Colosso, I have been up against death many times and have never had fear of it. It is the natural consequence of life and it fascinates me how people like you have such a fear of it. Que cobarde[5]! To struggle and make positive impact is what one must try to do with his destiny. Destiny can be controlled by audacious, well planned and timely action. I previously failed at a critical point of my life but I will not now. You are going to feel what it is like to be defeated and lose all of your dignity. For you it can be a gift if you learn from it.

President: *(With less fear in his trembling voice.)* Then you are not going to kill me?

Emilio: I never said that. I am simply stating I will not fail again in a critical moment. I am not going to allow you to go out and destroy this university, Tuffy and the elected board members that see you for the creature from hell that you are. There are times in a man's life when he must make an irrevocable decision that will forever change him for better or for worse. In such a situation some years ago, I failed and my life has been hell. Rarely does a man receive a second opportunity. This is my time to redeem where I have failed in the past. It will be done at your expense. *(With kind of a jovial tone in his voice.)* Colosso, I actually owe you a favor. I would have probably just lived and died trying to forget what I have done in the past. It would have been a lifetime at the oars in Ben Hur's boat. Instead of that, I now have an opportunity to make up for what I have done by destroying you and letting people know what an abominable creature you are. I will not fail this time; I promise you that on my mother's grave.

President: Emilio, please listen and I know we can....

(Colosso is again hit by Emilio and thrown on the ground. He lies whimpering and cowering on the ground.)

Emilio: You still do not get it. You have no power at this time at all. Your life is in my not so very gentle hands and I am going to make sure it is destroyed. Now just stay there and think about how your life is different because of what is happening today. You no longer have control over

---

[4] Que pocos huevos tienes tu! You have no courage (or balls)!
[5] Que cobarde! What a coward!

things. I am in control. With one squeeze of my finger I can kill you and end it all. With many slowly paced squeezes, I can put you in excruciating misery long before I have you pray and beg for el tiro de gracia[6]. Give me a reason why I should not kill you at this moment?

President: Because I promise I will immediately tell the truth and end this horrible thing that has occurred. Oh God Emilio, have mercy on me!

Emilio: There will be the type of mercy you show those who disagree with you when you have power: none! Now, what would you admit and how would you do it?

President: I would admit the AD/Coach issue is as irrelevant as you say. I would admit it is about power. I will admit I chose the issue to destroy my enemies and make me overwhelmingly powerful at State. I will admit how I cynically move the people to get what I want. I will admit how I will destroy anyone or anything that gets in my way. I will go public with this information if you only let me live.

Emilio: Very good; very good indeed! But why would I believe you would do that when you have never done anything of this type in the past? Am I ready to believe you would do such a thing?

President: Oh, I promise. I will definitely go forward and tell the truth. I would not lie about something like this. Please give me an opportunity. Let your compassion stand out in stark comparison with my self-serving behaviors. I will not fail you.

Emilio: Tell me again what you have been doing wrong here at State? My patience is wearing thin and I need to be convinced you are telling the truth.

President: *(With tears and the appearance of contrition.)* I have definitely been trying to destroy this university. You know that and I know that. It has been done to my gain and I understand that also. I have done what would give me power and destroy anyone or anything that stands in my way. I have been out to divide and destroy a constitutionally governing board of trustees and destroy the reputation of them as well as any sports persons and followers of those persons that disagree with me. I will say this, then quit and leave this university.

Emilio: Ha! Ha! Ha! Colosso, you are really good. You and I know what you are saying is very true; but we both know you have no intention of

---

[6] El tiro de gracia. The bullet shot through the head to guarantee death after the person has been shot at the firing wall!

giving up power. That is the furthest thing from your mind at this time. It is maybe not surprising that a man of words tries to come back to words when he is in tremendous crisis. Here I am, the janitor and I have life or death rights over you at this time. It is hard to not want to kill you slowly, taking into account the despicable and disgusting piece of mierda that you are. I had hoped you would try to fight back or try to continue defending your absurd positions; but in the end, you are just a lying scoundrel. The world would really be a much nicer place if you were not in it; and I am in a situation where I can make the world better. Now, Colosso, you know I do not believe you will just go forward and say everything you have been doing is wrong and then just leave the university. I know that and you really know that. Tell me what I can do short of killing you today to have you do what is the right thing to do? I also have the possibility of hurting you or shooting you to the point you are not able to function in your role either as President or sissy lover. You know I could do that easily and maybe that is the best idea. What do you have to say Colosso?

President: I may be all of the things you say I am, but I do want to live and do not want to be hurt. I promise if you let me go, I will make personality changes. I am the kind of man that learns from his mistakes; you can have confidence in that.

Emilio: Oh Colosso, you are incredible. Here you are again using words and trying to sort out my mentality. You know I see you as a pathetic and weak scoundrel: Un pajaro sin huevos[7]. Sadly, you do not know I respect somebody who is strong and will stand up for himself. I think it is time

---

[7] Un pajaro sin huevos! A queer (homosexual) with no courage (or balls)!

we stopped all the play acting and playing with words. It has actually been for my amusement to see a scoundrel such as you humiliated in front of me down to the pathetic snake level that you are. I know you have no intention of changing and that you really cannot change. You have really no sense of right or wrong and your changing would only be done to the point that it would serve your needs. Your needs are not to change at all but to try to turn this into some type of victory. Before I even let you think of doing anything Colosso, think of what a fool you are. I am somebody who knows no one here; I have no family anywhere; I have no friends or contact with anybody; I talk to no one and you have not had the least bit of interest to know why or learn anything of my background. A wise prince always knows who is or might be his adversary and thus is able to not have any surprises. Castro survived more than thirty years by doing as we say in Spanish-matando las sombras; or in English-killing anyone who might be a present or future threat to the prince's power. You have been foolish and you are going to pay. You are utterly untrustworthy and really a horrid virus and disease on this earth's surface; but I must thank you because the God I so long denied, gave me the opportunity, through you, to really make up for a time I failed as a human being very miserably. Colosso, I will not fail this time. I am weary of life and do not really have strong purpose for living anymore. If I know human nature, what I am doing today is going to lead to your demise and your time on earth is very small. These events will stick in your mind and you will have to deal with them at a later unforeseen time; but you are really very stupid and maybe killing you now is the only solution that is best for you.

President: Oh please, do not kill me. Do not hurt me and I promise I will do everything I said I would. You have helped me today. I will admit what I have done....

Emilio: Oh, shut up Colosso. Your pathetic little murmurings are bad enough, but to continue saying them over and over again is too much. But again and in a grotesque sense, I thank you for the opportunity to do what has to be done today.

President: Please do not shoot me; I beg you to put the gun down in the name of God himself.

Emilio: Colosso, you do not get it. This gun is not for you. This gun is for me and you will have to live with the consequences. Death would be ashamed to have you join its ranks and I think now death will finally be proud to receive me. I fear not death and seek it with intense desire.

Whatever is the next state, I seek it confidently with the belief that a man of cleansed spirit has nothing to fear in life or death.

(Emilio then points the gun at his chest and shoots himself through the heart and immediately collapses to the floor. Colosso looks at him in a state of shock and then stands up and begins to walk around trying to put himself back into a normal emotional state. He also quickly goes through his office drawer and takes a nitro tablet from its bottle and puts it in his mouth.)

President: *(With passion and glee in his voice.)* I knew that destiny would not let me down. I knew this was going to work out and I would again end up as the leader and winner at State. This has only proven that even greater things are ahead of me at this time. What to do now? He says he knows no one; he has no family; has no friends and contacts; talks to no one and therefore wonders why I know nothing of him. I think this is very good that neither I nor anyone else know anything of him. Because what he is and what happened here will be what I create. Yes, Emilio, you stupid spic fool. You are going to work into my hands and be a major part of destroying the Board and that idiot macho man, Tuffy Norkas. You are going to help me get rid of all my enemies at once. Oh, yes. I think I will call my good friend, the police chief at the university, and will indicate what has happened here today. Then, I will prepare a spectacular talk on the matter for tomorrow. Cicero's bones will wilt in frozen and forgotten neglect when his weak and pitiful words are compared with mine. Emilio, what a fool; what a fool; what a fool you are, but I will turn you into a useful tool for my purposes. As Castro turned Che Guevara into a hero of the revolution after he died, I will personally turn you into the great martyr that allowed me to save State University of America. Oh, Emilio, what a splendidly stupid fool you are. Whatever unpardonable sin you think you did in the past, your death today will make up for it! Stories will indeed be told forever about how your martyrdom allowed me to save State from those who would destroy it. That is a promise over your mother's grave; oh you stupid, stupid, stupid fool! The outcome of your idealism will indeed be remembered forever. Ha! Ha! Ha! Ha! Ha! Ha!

End of Scene

Scene 8

(Colosso is in his university office. He is excitedly preparing to give his talk to State University and the media the day after the suicide of Emilio. He has waited a year to have the right environment to bring a new Board of Trustees vote to get rid of Tuffy completely and totally destroy his supporters. Of course, Colosso will end up magnificently powerful after the vote. Colosso feels the moment is at hand for his great victory. He takes a nitro pill, relaxes himself and begins to speak as the cameras and lights go on.)

President: Emilio Gomez: A name we all must remember. A martyr who died in my arms after shooting himself. His warm blood now nourishes my soul to give me the strength to come to you and ask that the evil deeds that have so horribly wronged our university and led to the death of Emilio be made right immediately. He was a patriot who loved America and State University of America. Emilio escaped from Fidel Castro's brutal dictatorship and thus knew the effects of tyranny in a way most of us do not appreciate. Before I go any further, I state my purpose today is not to fan the fires of legitimate hate and rage; I come only to report the truth to you as your President and spokesperson. With that said, I will go on with my feelings about Emilio and how his martyrdom has forced me to present an action plan to save State. That was the purpose of his martyrdom and it must not go in vain. Oh Emilio! If only you were still alive; but we must accept you are not. I believe God's divine plan was that this martyrdom would lead to a more just and gentle earth; and of course, this includes our beloved State University of America. I want to share what Emilio told me right before he died. He told me he could not live while Tuffy and his nihilistic negative forces tried to destroy his beloved State University of America. I first pleaded with him not to kill himself when he pulled the revolver. If you look at the marks on my face, you can imagine what then happened. I tried to take the gun away from Emilio, but this tough proud old Cuban warrior was too strong for me and he pushed me away. We both looked at each other with respect through our eyes clouded with tears. As he put the gun to his chest, I begged him to tell me if his dying were worth it and he said yes with a voice loaded with such passion and pathos. I told him we needed men like him alive to fight to make State the greatest university in the world. I wanted him to know whether one is a student, bricklayer, custodian, professor, psychologist or world famous scientist, we all are one and must vigorously fight for right. I told him to live for all of you. Emilio said he could no longer go on. With tears streaming down his weather hardened face and my eyes feeling like a hot waterfall, I begged him to live. With great emotion etched over his tensed body, he said he had to die and he begged me to use him as an example of someone who died so that State University of America might live. I ask you, is a football game more important than Emilio's life? I ask you if you want people in power at our beloved State who would force an honorable man like Emilio to the fierce belief he must kill himself to try to save it? Is our business at State about life and academics or death and winning football games at any cost? I ask you, is our purpose to create an environment whereby Emilio and similar patriots of this university will die or to create an educational environment whereby death and illness will be beaten within the limits our God sets? I ask you, is our purpose at State University of America to create the will to live and succeed as human beings or to destroy life and the will to succeed in life? Bear with me a moment as these damn tears blind me. A strange feeling that mixes hurt, pain and rage is overcoming me. The image of Emilio telling me how much he loved you, State and saw me as the only person who could save State is overwhelming my senses. To be called the champion of the people at a time I could not help him tears at my guts and psyche in a way few could understand. Oh God, please give me the strength to carry on! Again, I plead with you not to think poorly of me because I am overwhelmed with feelings and I am sharing them with you; but I do believe you have the same feelings. Poor Emilio! Poor Emilio! Oh, poor Emilio!

But enough of that for now. It is the time for us to have destiny and God's plan implemented with vengeful and perfect haste. In your name, I have demanded a statewide televised Board meeting tomorrow in this very room at 8:00 p.m. I also will be having a statewide television interview in this room at 7:30 p.m. with Jim German to talk about your response to this talk tonight that I am giving to each and every one of you. The televised Board meeting will immediately follow the interview. I will report what you have told me. The meeting in your name is to deal with this tragedy and finally to right the wrongs that Tuffy and his clique have perpetrated on our beloved university. *(With disgust in his voice.)*

However, be aware I have been told I do not have the authority to call this board meeting tomorrow evening. So you know, I was told this by Board Chairperson, Terry Moore, that great supporter and apologist for the sports empire at our beloved, and yes, even sacred State. I also want all of you to know that with great anger and passion in my voice, I told Terry I have the blood on my hands of trying to save Emilio while he, Tuffy and Tuffy's other supporters on the Board have the real blood on their hands for having in effect caused his tragic death. Oh vengeance, do not be weak tonight! In that it is you, the citizens of this great state, that determine what is done at State University of America, I may have gone too far in that I said you are demanding this meeting; but if I am right and you want me to make our beloved university — State — number one in the world and cleanse it of the sports carpetbaggers who are out to destroy it as a world class academic institution, then demand there be a meeting tomorrow at 8:00 p.m. in my office to redress this most tragic of situations. We are all citizens and accountable to you. Call your newspapers, call your radio stations, call your television stations, write telegrams to voice your opinions, and call me and let me know what you demand. I will not let you down! The death of Emilio must be a noble tragedy to pull us all together. This period of mourning and grief for this proud Cuban-American warrior who died for us and who loved State so very much, must pull us together to put academics back on top and sports in a distant second place. The following is what I plan to do tomorrow with your consent: Fire Tuffy Norkas as coach and athletic director; let all his coaches go; have my close associate at Big State University, Wesley Smith, immediately become athletic director; have Big State's head football coach, Chump Cullihan, become head football coach. An emergency environment requires immediate action! These are two men of unimpeachable ethics who will know they work for you and that I direct their actions as you demand. This will get rid of Tuffy, damage the sports empire hopefully to the point of extinction and bring in some great persons to help save the situation at our beloved State University of America. As your servant, I will do what you demand. While I plead with you to do what you think is morally right, I want you to support me only if you believe strongly with me the following:

1. We believe our primary mission is to create the greatest university in the world.

2. We believe academic integrity and its growth are essential and not the feeding of the monstrous prostitute like sports empire which will gravely wound academics at State whenever given the chance.

3. We believe the President at State University of America must be allowed to manage the university without interference from the football coach and his clique of supporters on the Board and in the sports empire.

4. We believe the people must demand its Board members do what they demand and not what the worshipers of the football coach and the sports empire demand.

5. We believe our children deserve the best possible education imaginable on this earth.

6. We believe students and faculty at State University of America have priority over the football coach and his cronies in the sports empire.

7. Last and most important to me, *(his voice cracking with emotion)* in that Emilio died in my arms crying and begging me to save State with your help, we believe we must cleanse our beloved State University of America of its sports empire filth to mercifully avenge this martyr's death out of his uncompromising love for you and his beloved State University of America. I pray to our God on high that you believe what I believe; and that you will force all the positive forces that love State to rise up verbally, personally and in writing to destroy the negative jock loving forces of the horrid sports empire that are out to destroy the academic present and future of our beloved State University of America. *(With a somber tone.)* If you do not believe what I believe, then I will quietly leave and wish you the best. My memories of State will always be the very best of my life. I know I will be remembered as a man who failed in convincing the forces of light and truth at his beloved State University of America that Tuffy, his cronies on the Board and all the other members of the hateful sports empire had to be put out of power and replaced by those who would help make State the greatest academic university in the world. While I will accept your verdict, I pray that the God we love and trust will not let that occur and that he will inspire you to demand light and truth rather than darkness and lies. For now, God bless you, your children and those you love and know I am waiting for your response to my talk and the martyrdom of Emilio: A man who loved you and State University of America to the point he was willing to die for us in the hope his martyrdom would inspire you to save our beloved State University of America. His spirit is waiting for your response and may our just God guide your thoughts and actions.

End of Scene

Scene 9

(The setting is the university office of Colosso. The 32 hours since Colosso gave his speech to the public have seen overwhelming support for him as well as rioting on campus. All the major newspapers of the state and beyond have written blazing editorials and articles attacking Tuffy and his followers. All are demanding that every last recommendation of President Assassino be approved and implemented immediately by the gravely humiliated and wounded Board of Trustees. Colosso very belatedly sent university police to the football building after students and other protesting rioters began breaking windows and throwing paint all over the building. The hate for Tuffy and his followers is so great that the students were actually throwing paint on the building the colors of the hated University of America. As passions rage with various protesting actions occurring, there is a great anticipation in the air as everyone waits for the interview and then the Board meeting on television. Colosso has set up TV monitors all over campus. The most bizarre incident has to be that of Skip Goon. At 11:30 p.m. last evening, he was at the ice arena dressed as a symbol of freedom in America. He

was leading a torch light rally in support of President Assassino. With his torch, he accidentally set his oily beard on fire and in diving on the ice in a panic to put it out, he got a severe concussion and broke his jaw in four places and is hospitalized at a local hospital. He is excitedly awaiting the outcome of Colosso's great victory at the Board meeting tonight. The setting is President Assassino's office at 7:30 p.m. He takes a nitro pill and the interview with Jim German is just beginning.)

Jim: President Assassino, your willingness to do this interview at this most difficult time is greatly appreciated.

President: It is the right thing to do for State and all those who love it as much as I do.

Jim: You agreed to this interview at a time you had no idea what level of support you would have now. All could have been against you. What a risk of disaster and humiliation you took.

President: It was not a great risk as I am one of the people with the people. I am the one who represents their dreams. I knew what they were thinking, what they wanted and what they would do. *(Looking into the camera with a most sincere look.)* The martyrdom of Emilio forged us together in an unbreakable bond and alliance. How I love all of you and how we will fly tonight in a state of exquisite victory. Trumpets will blare on high and blast Tuffy and his cronies into oblivion.

Jim: If we did not before, we all know now how much you are loved by the supporters of State.

President: You are very kind.

Jim: In your words, how do you feel?

President: The hurt, rage, humiliation and powerlessness that have been relentlessly trumpeted into my psyche full blast since Tuffy and his power hungry clique took over our beloved State are only now beginning to subside. But my anguish from not being able to help all of you until tonight will be a slow burning acid that will torture my soul as long as I live. At this moment, I am being reborn with a rejuvenation of hope and purpose for the future at our beloved State.

Jim: Will the Board of Trustees do what the people are demanding be done to help alleviate some of the torture you have been through?

President: Oh, yes, but only a brutal rape victim knows the horrid memories last many years after the deeds of the depraved monster occurred. I have been raped and so has everyone else who loves State.

Jim: Are the wounds that deep?

President: Personally and at a very frank level, there were times I felt death would have been so easy and I even longed for the warmth it seemed to offer. I must say when Emilio martyrized himself, I wish it had been me. But very shortly after he died for all of us, I knew with conviction how I must go to war on this issue to make possible the fulfillment of the dreams of all those who love State. I knew it was my destiny to go forward as the example of what State could be and would become through my actions on behalf of the people. Oh, how I love them as one with myself. Love thy neighbor as thyself has true meaning to me now.

Jim: Your courage is a model to all of us now and forever. How have you felt seeing thousands of students demonstrating for you as well as total support from a mighty phalanx of the most humble and powerful persons in this state?

President: Tears of unexplainable and inextinguishable emotion and joy overwhelm me as this son of Italian immigrants realizes he was given this great opportunity by God to rid this great university of the vermin that have taken it over.

Jim: The people have told you they support you in the form of an avalanche of telegrams, phone calls, newspaper articles, comments on radio and television call in shows, as well as by the thousands of students and others demonstrating today. They clearly and overwhelmingly say they believe in you as their leader and want you to take control decisively. Do you agree?

President: What more can I say? I humbly recognize God's involvement in all this to have me be the punishing and purifying tool to eradicate the sports empire that has been destroying State. Tragically, this only is occurring due to the martyrdom of Emilio. He gave his life and died in my arms so State and the dreams of all of you can live. For me, the tears are still so close and the nerves so raw.

Jim: President Assassino, I hope this interview is not too much with what you must do in just a few minutes.

President: *(Decisively.)* This must be done! Truth must be brought forth tonight. Falsehoods and anyone who desires to destroy the great academic future of our beloved university must be publicly put out of power and shown for what they are; half measures will soil the memory of martyr Emilio and bankrupt the dreams of the next generation of State University of America students.

Jim: You of course are talking about Tuffy, his cronies and his group of supporting Board members.

President: The answer is clear. The people have spoken and as I have said, God has given me this great opportunity to do what must be done at State. I need not say any more than has been said before on this most wretched of tragedies at a public university. Emilio's martyrdom will not go without being avenged; his spirit is with us today asking for a fair and most thorough destruction of those who would destroy our beloved State University of America. He must be the standard for all of us!

Jim: Are you worn out by all this?

President: Too much so I am afraid; but I cannot rest until State is firmly set on the side of light, justice and superb academic endeavors. There can be no compromise at this time. The time is late and the human and social destruction have been incalculable; but this just war will be won this night. As Satan fell due to his great pride, God is now demanding the fall of Tuffy for the same sin of pride that took light and goodness from Satan and his cronies in sin. For now, Tuffy fortunately need not worry about eternity in hell for his grave sin of pride.

Jim: Why are you allowing the administrative building to be open to the public now? We can surely hear them outside this room supporting you with great zeal and devotion.

President: I want the people here tonight to keep an eye on their elected officials. They failed them before and a spotlight of justice will be overseeing their actions this evening.

Jim: Are you not fearful some acts of violence may occur to Tuffy or Board Members who acted most inappropriately?

President: Of the people there can be no fear. I have asked them to not harm the Board members or Tuffy. This is asked out of a desire they live and have a chance to repent for what they have done, rather than receiving now what they rightly deserve. The people can hear me now and that is what they also desire.

Jim: Did you say Tuffy is coming?

President: Yes, I did. I ordered him to be here this evening. He works for me and will be here or be fired for insubordination as the first act of business.

Jim: Would you like him not to show up and be fired for insubordination?

President: It would be best for State and Tuffy. It would also make Emilio's martyrdom have the positive result of chasing away the prideful Tuffy without the need for Board action. He would be acknowledging his grievous errors and begin his rehabilitation. Fierce and appropriate anger and rage would more readily be put to rest to some degree.

Jim: Mr. President, do you have any final comments before we move to cover the Board meeting? *(Persons are clapping their hands and whistling in the outside hall.)* I hope the clapping and whistling in the background does not bother you too much.

President: There is no problem with the noise. The people are communicating with me and I am listening before I speak. *(Colosso then pauses.)* These final comments are to the people of this great state who love our beloved university as I do. I am just overwhelmed and humbled with the astonishingly positive response you have given me; this was consistent throughout the state. I really feel God has given me the destiny to continue living to complete this important task. To this end, I again take a nitro tablet to open my heart for tonight's just actions to keep destiny alive and to fulfill my role at State University of America. *(He puts it in his mouth.)* I really am excited about the prospects of what is going to occur at State. I also feel very secure that Emilio's martyrdom will not go unforgotten and shortly the truth will shine forth in trumpet like clarity and State will move forward due to his death for the university he loved so dearly. I am with you and destiny is on the side of you and State University of America becoming the greatest university possible with all of your dreams coming true. To be the greatest university in the world is our goal. God himself is with us at this moment; he is demanding vengeful justice! As Satan was banished to hell for his pride, the same will occur for anyone who will not repent for sins committed in this sordid tragedy. Oh, I feel faint. Oh, I feel more than faint. Oh no, Oh God! *(He alternately clutches his stomach, throat and chest and has a contorted look of pain on his face.)* Oh Emilio, Emilio, you really did get revenge and I am dying. Oh Emilio, you really knew what you were saying when you said my time on earth was small. Now I know what you were doing at my desk. It was something you put into my nitro bottle, was it not? You have gotten your revenge and I am

dying. You bastard Spic! You wanted me and you got me; but I will see you in hell. Ah!!!! Ah!!!! Ahhhhhhh!! *(He falls and dies.)*

The End

Appendix A

Selected Character
Personality Descriptions

Colosso Michelangelo Assassino - *President of State University of America*

Colosso Michelangelo Assassino is currently the President of State University of America. He has held this position for over six years. He previously was President of two similar land grant institutions and additionally held various posts at other universities. His doctorate is not in an academic area but in an applied area. He holds no degrees from State University of America but does have degrees from other universities in the State, including The University of America. Colosso is very active in organizations at a national and international level. His critics say this is far more important to him than State University of America. He dismisses these arguments by stating his national and international glory transfers to State through him. Colosso has been President of the most prestigious International Council of University Presidents for the past five years. In more than a century of its existence, no one has been president of this organization for more than one year until Colosso. The unwritten tradition was that no one would be President more than one year. Through eloquence, charisma, infighting, character assassination and surreptitiously creating a constant crisis environment, he has remained as president with total control over all aspects of the organization for five years and shows no sign of stepping down or aside. Colosso is also on the boards of many prestigious organizations as well as on powerful national and international corporate boards. He is a legend among his peers for being involved in so many organizations at a wheeling and dealing impact level. His most prestigious role is that of Chairperson of the Justice Z. God Council of Select University Presidents. This select group of ten university presidents is reviewing the role of athletics in higher education. Colosso has eloquently championed the position of total power of the presidents to control all aspects of sports. He of course has given no acknowledgement of the governing role of Boards of Trustees or Regents over the Presidents in any way whatsoever. Colosso has also championed the view that university presidents should be publicly elected for life in the same way as are Supreme Court Justices. Colosso is the son of Italian immigrants and grew up in a relatively nice area of Big Town, USA. Even though he grew up in a middle class environment, he has created the myth that he grew up in poverty and made it to the top on his own perseverance. He is both the oldest child and the first born son. Being the first born son in the Italian culture often leads to tremendous power within the family. This was clearly the case with Colosso. He was the grand hero of both his parents and even has great sway over his brothers and sisters. Initially he suffered some type of discrimination simply from the fact he grew up in a tough city and derogatory names for Italian-Americans were still in vogue in his elementary and high school years. Colosso is fifty-eight years old and has not accumulated a lot of money in his lifetime and lives off his very comfortable income, palatial like lodgings and the many perks he receives for being President of State University of America. He has never had a developed sense of right or wrong but only wants what is right for him. People either see through him and despise him or fall completely under his huge charismatic sway. Fortunately for him, he influences the vast majority of people in a way that is only possible for the great prince without morals or principles. Colosso's early heroes were Adolf Hitler, Benito Mussolini, Juan Peron and more currently Fidel Castro. He never mentions this as he adroitly manipulates minorities and liberal groups. He actually despises them all but uses them to help him to be even greater. Colosso has superbly catered to the giant egos of the media chieftains in Big Town and throughout the State. They know each other well and give Colosso great and unflinching support for whatever his tiny and frigid heart wants. This is a reason he is often called a media hog and media magician by his detractors. These contacts and friendships serve him magnificently in his great battle with Tuffy and his governing Board of Trustees. One of the great attractions to him being in the university environment was the enormous prestige and power that goes with being a President. He has chuckled how foolish academicians, the public and the media are in that they assume the best of motives for the person who strives for the greatest position of power in the university and question the motives of sports persons who strive for far less power. Colosso's great charisma and pure sociopathic personality were perfectly matched in his role as President at State University of America. Colosso sees his power as analogous to the power of the Pope to his appointing College of Cardinals. Of particular use to Colosso was the glorious thirty years presidency of John Vandenberg at State that allowed future presidents to be far greater than were the elected officials that constitutionally they worked for. The weakness of his successors only led to a greater desire to find one like him. Succeeding board members never realized it was impossible and inappropriate to seek an employee to dominate them in a university constitutionally governed by its Board. But this did not stop them from trying to duplicate the times of President Vandenburg as well as the great

John Vandenburg himself. Of course Colosso knew this, but he never let them know. He promised them everything and all they had to do was unflinchingly support him 100%. As with many sociopaths, Colosso is not able to stay on one task for long periods of time. He needs to constantly be on the go and to be the center of attention. Thus, the focus of his leadership style is to have a Provost who pretty much manages the university and he functions more as a commanding board chairperson and is constantly traveling the world. Of course, he only goes first class and sees the heavy expenses he incurs as totally necessary for him due to his important work. At a general level, he is dynamic, charming, witty and very friendly. He is aloof to most persons at a personal one on one level and his personal friendships and relationships are always geared for who can help him. Colosso has nothing but disdain for the very weak board members that only live to be vicariously part of his glorious life. They, of course, do not know his feelings about them and to their face he lets them know how important their support is for his great deeds. To be near him and hear him say their names is all they want. Tragically, political parties have traditionally picked very weak and minor political figures to be on the Board. Only recently have some board members joined the Board who are very successful and who appropriately see Colosso as an employee of the Board and not vice versa. He has been somewhat paranoid since these new board members are definitely not going to do whatever he wants them to do. He has fought them with great energy and this has led to a tremendous power conflict on the Board. The issue over whether or not Tuffy Norkas should be coach and athletic director allowed Colosso the golden opportunity to fight an audacious battle for power by magnificently making the issue into one of sports versus academics. Of course, the issue was power and not at all academics versus sports. Colosso has no superego or conscience in the psychodynamic sense. His conscience and sense of right and wrong are really a rotting and putrid moral wasteland. His whole goal is to have great power and to win at any cost. In his own mind, Colosso has clearly merged his life with that of State University of America. To him they are one and he is the great charismatic champion that alone can help it be great. Without him, Colosso "knows" State University of America would be just another large and mediocre state university. There are many people that see him as the great academic champion of State and are overwhelmed by his tremendous presence and charismatic personality. Colosso's enemies or persons who see him for what he is, are either demoralized, afraid to speak or have nothing to gain from such public statements.

Tuffy Norkas - *Head Football Coach and Athletic Director*

Tuffy Norkas is the heavy handed, hard nosed and non-compromising football coach and athletic director of State University of America. He loves State University of America and proved it by three times turning down multi-million dollar professional football contracts to stay at his alma mater where he met his wife and knew and worked with two of the greatest coaches in the history of State University of America. He is condemned in the media for talking to the pros. Tuffy says he will talk to anyone who might offer him a job. He says this is America and his detractors are hypocrites. They got ahead by looking for better jobs or using potential jobs as leverage to improve their jobs. With them it is good, but Tuffy complains with him it is said to be wrong. He could give a damn what they think. Like Colosso, he also grew up in Big Town USA and is the son of immigrants. In his case, they are from Lithuania. Tuffy grew up in a tougher section of Big Town than Colosso and has the heavy body, square jaw and large head that is typical of many Lithuanian rural persons. He does not have the finely chiseled features of Colosso nor the tremendous charisma and speaking abilities that have given Colosso the tremendous charm to overwhelm anyone that goes against him. Tuffy is also not a media hog and has made many prominent enemies in the media in total contrast to Colosso who has totally catered to them and does whatever he can to have them on his side and under his sway. Tuffy is noted for tremendous loyalty to good friends and demands the same from his friends and associates. While Tuffy is not a compromiser, there are people he has respected over the years that have given him a tremendous sense of loyalty and commitment and he would never do anything to hurt them in life or tarnish their reputations in death through inappropriate actions on his part. Tuffy came to the college ranks from the professional ranks where he created some of the greatest defensive teams in the history of football. His coming home to his alma mater is based on total commitment and trying to eliminate the low self esteem that had resulted from total domination from The University of America over nearly a twenty year period. Coming back to State to try to resurrect the pathetic football program was extremely difficult due to the enormous stature of The University of America as well as its incredibly successful and powerful coach, Chuck Schultz. Schultz, in spite of being tyrannical, has always had the media from Big Town totally under his sway and he has most effectively worked with them to help keep State as low as was possible; that was low indeed. Unlike Tuffy, Chuck has no credibility as a pro coach and thus has never had the multiple million dollar contract offers that Tuffy regularly receives. Tuffy's approach to unfairness in the media and constant attacks to him and the program has been one of defiance and a single minded dedication to turn State University's football program into a top notch winning one. Tuffy's demanding for loyalty goes well with his single minded energies to help State. His willingness to fight anyone who is unfair and unwilling to help State has made him many enemies and he really accepts their enmity as the price he will pay. Such a powerful personality has inevitably led to some scrapes and run-ins with faculty at State who are either intimidated by him or not able to relate to such a rough and non-academic appearing no nonsense type person. Tuffy's great strength and potentially his greatest weakness is his unwillingness to compromise, regardless of the odds.

William Percival - *Provost of State University of America*

Provost William Percival is a forty six year old who was born in London and was trained in British universities. He is an internationally known chemist who came to State University of America as a special scholar in this area. He is perceived in the university community as a very honorable man and is loyal to friends and colleagues. Colosso chose him as the Provost in that he in effect can effectively manage the university; and by personality, he is not a "would be Caesar". Additionally, Bill has proven himself capable of defusing difficult situations and making Colosso look even more charismatic and magnificent due to great compromising skills and making friends and enemies feel at ease with him. He is of light complexion, has blue eyes and has a slight delicate figure with finely chiseled facial features. While nothing has been said publicly, there are unproven but whispered rumors about Bill having an intimate relationship with Colosso. Bill has been caught off guard by the tremendous conflict between Tuffy and Colosso and is not at all comfortable being placed in the middle of a political war that is really based on power and not academics. His sense of right and wrong is being challenged by his greatly enjoying his position as well as his career advancement. Additionally, he has the problem of loyalty to Colosso versus ethical behavior. It is his job to evaluate Tuffy in his placement as both athletic director and coach. His respect for the authority of Colosso and his growing respect for Tuffy, due to his commitment to State University and effectiveness in his dual role, leads to tremendous internal conflicts with him as a person. Bill feels he has probably overlooked Colosso's perverted sense of fairness due to his enjoying his job as well as being overwhelmed by Colosso's sheer presence. In effect,

Colosso has overwhelmed his passions and sense of reason at least until the crisis with Tuffy and the Board began. However, in the end, his loyalty to Colosso and his desire to stay in his position win out over ethical issues of right and wrong. By using the defense mechanisms of denial and repression, Bill is not able at this period of time to release himself from the great charismatic influence of Colosso over him. Fortunately for him, the final struggle between Colosso and Emilio makes it not necessary for him to plunge the knife into Tuffy when he least expects it.

Emilio Gomez

Emilio Gomez is a man in his sixties who grew up in the province of Oriente, Cuba, where his family owned a large plantation and lived near the plantation of the family of Fidel Castro. He grew up with Fidel and went to school with him in Santiago de Cuba and Havana. They were associates at the University of Havana and comrades in arms from day one of the revolution. Emilio studied political science and the English language; he became proficient at both. He was with Fidel in the Sierra Madre and heroically fought against the forces of Batista. Emilio was with Fidel when he first made a willing fool of Herbert L. Matthews of the New York Times. Matthews longed for a bigger than life hero and Fidel gave it to him. Emilio became a confidant of Fidel and took part in the "Great March" to the liberation of Havana. Emilio was with Fidel and Antonio Del Pino in the victory over the CIA backed invasion of exile Cubans at the Bay of Pigs. He was, for many years, an ideologue and could not see any wrong in Fidel. He was completely under the sway of the great charismatic field commander as is Provost Percival with Colosso. Over the years, as Emilio saw the total misery in Cuba, he began to sour on Fidel and see him for the despot he really was. He also saw many of his close friends killed or sent off to prison due to not being pure and obedient followers in the manner demanded by Fidel Castro. On a personally momentous day in 1982, he spent the evening with Fidel at his home in Veradero Beach. Emilio planned to kill Fidel as he slept that evening and thus end the horrible misery in Cuba. As a weathered heroic type figure, with strong manly features given him by his Galicia born father and Cuban born juajira mother, he really looked like he could do the part. In fact, he really felt it was his destiny to do this country saving act. It also would redeem him from the great wrongs he had supported by being blindly in league with Fidel. But at the critical moment, he was not able to do what he had done to so many other

117

persons during the turbulent war years before and after the fall of Batista. That night as Fidel slept, he had the revolver pointed at his head and only had to squeeze the trigger. The knowledge Cuba could be free excited him to fire white passion. Years of the horrible memories of the great misery and countless psychological and physical assassinations he had seen, flew into his mind at breathtaking speed as he thought to pull the trigger; however, he could not do it as he froze. It was inexplicable to him as he put the gun down and despair came over him in great overpowering waves. Shortly thereafter, Fidel briefly awoke and gave him a calm knowing smile that was loaded with sarcasm. Somehow he knew and he went back to sleep in a peaceful way. Feeling great despair and knowing he had failed at this critical moment destiny had given him, he wildly ran off and rashly took a small boat and left Havana in the direction of Florida as Fidel was calmly sleeping. Emilio never antici- pated making it but miraculously did survive. Because of the suffering his misguided blind allegiance to Fidel has caused them, he was not comfortable in the enormous and hugely successful Cuban exile com- munity in Miami and immediately chose to move far away and blend into the environment and forget his past. Due to the excellent English language skills he had learned as a young boy when he studied in the United States and then at the University of Havana, it was not hard for him to do this successfully. Emilio came to the town where State University of America was and settled down. He was able to obtain a job as a custodian at State University of America. Emilio has hid his education and has just worked his days in an efficient but mindless fashion. He has spent some years working and has tried to blend into the environment, to do a good job and forget his past. Emilio never had a wife and family due to his total commitment to the revolution. The affairs and short term relationships of the warrior revolutionary are now far behind him. His parents died long ago and his brothers and sisters know nothing of him. They are now all prosperous in Miami and know nothing of him as he dropped them all for the sake of the revolution. Emilio has learned to be alone and feels it is best he just live out his days in calmness and working in seclusion. He has a small apartment and almost never says anything more than hello to his neighbors. To his co- workers, he is communicative at a work level but not at a personal level. Emilio takes a liking to Charles, the young student janitor who works with him, and tries to be helpful to him. Unfortunately for him, his most effective detail work has led him to a position where he works directly for the President. Working with the President has led to tremendously negative feelings in him in that Colosso is a charismatic prince in the same sense as Fidel Castro. He sees the same sociopathic behavior patterns and manipulation of the masses through a very willing media and a population always ready to seek out the great prince. Emilio realizes this and he has a really great and total lack of respect for Colosso. Colosso can be very friendly to him when he is trying to impress people; but really is very indifferent and usually does not even realize he is there when he is cleaning or helping out with menial activities and no one is near. Emilio even heard Colosso one time saying he was glad that his Hispanic was white and not black or brown like many of the other Hispanics. This again only showed the tremendous hypocrisy in the man who often eloquently speaks of fair hiring practices and the need to help all persons of all races. Even from his custodian position, Emilio knows how Colosso often hires his own friends through sham interviews. One time he even picked a vice president friend of his with no interview. Emilio is an open man in spite of his great bravado and military past. He has been able to overlook these failings of Colosso as well as not judge too harshly the pretty and delicately featured male advisors that idolize Colosso and constantly surround him. However, because of what Colosso is doing to State at present, he is very distraught over the very giant flaws of Colosso and the lack of knowledge of them by his many supporters. A major reason Emilio has very little respect and even contempt for Colosso is that he is not at all bright and has severe delusions of grandeur. Colosso really knows nothing of Emilio's background and is not aware how easily he can read him and is in position to expose him. Emilio is just so distraught that this could be happening now. The memories of Cuba are too close and the great collision between Colosso and Tuffy with all the tragic effects is forcing Emilio into another critical period where he must decide if he will or will not do something to make a difference.

Norma Norkas - *Wife of Tuffy*

Norma is a point blank and up front woman in her mid fifties who enjoys the life of the wife of a football coach. She can have great talk with the toughest of characters and generally out puns any man or woman. As she says, she is able to "see through all the damn bullshit to see how people are and what the hell people are up to". She is extremely loyal towards Tuffy but is completely able to put him in his place and give him tough but necessary advice when needed. Norma's insights into people have been a great asset to him due to the blindness that can result from his great loyalty and single minded determination and toughness to get done

119

what he sets out to do. Norma loves State University of America but would have been more than happy to move with Tuffy if he had chosen to go into a big time multi-million dollar a year professional football contract as he has again had the chance recently. However, she is loyal to his commitment to stay at State and sticks with him through thick and thin. Norma really sees Colossal, as she puts it, as a "scoundrel and a revolting little fairy"; she would certainly know how to deal with him if the opportunity ever came up in a face to face confrontation. No one ever underestimates her brightness or determination.

Skip Goon - *Sports Editor of The University Town Journal*

Skip is kind of a pathetic lost hippy who is still living in the 1960's. He is really very shallow and looks for a cause or someone to worship. Colosso has been perfect as a hero for him with his great charisma and always adroitly saying the right jingoistic praises and thoughts that turn Skip on. Skip actually hates State University of America and does not at all get along with most of the sports coaches. His hatred and jealousy of Tuffy makes David Egan's feelings about Ted Williams look like great respect and love. Skip's thin body frame and his delicate and feminine features belie a very crude, judgmental and petty personality. Colosso has been able to completely manipulate him by giving him praise and inviting him over to the university mansion for discussion in a grand and opulent setting. Colosso basically is able to put all of his thoughts into Skip's mind and convinces him they are his own. Skip then goes out and in effect writes whatever Colosso wants him to write. Colosso then calls him and praises him. Skip even can get tears of happy and grateful emotion in his quivering high pitched voice as Colosso tells him how great and important is the work he has done and continues to do. Such hero worship from a person in his position is indeed rare and very pathetic. He is duped by Colosso in much the same way as was Herbert Matthews of the New York Times with Fidel Castro. To be despised by those you idolize is sad enough; to not know it is a blessing to the ego but a true personal tragedy. Such is the reality of the mean spirited, unfair and spineless Skip Goon.

Terry Moore - *State University of America Board of Trustees Chairperson*

Terry is a highly sophisticated political operative in the State and additionally is a successful businessman. He joined the Board through appointment by the Governor and has worked hard to try to develop a strong professional managing role for the Board of Trustees. He and Colosso have been on a collision course since they first came together and Terry tried to have Colosso be accountable to the governing Board for the first time. Colosso has told Terry that once he was hired, he could do any damn thing he wanted as the "administrator" of the people. Terry has told him this is absurd and he will report to the Board. Of course, Terry has found Colosso will not accept control of any kind and will battle him and the Board whenever it does not let him do what he wants. Colosso has most effectively stopped all attempts to develop a job description under which he would be evaluated. Terry sees this; battles Colosso, but is not strong enough to take control. He foolishly believes Colosso will ultimately do what is right for State. Colosso will do everything he can to not meet with Terry and also to sabotage any of his ideas. Terry has been willing to confront Colosso but does not have the charisma to effectively confront him publicly. He cannot fathom the enormous ability of Colosso to get what he wants through the media and the spectacular manipulation of powerful persons he has under his sway. To him, Colosso's flaws and insubordination to a governing board are so obvious he really believes people of good will will eventually recognize them. Terry has a great love for State University and as a result is willing to go along with certain things Colosso does if they are good for the university. This of course is a disadvantage in that Colosso has no sense of right or wrong and is willing to do things that are right for the university only if they are right for himself and advance him personally. Terry is surprised that Colosso's personality is not interpreted appropriately by people and underestimates Colosso as well as overestimates the ability of the people to ferret out the truth and do what is best for State University. Terry had a choice to make after the initial vote that made Tuffy both the athletic director and coach. Colosso went to war with him in the media and attacked the individual members who voted against his recommendation. At that time, the choice would have been to fire him or hope that things would work out with time. The decision was to try to work things out. Terry believed it would not have been good for the reputation of State to have fired Colosso at that particular time. This of course turned out to be a grievous error in judgment that would work into Colosso's devious and self serving hands.

Harry Boylen - *State University of America Board of Trustees Member*

Harry is a single man in his late forties who comes from a long time political family. He is basically very depressed and has a number of health problems including ulcers, obesity, poor circulation and a bad back. His whole life revolves around State University of America. Even though he often complains about it and the responsibilities on him as a trustee, he basically has no other life but State and does not realize that what he needs to do is get away and become a full person. Harry is the ultimate of president hero worshipers and has been the most servile of all boot licking board members to the omniscient power of his employees: The Presidents. Harry has even battled with board members that wanted to see itinerary and expenses of Colosso. Colosso has constantly fed his ego and always mentions the essential and important work he does. Harry often invites Colosso to little parties with insignificant people at his house and Colosso rarely appears. Harry excuses him and has no concept that he works for him. On the other hand, he is periodically invited into "The Kingdom" and just feels honored and happy to be a part of the greatness of Colosso. The glow helps to alleviate much of his depression and physical problems during his ventures into "The Kingdom" to bask in the glory of Colosso. Even though he worshiped previous presidents, no one can match Colosso in the estimation of Harry. His level of obedience and support has probably never been superseded by a human being for another human being in the history of mankind. Harry has even said his death would be insignificant to Colosso not winning this battle with Tuffy. He has no idea that Colosso has nothing but contempt for him and sees him as the sniveling minuscule person that he is in fact. When Harry is not near, Colosso loves to mock him by hobbling like him, imitating his grotesque hero worship look and mimicking his stupid little nothings in his pathetic voice tone.

Carla Barglor - *State University of America Board of Trustees Member*

Carla is a mid-fifties married woman who lives in a strong agricultural region of the state. She is an exceptionally opinionated person who loves to be in control but perceives Colosso as the personification of State; and thus she does all his dirty battling in the press and in other areas to support the whims and desires of Colosso. For an analogy, she would be the judgmental Cardinal condemning any Bishop or Priest who challenged the Pope even on a tiny secular point; and would then slovenly kiss the Pope's ring and ostentatiously defend even the most unchristian dictates of a senile or lying Pope as God given. She is actually not very bright but is part of a very wealthy long term agricultural family. She stupidly perceives the deference to her power and money as a deference to her intelligence and cleverness. Colosso is able to build her up as a brilliant strategist whose very activities make the difference between a great State University of America under his control and a horrid, despised, low level university under the control of Tuffy and the sports clique. Rarely has a person had this type of cantankerous, influential, effective and loyal type of servant as Colosso has with Carla.

Karen Wood - *State University of America Board of Trustees Member*

Karen is a mid-forties married woman who long ago was referred to as a woman of high potential. Her role in her political party has never been major and when put on the Board of Trustees, it was simply seen as something to do for a long time loyal but basically ineffectual person. She sees herself as an instrument to help Colosso reach his greatness through unity with the greatness of State University of America under his total control. Karen has a minor bureaucratic position in an organization with a big title and no authority. She greatly enjoys being invited into the "great kingdom" of Colosso and loves to see herself as a strategist as she blindly does whatever is the desire of Colosso. Rarely has a chief executive had such a loyal and obedient person doing his biding as Colosso has with Karen. The greatest thing that can happen in her life, as with Harry and Carla, is to be near Colosso, receive praise from him and do what he desires without question.

Appendix B

May 1, 1990 *Detroit Free Press* article of Charlie Vincent

MSU is tarnished by Perles-DiBiaggio fued

At Michigan State University, they keep wallowing in their own sludge pit.

And when they tire of rolling around in the muck and insulting each other and pointing fingers at each other, they say the press, too, is to blame for their sorry state of affairs.

They say the press exacerbated the polarization between football coach George Perles and president John DiBiaggio.

I knew exacerbating was a bad thing to do, but I wasn't quite sure what it meant until I looked it up and found it defined as "to increase the bitterness or violence of…"

DiBiaggio received almost unanimous media support in his attempt to block Perles from being named athletic director as well as head football coach. I joined in that support, not because I think it is immoral to hold both positions, but because I thought it was important that the president's authority not be undermined.

DiBiaggio lost; Perles won.

It's over.

Life goes on.

It is time for the president's office and the athletic department to mend fences and move on together, in unison, in a fashion that would benefit the school, the athletic program and the young men and women student-athletes.

That is the reasonable thing to do. The proper thing. The civilized thing.

But it is not the way business is conducted at Michigan State these days.

DiBiaggio's pride has been hurt. He has lost the game, and now he has taken his ball and gone home.

And he's not talking to the guy who beat him -- his football coach and soon-to-be athletic director.

Perles turns tables on DiBiaggio

They exchanged letters recently. Perles asked for a meeting, and DiBiaggio responded: "I must advise you that I feel it is in the best interest of the university that I distance myself from intercollegiate athletics and particularly from the football program. My participation will be very limited."

The most vehement of DiBiaggio supporters make a case for such a position, noting Perles' football program is under an internal investigation because of the reported use of steroids by Tony Mandarich and others. Some say DiBiaggio was too involved in sports and only now is normalizing his relationship with the athletic program.

But it seems communication, if not observation, is the best way to prevent violations. If DiBiaggio locks himself in an academic closet, will it improve the Spartans' image or their perceived behavior?

Not only does he come across as a poor loser, but as a man who has already judged his athletic program to be guilty of something and cannot distance himself from the mess quickly enough.

So he's holding a grudge and driving the wedge deeper between academics and athletics.

And how does Perles respond?

He responds by allowing the personal letter from DiBiaggio to somehow slip away from him long enough to be copied and passed around.

Perles probably did not do it himself, but the letter could not have been circulated had he not allowed it to be.

And why not? It makes Perles look good. Didn't he try to patch things up? Didn't he come offering the olive branch of peace?

And DiBiaggio refused it.

So who's the bad guy now?

Michigan State deserves better

Is DiBiaggio the villain because he refuses to meet with Perles and set the MSU athletic ship back on course together?

Is it Perles because he failed to honor the confidentiality of a personal correspondence that made him look good?

No!

No, it is the media for printing the story. DiBiaggio, the beneficiary of an almost unanimously supportive press, said so in his letter to Perles.

"I think the integrity and the credibility of Michigan State University have been compromised, a situation that has been exacerbated by the manner in which the media has handled the entire situation," he wrote.

Well, I'm sorry, I reject the notion. I plead innocent.

The guilt does not lie with the media.

It lies with two grown men, who are supposed to be among the leaders in their professions in this nation, who have refused to deal with each other in a civilized and honorable manner.

Between them they have dug a sludge pit around the school both profess to love, and now they are wallowing in it together.

It is a shame.

It is a waste.

It is a situation that should not be allowed to exist.

The board of trustees proved its strength when it overrode DiBiaggio's desires and named Perles athletic director.

Now the trustees can reaffirm that strength and do something beneficial for the school. It should demand DiBiaggio and Perles meet with them, shake hands, join forces and move on to the future instead of holding grudges over the past.

Michigan State University deserves that.

It surely does not deserve what its two most visible leaders have been giving it the past four months.

127

Appendix C

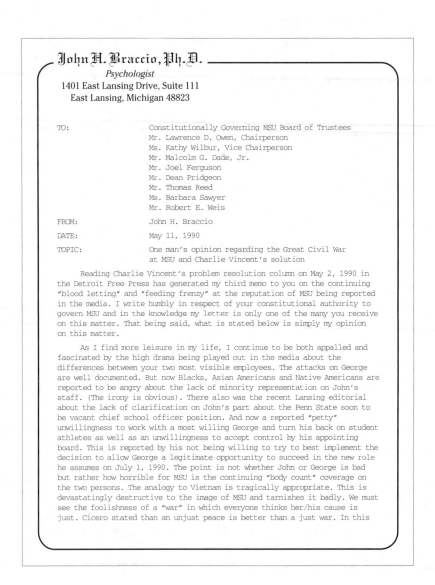

John H. Braccio, Ph.D.

Psychologist

1401 East Lansing Drive, Suite 111
East Lansing, Michigan 48823

TO: Constitutionally Governing MSU Board of Trustees
                              Mr. Lawrence D. Owen, Chairperson
                              Ms. Kathy Wilbur, Vice Chairperson
                              Mr. Malcolm G. Dade, Jr.
                              Mr. Joel Ferguson
                              Mr. Dean Pridgeon
                              Mr. Thomas Reed
                              Ms. Barbara Sawyer
                              Mr. Robert E. Weis

FROM: John H. Braccio

DATE: May 11, 1990

TOPIC: One man's opinion regarding the Great Civil War
                              at MSU and Charlie Vincent's solution

Reading Charlie Vincent's problem resolution column on May 2, 1990 in the Detroit Free Press has generated my third memo to you on the continuing "blood letting" and "feeding frenzy" at the reputation of MSU being reported in the media. I write humbly in respect of your constitutional authority to govern MSU and in the knowledge my letter is only one of the many you receive on this matter. That being said, what is stated below is simply my opinion on this matter.

As I find more leisure in my life, I continue to be both appalled and fascinated by the high drama being played out in the media about the differences between your two most visible employees. The attacks on George are well documented. But now Blacks, Asian Americans and Native Americans are reported to be angry about the lack of minority representation on John's staff. (The irony is obvious). There also was the recent Lansing editorial about the lack of clarification on John's part about the Penn State soon to be vacant chief school officer position. And now a reported "petty" unwillingness to work with a most willing George and turn his back on student athletes as well as an unwillingness to accept control by his appointing board. This is reported by his not being willing to try to best implement the decision to allow George a legitimate opportunity to succeed in the new role he assumes on July 1, 1990. The point is not whether John or George is bad but rather how horrible for MSU is the continuing "body count" coverage on the two persons. The analogy to Vietnam is tragically appropriate. This is devastatingly destructive to the image of MSU and tarnishes it badly. We must see the foolishness of a "war" in which everyone thinks her/his cause is just. Cicero stated than an unjust peace is better than a just war. In this case, only a Pyrhic victory could result. An old African saying says that when two Rhinoceros fight together only the grass is destroyed under them. (no explanation is necessary). Please put your honest disagreements apart and insist that your most visible employees get together and work things out. George must continue to be conciliatory and John has an ethical obligation to leave or implement as best he can decisions the Board makes. Majority rules and he cannot only implement unanimous decisions that support him. You are the Constitutionally Empowered Board to govern MSU. Regardless of public opinion, you must call "the dogs off" and either make your two most visible employees work together or make some tough but necessary decisions. Like John, I want Eastern Europe back in the news and "body counts" for John and George out of the news. MSU must again have everyone pulling together.

The following solution of Charlie Vincent of the Free Press seems reasonable and acknowledges you as the Constitutional Governing Board of MSU and the responsibility that goes with it:

"The board of trustees proved its strength when it overrode DiBiaggio's desires and named Perles athletic director. Now the trustees can reaffirm that strength and do something beneficial for the school. it should demand DiBiaggio and Perles meet with them, shake hands, join forces and move on to the future instead of holding grudges over the past. It surely does not deserve what its two most visible leaders have been giving it the past four months."

On May 6, 1990 in the State Journal, Jack Ebling said the following:

"Michigan State Unbiversity is and always will be bigger than John DiBiaggio's ego and George Perles waistline…DiBiaggio and Perles are both supposed to be MSU leaders. It's time they lead it or leave it!"

On the same date, Neil Koepke said the following:

"DiBiaggio and Perles are leaders and the school deserves nothing but their best efforts. That means working together to address the issues. They don't have to be buddies. But they do have to be professionals."

While I believe tongue in cheek, I hope that what Mark Nixon suggested on May 6, 1990 is not the only solution if the Baord does not take a stronger role in this matter:

- 2 -

131

"My first reaction is to give them both a set of brass knuckles and lock them in a toilet stall for the night."

Detractors of George would seem to see him as a combination of Genghis Khan and Attila the Hun. He is perceived as a person who has ruined education in America. Others condemn the football coach for talking to the New York Jets about a job that would pay millions of dollars when he had said two years before he would not leave MSU. They say they would never even talk to another employer for a 600% salary increase under similar circumstances. There are those who believe he cannot be forgiven for his ambition and grievously he is suffering is deserved and he has not had enough yet. When John and George could not agree on the joint Coach/A.D. position, the football coach actually went to both of their employers (MSU Board of Trustees) and asked them to resolve the difference of opinion. The detractors would say, imagine what would happen in Public and Private America if employees thought they had the right to take concerns they cannot work out with their managers to higher levels. The critics say the football coach did this. The critics condemn the democratic debate the Constitutionally Governing Board had when George was chosen as the new A.D. to take effect July 1, 1990. Still other detractors condemn the football coach for noot winning enough and thus giving him the A.D. job was inappropriate. Still others have said it was un-American for the football coach to use one possible job as a "wedge" to get additional duties. This is not done in Corporate and Public America the detractors say. They would not do it and then the football coach did.

Detractors of John DiBiaggio would say that after you peel away his tremendous polish that what you have is a Petty Nonelected Charismatic Field Commander who has taken a populist issue and is skillfully manipulating popular opinion to have supreme powers and destroy the divided Constitutionally Empowered Governing MSU Board of Trustees. Analogies might be to Caesar destroying the Roman Senate/Roman Republic to give the peasants land or the attacking of the Constitutional Authority of Truman by MacArthur when he said in effect he was "defending the honor of the American Eagle" in Asia. Detractors with a Roman sense of history daily say the following: "Delenda est DiBiaggio". Detractors not that Constitutionally Empowered Boards often have been divided and sadly confused by the Nonelected Charismatic Field Commanders with a populist issue. Other critics would say that John is a media magician in the best of the Reaganesque tradition. It would thus be impossible that John does not know he could end the horrible tarnishing and bludgeoning of MSU by simply calling a media meeting with George and his Board and saying sincerely that the blood letting is over and all will now work together and that he is a member of the team. But then John is not perceived as a team player by his detractors. An ego bigger than the universe is the complaint. Critics would ask if we are really to believe he is doing his job by not dealing with George or being seen with him? Will he or the Board be accountable in 1991 when permanent appointment time comes and George cannot have possibly been given a chance to succeed? For example, did John meet with George and look at the Auburn and Illinois models to best implement the Board decision? This had to been have done months ago. But then this chief public school official will not talk to George. Is Scott able to evaluate George better than the long term MSU employee Roger Wilkenson? Was Roger's removal petty or useful? Is he being punished for supporting George for the A.D. position? Still other critics would say his ego is more important than getting all Spartans together again. There are still other detractors who would say John has failed miserably in his major diplomatic role of channelling all the powerful and yes even less powerful forces that can help MSU in the same direction. Instead John sees them as competing power sources. They ask if Michigan became great by having its chief public school officials fighting persons that could help it? Other critics believe that John's pride is legendary and he has not suffered at all. Amazingly, still other detractors would say because John wants to be a Board President, he rejects his Board as a Governing Board and he functions like a Board President and Dr. Scott in effect manages the University!

Personally, I could disagree with manyh things the detractors say. I think John has done some good in his five plus years at MSU and for that we are all grateful. The future changes in the core curriculum are positive among other things he has been able to convince his Governing Board to implement. As far as George is concerned, this son of an Italian immigrant who learned loyalty at his father's knee must look at George's commitment, loyalty and service to MSU in the 1950's, 1960's, 1970's as possible, 1980's and the the 1990's prior to passing judgment on him for the things his detractors would have us believe he has done. When I do think, compassion, appreciation, concern and genuine caring come to me for this man I do not know other than to say hello. The bottom line is that these two tought old Detroiters who are children of immigrants must work together. Thus the recommendation of Charlie Vincent is what would seem extremely logical for the Governing Board to implement.

Even though I fully support the solution oriented suggestion of Charlie Vioncent metioned above, I would like to give a "dream" of how I would love to see this tragic chapter in MSU history resolved. My dream is related to my belief that John,as an appointed employee of the Constitutionally Empowered MSU Board of Trustees to Govern MSU, must be able to diplomatically work and represent a Board made up of many diverse individuals. As Churchill said, democracy is inefficient but it is the best system we have. The dream is that a smiling and gracious John would meet the media with a smiling George, a smiling Board and sy it is over and we are again a team. John would say even if he disagreed, he will do his best to give George the best of chances to succeed in the Board's decision to have him be Coach/A.D. He would graciously acknowledge the supremacy of the Board. Then these two

Detroiters and children of immigrants would have tears of joy in their eyes as the Great MSU Civil War ended. Many of us would join with tears of joy. Greater meaning and pride would be in place for persons saying "I am a Spartan" then when Cicero long ago pridefully stated the immortal statement that said it all in Rome -- "I am a Roman Citizen".

Best to all of you in your important work and may the future be so bright in diplomacy and harmony at MSU that the sad recent past will be gradually forgotten. You need someone who can with great diplomacy now channel all the positive forces that care for MSU in the same direction. I believe with your direction this can occur. The citizens of Michigan are pleading for it and you have the power and responsibility to do it. This is an historic moment of opportunity for ordinary persons to do an extraordinary act for the common good of MSU. What an opportunity!

cc: Charlie Vincent
      George Perles
      John DiBiaggio

A Man Through the Ages
or
A Man Who Walked with Caesar and Byron

A family fantasy

Written By:
John H. Braccio, Ph.D.

Table of Contents

A Preface To

"A Man Through The Ages
or
A Man Who Walked with Caesar and Byron"

Even a psychologist can speculate on personality development in a person who does not follow a normal aging process. I have always been intrigued by how a person would personally develop who lived for centuries. I chose the age of thirty-five for the person in this family fantasy because he would still be in the flush of life with all of life's passions in full force; however, he also would have lived long enough to develop sufficient maturity to hopefully be able to adapt to change and survive over the centuries. In that I have been fascinated with the lives of Caesar, Horace, Ben Johnson, William Shakespeare, Ovid, William Hazlett and Lord Byron, periods of time and anecdotes were easy to put into the dialogue. More difficult was deciding on what type of personality the thirty-five year old would initially need and then evolve into so he could have survived over more than two thousand years. An additional interest would be his impact on persons he knows who find out how long he has lived. That is enough said prior to your reading my conclusions on how I have addressed these points. I have chosen to put two main characters into the fantasy drama over seventy years old. Too often, persons of this age, and even much younger, are not given credit for having minds greatly enhanced by experiences and philosophically having come to terms with the obvious changes in adjustment that result from aging and preparing for both death and an afterlife. Instead we see persons, even sometimes only over sixty, excluded from public consciousness or presented as ill, stricken with dementia, alzheimer's disease or childlike and not able to think for themselves. I wrote this to give a more accurate picture of reality as well as a tribute to many remarkable, clearthinking and perceptive human beings, well into their lifespaces, with whom I have had the pleasure to work in therapy and/ or know as family and friends.

List of Characters in Order of Appearance

Guido Bucciferri - Professor Emeritus of Ancient Roman History at State University of America.

Mary Quigley - Professor Emeritus of English Literature at State University of America.

Benjamin - Professor of English Literature at State University of America.

Mark Fredericks - Professor of Ancient languages at State University of America.

Janice - Professor of English Literature at State University of America.

Maria Leonardo - Professor Emeritus of Ancient Roman Archaeology and History at the University of Rome.

Francesca - Secretary to Maria.

Dr. Judy McIntire - Private Practice Psychologist.

President Klemczak - President of State University of America.

Secretary Haddad - Secretary of Historical Affairs of the United Nations.

Dr. DeGaulle - Professor of Latin Studies at the University of Paris.

Charles Smith - Professor of English at State University of America.

Harry Root - Professor of History at State University of America.

Scene 1

(The setting is the family room of Professor Mary Quigley of the Department of English at State University of America. A small group of professors are discussing academic subjects. With the exception of Mark Fredericks, Professor of Ancient Languages, all are experts in the literature of the English Romantic period. At this moment, Mary is greeting Professor Guido Bucciferri, Professor Emeritus of Ancient Roman History, as he enters into her family room.)

Guido: Mary, it is not often you invite me over to a get together at your home with the English Lit folks. What is going on?

Mary: I am glad you could make it.

Guido: Well, I had no trouble doing that; but why am I here?

Mary: Old friends like you and me deserve to see each other from time to time. However, I do have another reason I wanted to talk to you.

Guido: I knew it; and what is it?

Mary: Guido, I am really fascinated with Mark Fredericks. He has a grasp of English literature that amazes me.

Guido: Sometimes you make it sound like because we are more interested in Ancient Rome than modern times that we could not know anything about anything else. Remember, we study all literatures since Rome to determine the influence of both classical Rome and Greece. The result is very broad based literary knowledge. Have you forgotten Mark was married to Judy Thomas, a topnotch Byron[1] scholar?

Mary: No, but it is much more than that. He really seems to know things I would not expect anyone to know that was not there at those times.

---

[1] <u>Byron</u> - (1788-1824). George Gordon Lord Byron. Flamboyant British poet who created the Byronic hero based on his own lifestyle.

Guido: *(With a smile and said with lightness.)* Again, I say we are a great and very knowledgeable bunch that study Ancient Rome.

Mary: *(Said earnestly and slightly annoyed.)* I know you are seeing this in a kidding sense, but I tell you he knows things he cannot really know without having been living there at those times.

Guido: You are being a little too vague for me; of what time period are we talking?

Maria: Most specifically, the early 1800's up to the death of Byron in 1827... as crazy as that seems.

Guido: Oh please, are you now going to say he has been living for centuries?

Mary: Well obviously I am not saying that, but I am curious how he knows what he knows. I am just baffled and intrigued.

Guido: You are still being too general and vague with me with this wild tale; be more specific.

Mary: Okay, let us take Lord Byron. A few weeks ago I was looking through a recently discovered diary by a friend and contemporary of his during the time he was living in Italy. The diary gives specific quoted statements of Byron about William Hazlett[2], the literary critic, Napoleon Bonaparte[3] and many of the leaders of that period. It is a goldmine of anecdotal information on him over a period of two years. Do you know who William Hazlett was?

Guido: Yes, I do because Mark and I have talked of him many times. You also might remember Mark and I did a paper on the impact of Ancient Rome and Greece on nineteenth century Romantic Literature.

Mary: I do....so at least you are aware of the period I am concerned about.

Guido: Okay, and while the diary sounds like a great find, I still cannot see what this has to do with Mark.

Mary: Guido, nobody knew the scorn Byron was feeling in relation to Hazlett at that time. He was boldly ridiculing Hazlett as an emotional midget in relation to what he knew of his views about him and his works. Mark has always said a visiting Englishman named Mike Johnson was

---

[2] William Hazlett - (1778-1830). British literary critic and painter who was a good friend of many key literary persons of his day.   [3] Napoleon Bonaparte - (1769-1821). Brilliant general and Emperor of the French.

at some of these previously undocumented parties and told Hazlett what Byron was saying about him. Mark also said it was these reported statements of Byron that offended Hazlett at that time and he never forgave him. This really explains why Hazlett never praised Byron the man or his work to the level he deserved. Hazlett's notorious problems with real or perceived criticism would explain what led to his unfairly judging Byron the man and his work.

Guido: While I am not a Byron scholar, this does not seem so exceptional. Mark must have guessed. Also, as I said before, remember his late wife was a world class Byron scholar who uniquely interpreted and discovered many things about him.

Mary: Two things.

Guido: No one knew of a Mike Johnson until this diary became public. And second, I now question who made the discoveries. Her best insights and great discoveries were done after she met Mark. I believe it was somehow his knowledge or insight that led to her greatness.

Guido: Oh Mary!

Mary: Let me be more specific. The diary in question was of a Count Finelli. As a specific example, he describes in detail a party that Byron attended at his residence with a previously unknown Mike Johnson present. He stated that under the influence of heavy drinking and earlier in the evening amorous activities, Byron was brutally mocking and blasting Hazlett as a person, painter and literary critic; and told Johnson to tell him what he was saying that evening. Finelli said that Johnson, also under the influence of drinking, said he was already writing to Hazlett and telling him about similar statements of Byron and that he would tell him all when he was with him in two months. Finelli then wrote Byron dramatically smashed the glass he was drinking out of and demanded it be done. Johnson nodded in agreement and smashed his glass to cement the agreement; then the two drunk men embraced each other and went to pour another drink. He described the setting, who was there and what was discussed. Oh yes, he even described the weather.

Guido: And...*(There then is a pause.)* What more is there?

Mary: Some time ago, Mark described this specific party in detail to me to justify his views on why Hazlett so strongly criticized Byron the man and his work; he had to be there to know what he knows. Guido, this diary was lost until three months ago and has only been available to scholars in the past thirty days. I promise you, this party, the persons who were there and what was discussed were not known three months ago. In a kidding tone, he once even named and described the previously unknown Count Finelli and his simultaneously amazing and annoying Byron by feverishly writing his detailed diary in his presence. How could he have known this; or about Byron and Johnson smashing their glasses to cement the agreement?

Guido: Oh please Mary, this sounds absurd.

Mary: There is more! Count Finelli also describes a congenial and for his age youthful looking man named Marco. He was a friend of Byron with whom he often spoke Latin and discussed the classics. He states the man's superlative grasp of Latin and awareness of things long before his birth were eerie to experience and he was compelling to hear by people who got to know him.

Guido: And you think this Marco of more than one hundred and fifty years ago is our Mark?

Mary: It would appear physically impossible but it seems so reasonable when one considers what he knows about Byron. For whatever the reason, Mark has information about Byron that no one else has. The level of knowledge and insight he has about Byron is unique and impossible to explain with logic.

Guido: So why am I here?

Mary: *(Said warmly.)* Dear friend, it is because I want you here; however, I would like you to listen to Mark and see what you think about what he seems to know, or maybe more appropriately, "divine" about people and times of long ago. I will steer the conversation in the direction so you can hear for yourself what he knows; he will not disappoint us.

Guido: Even though it is trickery, I am sure Mark would approve. While I am familiar with Byron the man and his work, I am clearly not a Byron scholar.

Mary: That is all the better from my point of view. You are more detached and can get a feel for him as a person interpreting or remembering the past in an area outside of your scholarship, but in an area you are familiar.

Guido: I will do what you ask, but it is senseless. I discuss and argue with him all the time. He is a magician with words and the logical construction of historical events into conclusions to prove his arguments.

Mary: Ah! Does he seem to know more than you would expect?

Guido: Yes, but so much of what we do is conjecture due to the many years that separate us from our study; but I will admit he is often remarkable in what he knows or seems to know. But most amazingly, he is often found to be correct when new discoveries are made. Mark even recently directed me to an ancient document that allowed me to complete a translation of a previously incomplete text of a work by Cicero.

Mary: Ah! Ha! Enough said. Your very words prove my point is not unfounded.

Guido: Oh Mary!

Mary: I again ask you to just listen.

(Guido nods in agreement and they walk over to where Mark, Benjamin, Janice and a few other persons are standing and talking.)

Guido: Hello to you, friends.

Professors: Hello, Guido.

Mary: Friends, what is going on?

Benjamin: Just more discussion on literature; join us.

Mary: Whenever I do, I end up arguing with Mark.

Mark: And you love it; admit it. Guido, my old friend, a personal hello to you and join us! *(He and Guido warmly embrace and he says with a humorous tone.)* Apparently, they desire to simultaneously pick our brains and verbally attack two Romans of current times.

Mary: *(Walking over and looking at Mark, she begins to speak.)* Mark, I want to argue with you on an old concept of yours. As we have discussed on previous occasions and I say again, Byron was a romantic[4] and not at all a classicist[5].

Mark: Oh God, the same "Carthage must be destroyed"[6] talk again. The unmatched beauty of Diana[7] and handsomeness of Apollo[8] would wilt into ugliness under your continuous assault. Only a God like Mars[9] could effectively fight you; but I will try.

---

[4] Romantic - One who is an adherent to the values of the late 18th Century European Movement that accepted individual expression of emotion and rebelled against many established social rules and conventions. [5] Classicist - One who is an adherent to the values that embody the study, customs and culture of ancient Greece and Rome.
[6] Carthage must be destroyed. "Delenda est Carthago" is the famous Latin statement that Cato the Censor said daily in the Roman senate prior to the destruction of Carthage.
[7] Diana. Goddess of female beauty and love in Roman mythology. [8] Apollo. God of the sun and masculine beauty in Greek mythology. [9] Mars. God of war in Roman mythology.

Mary: Do not use all those words to confuse me.

Mark: Okay. I again say I think not Mary. In fact, I think not at all. Lord Byron was a classicist. He loved the Latin language and cultures of classical Rome and Greece. It was a classicist who swam the Hellespont to equal or outdo Leander[10].

Mary: Will you rewrite history today? Do you not know he hated Latin?

Mark: I still think that is not true; he hated the way it was taught him in his school days in England; not vibrant and living Latin. He loved to practice speaking Latin whenever he could. He often bragged his Italian was derived from the Latin he initially suffered in learning and then thrived in learning while in Italy.

Benjamin: You may speak Italian and Latin, but how do you know that about Byron? No one else knows it, has said it or written it in the past one hundred and seventy years.

Mark: While I humbly acknowledge to not be a Byron scholar, I somehow know it from my Italian studies. I see the image of him speaking in animated Italian in Ravenna about how the modern Italy of the Post Napoleonic era must be free and return to the glory of Rome. To have this image in my mind of this heroically handsome Englishman with his alabaster skin glowing red under the influence of wine, flickering candlelight, beautiful women, Italian patriots and English expatriates cannot be forgotten! He would have made a great Roman and he died a noble Greek in the cause of her freedom[11]! He was a classicist or the sun circles the earth and God made mice to rule the earth.

Mary: There you go again. Consistent with Benjamin, I have spent my professional career studying Byron and what you say you know is not known. You behave like you knew him and were there!

Mark: Ha! Ha! Oh please Mary. As with the painter and playwright, creations of the mind are as real as any memory; but what do I know and how can we give scholarly credence to my obviously artistic images of the past? Ignore my images as you would the rantings of a madman.

Benjamin: *(Said in a pensive mood and to the group.)* Such false but enjoyable humility. Why do you think Mark says such things about

---

[10] Leander. The youth of Abydos in Greek mythology who swam every night across the Hellespont to visit his love Hero. Once during a stormy night he drowned and she then threw herself into the sea to die after his body was washed on the coast of Sestus.

[11] ...he died a noble Greek in the cause of her freedom. Byron died in Missolongh, Greece trying to free her from the Turks.

144

Byron and other romantics to us? For what purpose does he come up with examples that tantalize, are impossible to disprove and seem so logical? Maybe more so, why do we let him get us going? And worst of all, why do we like him so and invite him to bother us?

Mary: Besides the fact he has had too much wine, we know Mark and we love him as a friend and an almost English Lit colleague. As Benjamin has said, his great talent is his knack for logically presenting anecdotes that he cannot prove nor we disprove. I think he only wants to raise our scholarly ire, win debating points in a subtle manner and continue being invited to the homes of the most brilliant scholars on campus: we the English Lit crowd!

(General laughter by all.)

Benjamin: I would agree with that.

Mary: Amen. I think he knows Ancient Rome intimately and wants to know our Byron the same way; but conjecture and facts are confused. History clearly states he was a nineteenth century romantic and not a classicist.

Mark: Maybe you are right. However, I stand on my position he was a classicist; but as always, I defer to your greater knowledge and wisdom in this area. *(All laugh.)* Maybe I have not had enough wine; it might help me say less; but then it might help me share other things about Byron and our many horse rides and talks in Latin together. I also could tell you much about Shelley[12].

Janice: *(Said with strong emotion.)* Oh Mark! I have said nothing to this point and have just been listening; but now you will torture us with Shelley insights?

Mark: Maybe, if torture is what you call it. He was a liberal romantic at the level of the masses who imperiously cheated and hated many fine people at a personal level. While we know how Dan Henley went to jail because Shelley would not pay a fine given to him for doing what he told him to do, this was only typical of this supreme egotist.

Janice: I think your analysis of Shelley is very harsh.

Mark: And I am not done. Byron was a man of action with the people in the Roman sense, while Shelley only helped and loved the masses at a philosophical level. Byron was scandalous but honest with women; Shelley was dishonest and a despicable scalawag with them. While all

---

[12] Shelley (1792-1822). Percy Bysshe Shelley. Britain poet and friend of Lord Byron.

145

is still not publicly written, Mary Shelley[13] and Claire Clairmont[14] wrote and spoke this truth about him often and I suspect you know more about this than you admit publicly about one of your favorites; this is said suspecting what you have found in your recent research. I somehow believe you have found some until now long lost personal materials pertaining to Mary and Claire and their views of Shelley.

Janice: Mark, how do you know anything about what I have found out? I think you are guessing and trying to get information out of me.

Mark: Okay, you are right! I just guessed. But now, back to Shelley and also Byron. I still remember their fascinating discussions with each other. Even though those discussions taught me to hate Shelley and his petty arrogance, I still praised him personally for his putting into writing the contents of those discussions in his fine "Julian and Maddalo"[15]. He ignored my praise and looked through me with a very cold and distant look. Because I did not applaud his views and once criticized his selfishness in relation to people at a personal level, he was enraged at me. However, he only showed indifference to me because he knew Byron and I were friends; and he greatly respected Byron and would have offended him by being openly angry or hostile at me.

---

[13] <u>Mary Shelley</u> (1797-1851). Mary Wollstonecraft Shelley. British writer who married Percy Shelley in 1816 after his wife Harriet committed suicide. [14] <u>Claire Clairmont</u> (1798-1879). Mary Shelley's step-sister who went on Mary's elopement with Shelley. She later fell in love with Bryon and their daughter Allegra was born in 1817. [15] <u>Julian and Maddalo.</u> Written by Shelley in 1818 and published in 1824. It related to conversations between Shelley (Julian) and Byron (Maddelo).

Mary: Oh please! Byron was bad enough, but now Shelley too! You drive me crazy. What about Keats[16]? Why not Keats too?

Mark: My images are all gone now; please pass the wine. I now prefer to be a dull madman with no visions. While such men leave no impact on the world when they leave, their lives are happy and uneventful.

Janice: You do amuse me. How do you know what I have found out about Mary's and Claire's views of Shelley late in their lives?

Mark: As I said, I guessed; and you have verified what I believe. I have long had images in my mind of Mary eloquently describing how foolish and misled she was with Shelley and how disgusting and ungrateful he was to those who cared for him back in her youth. Of course, the same can be said of Claire Clairmont later in her very long life.

Benjamin: Maybe he intrigues us and that is why you have him over. Mary, let us admit he has us going again. He even included the always cool and unflappable Janice today.

Guido: Or, is it that he enrages you folks?

Mary: He does both and much more; and I love him!

Mark: Pour the wine and let us keep talking! Ah! I must apologize: The images of the artist are once again overtaking me. I am getting the image in my mind of two days I remember as clearly as today. The crystal clear days were essentially the same, but the two men I was with were so different. A difference is that I had known one of the men many years and the other, a young Englishman, for a shorter time. Each was being inspired to write about the snow-capped mountain Soracte. I rode with both men to the base of the mountain. Horace[17] was inspired by a long lost Greek poem and Byron by the ode of Horace as he worked on his autobiographical "Childe Harold's Pilgrimage"[18].

Mary: Oh no! From two hundred years ago to two thousand!

Janice: Amen.

Guido: (With a chuckle.) May Rome live forever!

Mark: Please let me finish. In each case, we stopped and talked in the same Latin. Except for the Italian that was spoken by the peasants near

---

[16] Keats (1795-1821). John Keats. A British poet. [17] Horace (B.C. 65-8). Quintus Horatius Flaccus. Roman poet of the highest order who desired to raise Latin literature to the level of Greek. [18] Childe Harold's Pilgrimage. A semi-autobiographical poem written by Byron in 1812-18.

Byron and me and the roughly two thousand years separating the two events, everything was identical. Byron actually talked to me some hours that day. I told Byron about my riding with Horace and he laughed and called me a wise fool who could convincingly create the past in words and images; you in effect do the same; and I contend the man who wrote a poem under the inspiration of the gentle and wise Horace was a classicist; and friends, he was definitely the same George Lord Byron about whom we are speaking. It was meetings like that and our talking in Latin that led to constant discussions from which I got to know him very well and most appropriately have declared him a classicist.

Mary: I give! Pass the wine.

Benjamin: I will, but me first; and what about you Guido?

Guido: I am fine as I watch the wondrous impact of the judicious use of wine. It either masks or creates madness and/or recollections the person otherwise does not share with anyone.

Mark: You are all too profound today. En vino veritas[19] or maybe wine brings out the fool in all of us? I have foolish visions and you press me for more.

Janice: Fools are often wiser than intellectuals because they have no pressure to be profound and they can observe and speak with impunity as wise persons stupidly tell all.

Guido: Ha! Ha! This is why I enjoy you folks. I never know what will come out of your discussions.

Janice: You surely seem to match us in our wisdom or folly.

Guido: Touche and probably true. First Mark is challenged for knowing too much personally about Lord Byron and his activities of something less than two hundred years ago. *(With a sparkle in his eye and said with humor.)* Not to be daunted, Mark then speaks of Shelley and then his friendship with a man who lived over two thousand years ago.

Benjamin: And amazingly, Mark always puts a tinge of doubt into my mind as to whether or not he is right or was even really there.

Mary: Me too. I even feel foolish I talked to Guido about this.

Mark: I love it; and remember, I speak too much to be wise and too little to be a complete fool.

---

[19] <u>En vino veritas.</u> Latin saying that when drinking wine, people often unwittingly speak the truth.

Guido: Mark, we must talk more about the horse rides and discussions you had with Horace. Such conjecture is fascinating.

Mark: We shall my dear friend; in fact Horace would have enjoyed and loved you a lot. Like Horace, even though your father did not have great education, he saw the talent in you and worked hard to give you the best education possible; and like Horace, you seized the opportunity with great gusto. Your dust is highly charged indeed!

Mary: To imagine I asked Guido to listen to Mark and evaluate what he said. He is as bad off as we are with Mark!

Guido: *(With a chuckle.)* I take that as a compliment.

Mark: *(With humor in his voice.)* I am glad someone defends me and my ability to put in dreams or thoughts what I deduce from known facts. *(Snapping his fingers.)* The difference between memory and dreams is less than a second.

Mary: Oh please Mark. You are falsely modest in that your dreams have too much meaning to them. Unknown names, dates, events and written documents to us, but known by you, give you an uncanny ability to almost divine things; and amazingly, many of your "memories" actually show up to have occurred in the life of Byron or others that died centuries ago. To be honest with you, I sometimes think you were living with Byron and your supposed dreams or delusions are really personal memories.

Janice: While I am new to these get togethers, I must agree with Mary. *(Said with strong feeling.)* Mark, you do amaze the hell out of me!

Guido: *(With a chuckle.)* Crude, but clearly makes the point. (Spoken seriously.) Is not the key to art that it mirror reality?

Benjamin: *(Responding to the statement of Guido and looking at Mary.)* I would say that is true Mary.

Mary: *(Speaking to Mark.)* Well, all I can say is that you still cause me turmoil and awe!

Mark: Mary, I thank you for the inadvertent compliment; and I suggest we work on my creating only awe for you rather than turmoil.

Mary: Oh, you really do Mark and you know it.

Mark: I hope you will permit me to leave. A professor is waiting for a translation I said I would do for her.

Mary: *(With a light voice tone.)* I permit you to leave because I have no other choice.

Guido: Mark, may I walk you to your car?

Mark: Does the Pope turn down the Sunday collection?

Mary: I assume the answer is yes.

Mark: Of course. *(Looking at Mary and shaking her hand warmly.)* And I thank you for the invitation to your home. Mary, I really feel fully alive and accepted with you and your friends. That is important to me and I thank you for that. *(She grabs him and takes a hug.)*

(Everyone says good-bye. Mary walks with Guido and Mark to the door.)

Mary: I care for you Mark and I took my hug! I thank you for coming. You keep my cardiovascular system in good shape.

Guido: That appears to be true for all the others here also.

Mark: I thank you for the hug; and please quit taking me so seriously!

Guido: Amen to that and I want my hug. *(He and Mary laugh and warmly embrace.)*

Mary: I am wacky or you are unique indeed.

Mark & Guido: Unique indeed; and maybe you are also wacky!

(They all laugh.)

Mary: *(With a smile and said warmly.)* Until later and again I thank you for coming.

End of Scene

Scene 2

(The setting is outside of Rome, Italy, in the large study of the family estate home of Professor Maria Leonardo of the University of Rome. Guido Bucciferri has been reviewing recently discovered original Latin writings from the time of Julius Caesar[1]. Guido is walking into the large study of Maria. They see each other, embrace and begin talking.)

Guido: Maria, it is so good to see you. I am so excited and ready to talk about this astonishingly incredible Roman find you have made. This is a discovery of such titanic proportions as to awe even mighty Jupiter[2] himself.

Maria: Dear Guido, even after all the years we have known each other, I always enjoy your enthusiasm and kind use of words to describe my work. Have you had a chance to see and read all the documents yet?

Guido: Yes, I have. In fact, it is hard for me to believe that after over two thousand years, the materials are still fully readable. I am so excited; the handwriting even looks familiar.

Maria: It is an ecological miracle. They were placed in the mountain in a way the temperature was constant over the years and miraculously no precipitation got in to destroy them.

Guido: To me, as remarkable and impossible as it sounds, it would appear these writings were written by a man that took notes for Julius Caesar on a personal day by day basis to the eve itself of when he crossed the Rubicon[3]. Am I right? Is that also your opinion?

Maria: *(Said with excitement.)* Guido, it is safe to say it is more than an opinion; it is absolutely true and so incredible that no one I know has ever heard of such a thing. The find is completely unique and absolutely overwhelming in terms of personal interest and historical findings.

---

[1] Julius Caesar - (B.C. 100-44). Gaius Julius Caesar. Great Roman general, writer and dictator. [2] Jupiter. King of the Gods in Roman mythology. [3] Rubicon. The famous river in Italy that Caesar crossed in 49 B.C. and thus declared war against the Roman Republic.

Guido: How did you ever figure to dig in that remote area near the Fiumicino River? I mean it is not so significant these materials were found near it, but how did you possibly know to go and dig in this otherwise totally secluded area? As an aside, this surely shows the Fiumicino, and not the Pisciatello or Uso, is the Rubicon of Caesar.

Maria: It actually is an old story. Even though we have known each other for many many years, there are family matters we have never really discussed. My father was sixty when I was born and when he was twenty-five, his father somehow was inexplicably killed or disappeared. My father said he told him the general area to carefully look to try to find materials such as we were seeking and found. As you know, his father was also a professor of ancient languages at the University of Rome, wrote many articles and performed much research in this area. My father was so busy over the years of his life on other finds and projects, as have I over the decades, that just in the past few years have I undertaken research based on those suggestions made to my father so very long ago.

Guido: I was not aware your father had been told this by his father.

Maria: I have really had no reason to talk about it. Along with many other suggestions similar to this, my father and then I have kept it a family secret since at least 1880...when my father last talked to his father and he was continuing an already brilliant career in this field for someone so young. My father said it was actually the last suggestion of my grandfather before he disappeared; and I really did the excavation out of memory to my father and his memory of his father. His spirit and presence have seemed very strong during this work and that has been helpful and warm to me.

Guido: How wonderful for you. Memories and images in the mind are often what we determine them to be with purposeful action on our part to bring them out in full bloom.

Maria: Spoken like the philosopher you are. What amazes me is that so much of what Plutarch[4] wrote and we know about Caesar is actually accurate. The astonishing thing is that we now know what he was thinking the night before he crossed the Rubicon and irretrievably changed western civilization. During my whole life time, I have often dreamed of knowing at a personal level what Caesar thought and

---

[4] Plutarch (A.D. 50-125). Greek moralist and biographer of famous Romans and Greeks.

actually said as he began the great Roman Civil War[5]. To now be able to read the first hand answers in the handwriting of an exact contemporary that was not only with him that night but who talked intimately about his decision, is inspiring and exciting at the same time.

Guido: *(Said pensively.)* To me, it is almost like what I have sought in my whole life has now been achieved.

Maria: *(Said with humor.)* Please Guido, you are only seventy-five and certainly in no situation to be feeling so old and ready to give up. Remember, I am seventy-eight years old and this discovery brings me closer to the memory of my father and actually makes me feel younger.

Guido: *(With a laugh.)* I am not feeling old or ready to give up; I am simply overwhelmed, awestruck and drained at the same time. This is just astonishing to me. Amazingly Maria, I actually have a colleague at State University of America that has spoken with me and has basically said the same thing that is written here. He has been able to understand what was going on in Caesar's mind way beyond what we know of him from any of his contemporaries until this time. He also has always strongly stated his belief the Fiumicino River was without doubt the Rubicon that Caesar crossed; he even says he knows the exact spot and can still smell the warlike red dust storm that swirled around violently and covered it as Caesar's invincible battle hardened legions somberly crossed it en masse as the venerable Roman Republic tumultuously exploded into cataclysmic civil war from which it would cease to exist.

Maria: Who is this man? Besides being somewhat dramatic, he sounds very interesting and prophetic.

Guido: He is both of those to the extreme. In fact, I know no one more accomplished in classical Latin, Greek and other languages of that period. I say this about a man whom I have known fifteen years, is no more than fifty and does not look a day over thirty-five. I hope you will have a chance to meet him when you visit next month. Unfortunately, he was out of town the last time you visited three years ago and also the two times before that. His name is Mark Fredericks.

Maria: I do not know him and am surprised he has not come to visit and meet with us; I have noticed you and a few others have made glowing acknowledgments to him in various research papers and books.

---

[5] <u>Roman Civil War</u>. Began in 49 B.C. when Caesar crossed the Rubicon and ended in 31 B.C. when Octavius Caesar defeated Mark Anthony.

Guido: He has been here many times but is a person who keeps to himself at a professional level. He actually has been working more as a resource to me and my colleagues and is just a brilliant language person. Amazingly, he also seems to have an astonishingly uncanny ability of knowing things about long dead persons that others just do not know. While a few see him as kind of an analytical and convincing bullshitter, most are amazed at all the things he seems to know; and no one questions his horizonless ability in languages and deducing major finds from very meager facts.

Maria: I would really like to meet him. He sounds like an interesting man; a very interesting man. *(Speaking in a pensive manner.)* I really am surprised he has not come to see us and I do not know him personally.

Guido: It is also very surprising to me, particularly in that he certainly knows of you and your work intimately. We have discussed you and your work often and he is very impressed with your life achievement to date. Also surprisingly, he enthusiastically surmised you might find something like you did when I told him last year where you and your team were digging; and why he never talked to you about this in trips to Italy is also surprising.

Maria: Do you remember what he said?

Guido: Yes. He said you were not far from where Caesar crossed the Rubicon and believed some very important historical written documents of the period were ready to be discovered. I did not take him too seriously and he obviously was right. I again say for such an easygoing scholar, he was very excited about your prospects for a major discovery.

Maria: What did you say to him when he told you this?

Guido: Not very much. Mark is always making predictions and presenting his views. I could never talk to him if I reacted to everything he said. But enough of Mark; I really would like to know more things about your father. In spite of all the time we have spent together, I only know of him by reputation and some personal stories you have told me and the fact he made many archaeological and historical discoveries of the Roman period that were really unique and ground breaking for the rest of us. While I know something of your grandfather, I really only know of him as a noted scholar of ancient languages and more of a behind the stage kind of a person.

Maria: That is because he was that kind of man. Would you like to see the only picture I have of him?

Guido: Very much so; and I apologize for not having talked to you more about your father as a person.

Maria: Apologies are out of order among true friends when no bad purposeful acts have occurred. We also can talk more about my father as you desire. But now please Guido, back to the picture. It is a family treasure and was taken of him and my father the day before his mysterious disappearance. *(Maria goes to a drawer and opens it, takes out a picture and brings it to Guido.)* Here, take a look Guido.

Guido: *(Guido carefully looks at the picture and then looks awestrucken.)* My God! This cannot be that old of a picture.

Maria: I certainly promise you it is.

Guido: It cannot be! It just cannot be!

Maria: What are you talking about Guido? I have known this picture since I was a young girl. It was a prized picture of my father and the one that has been so important in my family. I remember my father looking at it periodically for long periods of time. He would sit in that chair *(pointing to it)*, stare at it and say nothing. What he thought, only he knew. I now do the same thing and think of him so much and what we had together. Maybe he did the same thing about his father.

Guido: *(Said in a most earnest manner.)* Maria, please listen to me.

Maria: Guido, settle down; you really do look like you have seen a ghost.

Guido: *(Pointing with his finger.)* You see the picture of your grandfather here?

Maria: Of course I do; what are you thinking?

Guido: You know that man I was talking about at State University of America?

Maria: Mark Fredericks?

Guido: Yes......

Maria: Guido, what is going on? Tell me what is happening to you.

Guido: *(Said very excitedly.)* I promise you that that is he; it is Mark exactly; even the smile is identical. Except for the beard and hairstyle, there is not one difference between him and Mark. It is either the astonishing cosmic phenomenon of two duplicates placed more than a century apart or Mark is indeed your grandfather.

Maria: *(Said with laughing incredulousness.)* Guido, what has happened to you? I know you are not senile or a clown, but this is really too incredible to take seriously.

Guido: Would you believe it if I were to fax a picture of him right now? There is a picture of him and me on my desk that was recently taken at a presentation we gave together. *(Looking closely at the picture with a magnifying glass.)* The two even have the same clepped chin and slightly crooked half smile.

Maria: Oh, please Guido, my grandfather died long ago and certainly is not alive now. While we are historians, it is an issue of pure physics.

Guido: Then give me one possible explanation? You yourself said no one really knows what happened to him.

Maria: *(Said incredibly.)* But Guido, that was in 1880! One illogical but possible explanation is that he did not die and came to the United States and had a child very late in life; and this is his grandson. As I said, to me, this is illogical and very highly unlikely, but it is certainly more reasonable than this is the same person in an unaged state. *(With a smile.)* He would even be my cousin!

Guido: *(Walking nervously around the room talking and wringing his hands as if alone.)* I have always felt he was a different kind of a person. My professor friend Mary saw it also but I was too blind to see it. I was too close to Mark. He has always had too much information about too many things and people over too many periods of time to be possible for a normal human being. The only conclusion, irrational as it is, is that he in fact has somehow lived in many periods of time. A possible but very unlikely alternative is that he regularly uses sources available only to him to help with his seemingly uncanny beliefs that lead to so many discoveries of materials lost even since the time of Rome; but I do not believe that is the case. My disciplined mind is up to irrational thoughts; a new activity for a seventy-five year old professor emeritus. Ha! Ha!

Maria: This is absolutely ridiculous; incredible; remarkable; and indeed impossible. You should hear yourself!

Guido: Will you at least be willing to see the picture?

Maria: I promise; but that will still not convince me it is him. Guido, you either have been drinking too much or you need a drink; and you know I only approve of drinking wine in moderation with meals.

Guido: Hold the chariots! I am going to call my office in America and have the picture faxed by my secretary, Pat. I am overwhelmed but ready for battle! Bring on the picture.

Maria: *(Said with resignation.)* Wait just a minute, Guido. I will have Francesca call her and have it faxed; maybe that will be helpful to you. Guido, I have never seen you like this; and I have seen you in many, many moods indeed.

Guido: I have never seen me like this either; certainly not in many decades. *(Maria leaves the room to talk to Francesca. Guido is speaking to himself.)* What is happening? Could it be Mark is her grandfather and rode with Caesar himself as a personal secretary? *(He rubs his beard and is in heavy thought.)* How absurd but plausible under the circumstances.

Maria: *(She walks in.)* Guido, we hopefully will have it shortly. While all this is exciting, please let us talk about these findings of a lifetime. Rest assured, we will have an explanation of Mark.

Guido: Indeed we shall.

Maria: In a selfish, youthful and foolish way, I hope he is my grandfather; but at my age, reason and caution certainly win out over fantasy and irrational thinking.

Guido: *(Said with great passion.)* Oh phooey! We can give full reign to our intuitions because nothing is expected of ancient ones in this day and age and we have no socially pretentious inhibitions. To imagine a man I have known as a colleague, and yes even a friend for fifteen years, could have been an intimate with Caesar makes the chemicals that make me up bubble with the excitement one expects in adolescence when passions so often rule reason.

Maria: I wish you could hear yourself; surely you would not want anyone else to hear you.

Guido: *(Said dramatically and throwing his hands and arms in the air.)* I could care less. I have been proven right in my life many times when the facts were nowhere as strong as in this situation. *(Said with firmness and sincerity.)* Maria, I think he is what I believe him to be.

(Francesca enters with the picture and gives it to Maria.)

Francesca: Doctor Leonardo, this is the picture Dr. Bucciferri wanted to have sent.

Maria: Thank you Francesca. *(Holding it in the air and waving it.)* Well, here it is Guido; let us take a look.

Guido: Look! *(Pointing his finger at it.)* Is that not the same person?

Maria: *(Said with surprise.)* Oh my! I must admit they look remarkably alike; in fact, the resemblance is eerie; in fact, the resemblance in an imperfect world is perfect.

Guido: I do not know how, but it is the same person; I know it!

Maria: Guido, think of what you are saying; it just does not make sense. There surely is a reasonable explanation; but I must admit at least doubts come into this old head of mine.

Guido: Tell me something about the parents of your grandfather; tell me something about their lives.

Maria: There is nothing to tell. He was an orphan and had no family.

Guido: There, is that not something else to lend credit to what I am saying.

Maria: It simply shows my grandfather was an orphan and not that he is still alive.

Guido: Has it not surprised you your grandfather does not really look that much older than your father in the picture?

Maria: I must admit that has always been somewhat confusing to me and noticed by many persons. My father would laugh when told this and said it was an off day for him and an on day for his father. Contemporaries of my father and grandfather often commented on this; and a dear friend of mine, my father and grandfather, who lived well into her

158

nineties, said many years ago she felt he began to seem awkward around people a few years before he disappeared or died. She also said he was strange; and yes that was the word, in that he never seemed to age in the twelve years she knew him.

Guido: You are not supporting your case.

Maria: Oh Guido, I am simply explaining it is no secret how young he appeared. Another friend of my grandfather, Giovanna Rossi, who once had a discreet but I believe intense romantic relationship with him, told me how she aged and actually felt he did not age. From a romantic relationship, she later felt she additionally became like an older confidant to him as the years passed. She also said how he seemed to be very sad and preoccupied with something before his mysterious disappearance. Giovanna said she tried to talk to him about it several times but he would not tell her anything. She said this even though one night after a party at their home and under the influence of wine, he cried in her arms and said he was feeling he would be alone again and that she would never believe what he could tell her about himself. She pressed him about it, but he only wept into sleep and would say nothing. When Giovanna talked about this the next day, he was polite but coolly denied the significance of what he said and simply stated the wine was at work doing crazy things to his mind.

Guido: Then what happened?

Maria: Nothing. He disappeared a few days later.

Guido: You must realize everything you tell me only reinforces my beliefs. Tell me something of your grandmother; and did they always live in this area?

Maria: My grandmother was ill when she met my grandfather and died when Papa was thirteen years old. Apparently, she had some type of what we would call turberculosis at this time. What else did you ask me Guido?

Guido: I asked if they always lived in this area?

Maria: No. My grandfather came to the community of my mother and he moved here after she died and joined the university.

Guido: I thought so. Maria, can you at least admit the facts really do seem to be all coming together in support of my crazy idea? *(Said humorously and rolling his eyes like a comical madman.)* Maybe old mad Guido is wise indeed.

Maria: Guido, I must admit the circumstances are strange and I have often had questions about my grandfather that Papa really never answered. He seemed to know more than he said. It also was surprising how he seemed to always know where to dig and gather information that often led to great discoveries about Ancient Rome that no one else ever found or had any idea where to look. His command of Latin and its nuances were also singularly unique. While it was attributed to him, he always said it was because of his father. Papa even stated they often spoke in Latin and his father demanded he be able to speak it as well as any other language. While disappointed I did not speak Latin like he did, this never bothered him; he even said maybe that was better.

Guido: Maria, was there anyone in particular who was uniquely helpful to your father during his long career at a professional level?

Maria: What do you mean?

Guido: Well, if this crazy thing is possible, your father had to have known that Mark lived a very long time. And .....

Maria: Why do you think that is true?

Guido: Because your father was twenty-five when they were last together. There is no way he could have hidden the fact he did not age to his only son that he was with for twenty-five years. At least it would appear impossible and the picture of the two does not make them look that different in age.

Maria: You make sense even though I cannot believe two scientists that have lived one hundred and fifty three years between the two could be having such an absurd talk; *(Said with a chuckle and twinkle in her eye.)* and Guido, I love it!

Guido: It is a well documented fact your father made a series of sparkling discoveries over his brilliant long career. Assuming your grandfather had something to do with this and they kept in contact over the many years through correspondence, we should be able to find him in other roles with different names.

Maria: A reasonable conclusion even if absolutely incredible; but as I said, I actually am loving it. As I think about it, there were some men my father communicated with often over his lifetime. I clearly remember that in the last ten years of his life...and during a time I also was very interested in this field, there was a Professor Riolo in Argentina.

Guido: I thought so, but had no idea what names he would have used.

Maria: His full name was Carlo Horacio Riolo. He was at the University of Buenos Aires and they had an extensive correspondence during at least the last ten years of Papa's life. Guido, I really think we are on to something.

Guido: What do you mean?

Maria: When Papa was on his deathbed back so many years ago, he had me send a telegram to Buenos Aires with the goal of making contact with Professor Riolo. I remember how important it was for him that he see him before he died. I always thought of it as Papa simply wanting to make contact with a colleague that had been very helpful to him over the years.

Guido: And that would be reasonable. Did you ever see him?

Maria: Yes. I was twenty-one years old at the time. It was a very strange evening when a man came to our door; there was tremendous rain and the wind was bellowing outside. It was a frightful evening. It seemed Neptune[6] and Mars were in a rage. It was very late; probably around one in the morning. Earlier in the day, Papa had told me he wanted to talk to Professor Riolo with only the two of them there and did not want to be disturbed. I remember asking Papa if he were really up to this due to his health and will never forget the look on his face. He suddenly seemed very angry and stated he absolutely was able to meet with this man and did not like my questioning him. This was not at all like him and certainly showed a lot of emotion on his part. I immediately backed off and told Papa I would do what he wanted. *(Said with strong emotion.)* I still remember that look and statement as clearly as this moment...

Guido: Maria, tell me what happened that evening.

Maria: Again, as I was saying earlier, the night was horrible. I had been reading Juvenal[7] and was momentarily thinking about the horrible weather; and all of a sudden there was a loud knock at the door that startled me. The butler answered the door and a man said he was there to see my father. At that moment, I came out of the dining quarters to see who was there. Before the man said who he was, Papa, who had been able to walk only a very little over the past few months, was actually walking like a relatively young man to meet him. The man entered our home and immediately ran over to my father and the two of them hugged and began crying with intense emotion. All their words of endearment

---

[6] Neptune. God of the sea in Roman mythology. [7] Juvenal. (60 A.D.-136). Decimus Iunius Iuvenalis. The greatest Roman writer of satire.

were spoken in Latin. They then walked back to this very room and Papa closed the door. Within an hour and in spite of what he told me, I became worried and knocked on the door and called to him. Papa came to the door and opened it half way and reiterated in his customary friendly tone what he had said earlier in the day: He did not want to be disturbed while with his friend and colleague from Argentina. While this stranger to me still had his large coat and hat on, Papa introduced me to him; I remember Papa saying it was a pleasure having me meet him because he had been a great friend and support to him over many years. The man said in a melodious and flawless Italian he was charmed to meet me, had great respect and caring for Papa, and knew I would do great work in the future. He also said he and my father would be talking about things they felt I would be developing long into the future. I thanked him, said goodbye to Papa and left. It was rather apparent Papa did not want me to be there to share in their discussions, to see the stranger or get to know him better.

Guido: Did you get a good look at him?

Maria: No, the lighting was poor and he kept his clothes about him in a way I was not able to see his face; but everything certainly fit to convince me the visitor was Carlo Horacio Riolo.

Guido: Was there anything that seemed unique or different about him?

Maria: Only that his soft and warm voice seemed like that of a younger man than I anticipated; but then I never got a good look at him.

Guido: Was it like your father to in effect keep you away from a conversation with a professional colleague in your own home?

Maria: Not at all. In fact, it hurt my feelings then and has bothered me ever since. It was so unlike Papa. They spent the whole night together and my ill father walked over the grounds with Professor Riolo before he left in the morning as mysteriously as he appeared the night before.

Guido: How did you know they walked around the grounds?

Maria: I saw them from a distance early in the morning from my bedroom window.

Guido: Why did you not go down to see them?

Maria: Guido! Must you ask?

Guido: I apologize.

Maria: I accept your apology, dear friend.

Guido: I am just so curious.

Maria: Well, so am I. But in those days, and for me always, I respected Papa and let him have this time alone with his friend. What amazed and frightened me was the way Papa seemed so much younger again and was walking with energy I knew his ailing body did not have. He was obviously moving on nerves and pure willpower; his body alone could not have carried him.

Guido: Forgive me, but could not seeing his father under those circumstances create such an extraordinary energy source?

Maria: Oh Guido! *(After a pause, said with earnestness.)* I do believe we are on to something unbelievable.

Guido: Did you ever try to contact Professor Riolo after your father died?

Maria: Yes. Some years later I wrote to him...maybe two years after the death of Papa. I received no response. I wrote again to him with a copy to the department chairperson about two years after that. A Professor Mario Diaz, Chairperson of the Ancient History Department, returned my letter with a note stating he no longer worked at the university and there was no forwarding address.

Guido: Was a reason given?

Maria: Yes....

Guido: Well, what was it?

Maria: Professor Diaz said he had disappeared four years earlier while on a scientific expedition in Northern Africa; he was presumed dead. There is something more. He also sadly reflected his loss was inestimable because his Latin mastery was so perfect; his support to staff in their research was superior and irreplaceable; and he seemed to know so much about so many things that no one else knew. Again he stated the loss to his Department could not be measured. He added he was a good friend of Carlo and the loss of his gentle and perceptive self was a personal tragedy to him and he was still grieving him.

Guido: Is that all?

Maria: No. He also said some foolish staff members were saying Professor Riolo was not only still alive but had been living for maybe centuries. He said it was absurd, foolish, but asked me to let him know how much he cared for Carlo if ever I were to see him sometime in my future. Of course, I thought this was strange and not very scientific at the time; obviously an aging man still grieving the loss of a dear friend and colleague.

Guido: Oh my! I know it logically is impossible, but my seventy-five year old body is tingling like a young adolescent.

Maria: Mine too! And why not, with such an irrational discussion as we two old scientists are having...and enjoying?

Guido: People forget persons our age have feelings that are often deeply more sophisticated than those of the young. Youth is certainly wasted on the young! We can enjoy and better control the heights and nuances of these feelings because of what we have experienced. Dreams and fantasies reach their high point when based upon, but released from a solid base of experience.

Maria: I can only agree. What do we do now?

Guido: Hmm. Let me think. I have an idea, Maria. Let us compare the handwriting of the Ancient Roman with correspondence I have had with Mark about matters pertaining to what we are discussing today that I happen to have with me right now; and also with any correspondence from our Argentinean professor to your father. Later we can look at the handwriting of other names from your father's past.

Maria: Good idea, Guido. I actually have a lot of correspondence between the two of them I have kept for sentimental reasons and have never really analyzed. It is right over there in that large cabinet among the correspondence of my father.

Guido: Well, let us get to work and take a look. *(Guido goes through his attache case and brings out some sheets and puts them on the table. Maria puts some materials on the table that apparently are from the Roman find and goes to a large cabinet and begins looking in a drawer and going through papers. She pulls out some papers and puts them on the table.)* Maria, here we have all three of them. Let us take a look. *(Guido puts the written materials side by side. They both intently look at the documents.)*

Maria: They really look alike to me...in fact, identical.

Guido: I cannot tell them apart. Granted, they are written in different languages; but the similarities appear quite remarkable to me. But look here Maria. Carlo also wrote to your father in Latin. *(He compares one page with the ancient document.)* To me, they are identical. Please look Maria.

Maria: They do look exactly alike, but I have a way to resolve this matter...without emotion ruling. I do not think we can be trusted in this Guido.

Guido: I fully agree, Maria. What do you propose?

Maria: A good friend at the university is a handwriting expert and I could certainly have him check them out in a way he would not know the materials are from totally different time periods. I also trust him and know he is discreet to the point he would not even ask me the obvious question if what we are thinking is true.

Guido: There is a good chance we are just a couple of foolish old people, but I am fascinated and need to know more. I cannot wait until your visit to the university next month when we will confront Mark head on.

Maria: I have already been thinking about that Guido, and am absolutely ready to go. *(Said philosophically.)* Depending on what we want, time can punish and tease in both directions.

Guido: Maria, I want to ask you a question...may I?

Maria: Please Guido, of course you may. Go ahead.

Guido: Do you believe Mark is your grandfather?

Maria: I do and I also know it isimpossible.

Guido: At my age, because heaven and hell are concepts we fully comprehend as we come to the end of our lifespace, a Mark that lives for centuries or appears periodically over the centuries does not seem impossible to the heart; but logic says it is impossible. I must admit my heart is winning.

Maria: *(Holding Guido's hands and looking into his eyes.)* Even if we are only old fools and confused scientists, let us enjoy this period of time when logic, physics and the human life cycle are irrelevant; we deserve it old friend.

Guido: Yes we do. *(And they warmly embrace.)*

End of Scene

Scene 3

(The setting is the office of Mark Fredericks. Guido has just returned from Rome and has entered Mark's office, closes the door and is ready to talk.)

Mark: Guido, my boy, how are you doing today?

Guido: Very fine indeed, Mark. Do you have some time we could speak?

Mark: Always for you; you certainly know that. Old friend, you have a rather earnest look to you today.

Guido: In my seventy-five years, I have never been as baffled as I am at this time.

Mark: *(Guido sits down and looks intently at Mark.)* Does this have anything to do with our work together?

Guido: Indirectly, I believe.

Mark: Well, what is on your mind?

Guido: The thoughts are so strange I am not really sure where to start.

Mark: Why not start anywhere?

Guido: I have noted for a long time you never change; you look the same now as you did here at the university fifteen years ago.

Mark: Ha, Ha. You are really paying me a compliment. You are certainly aware of my physical regimen and it really is a compliment to me that you notice this. Let us.....

Guido: I think you know I have something else on my mind I cannot explain but which has me confused.

Mark: *(With a look of knowing sincerity.)* Guido, my old sincere friend, why not just say what you are thinking?

Guido: You really know, do you not?

167

Mark: I do.

Guido: I just do not understand it.

Mark: You are a wise man; a real Roman through and through. I am not surprised you figured it out. I will not try to fool you on this. Tell me how you first came to the conclusion something was wrong.

Guido: It probably began somewhat unconsciously as the years have passed. I used to think you were old for thirty-five and then recently that you are very young indeed for fifty. But consciously, I began to notice you knew so much about so many things that really no one could logically know. Whether we were talking about Ancient Roman history, Middle Ages history, Elizabethan England, Lord Byron, various histori-cally significant persons or time periods covering more than two thousand years, you often knew far more than you could possibly have known. I first thought you just had great imagination, even greater intuition and a splendid writing and speaking ability that together were really spectacular to me. I even compared your writing style in Latin and English to William Hazlett, the nineteenth century literary critic you have talked about many times and thus generated my interest in him and his work. You also know how Mary cannot figure how you seem to know more about Byron than even the greatest Byron scholars alive who have spent their whole professional careers studying him. But tell me, how long have you lived and how you have done it?

Mark: You really want to know?

Guido: *(Said strongly and with great determination.)* I absolutely have to know. It amazes me and I really cannot put an exact time frame on it other than so long it is awe inspiring and exciting to me at the same time.

Mark: But first Guido, tell me when you first figured it out for sure?

Guido: You really want to know?

Mark: *(Said jovially.)* I thought you were here to get secrets from me and not the reverse.

Guido: You are aware of Professor Maria Leonardo, are you not?

Mark: Yes, and I am very familiar with her excellent work.

Guido: Well let me tell you a story that finally convinced me you have lived a long time or somehow have been able to travel through time and appear for periods of time. The father of Professor Leonardo was also a Professor Leonardo of the University of Rome; his first name was Mario. Does that name ring a bell?

Mark: *(With a resigned and knowing look.)* You know it does, do you not?

Guido: I do. I have a copy of a picture here in my pocket that was taken of her father in 1880, when he was twenty-five years old. *(He takes it from his jacket.)* He was with his father and that is the only known photograph of him. Have you seen this picture or these two persons before? *(He shows it to him.)*

Mark: *(With a look of pained emotion, he speaks very softly.)* I have Guido; in fact, I remember that day as clearly as any I have lived. It was a beautiful spring day; the earth was so green as only Italy can be in the spring; the birds were happy and singing with carefree abandon, but I had to leave my beloved son; he was the treasure of all my family members over many centuries; he overwhelmingly was the most like me and the one person I probably loved more deeply than anyone else; I still miss him deeply everyday and grieve his death beyond words. I have sometimes felt drinking of the mythical forgetting waters of Lethe[1] would take the grieving for him away; but then I realize his memory is a continuous part of my past, present and future. He in effect is an integral and indivisible part of my essence. *(Looking very self-conscious.)* Please forgive my mutterings.

Guido: Oh God, I feel faint... I cannot believe this. Mark, how old are you? How have you done this?

Mark: Guido, at this moment you are one of no more than one hundred people I have known since I was born that has been aware of how long I have lived. No one has effectively betrayed my secret and I hope that will remain true with you.

Guido: I have no reason to misuse the information you give me, but I must know how long you have lived, how you have done it and just want to spend so much time with you discussing what you have seen first hand.

Mark: And you will my dear friend. I will answer all your questions. Guido, it is such an amazing story that even I find it hard to believe I have lived this long. I was born in what we now call the Before Christ period. Guido, old dear friend, as hard as it is to believe, I was born on January 1, 83 B.C.

---

[1] Lethe. A river in the lower world (Hades) where the souls of the dead drank and forgot all they had done or said in the upper world. (Earth).

Guido: Oh God! You are two thousand and seventy-six years old. I thought it was possible; but knew it was impossible. How have you done it? I must know!

Mark: You shall know all you desire; but first let me tell you my story. I was born in what we now call Tivoli, right outside of Rome. I really was raised away from most of the political activity of those last years of the Roman Republic. I was part of the wealthy merchant class and never went without while growing up. It was due to the wealth of my father, his personal contact and friendship with Caesar himself and his desire that I receive the best possible education that I studied at the best schools at Rome and also Greece; where I humbly and proudly state I completely mastered the Greek language and culture. In Greece, I actually had introduction papers from Caesar himself; and the doors were as wide open as the finite mind can imagine with such a man knocking on the door before you enter. I worked in the Roman government and was in the Gallic, Germanic, British, and Civil War campaigns. I was an officer and actually in the amazing situation of being one of the few persons with whom Julius Caesar confided and dictated his commentaries. In spite of our age difference and his colossal position in the world, he and I were friends and he had genuine affection for me as I did for him.

Guido: My God man, then you personally knew Julius Caesar and were with him on a day to day basis?

Mark: As incredible as it sounds, I knew him as well as anyone and he really treated me like a son. He chose me to work with him because my father had done business with him and had fought with him in many previous campaigns. If you can imagine, my father actually saved Caesar's life when captured by the pirates who held him for ransom. In the brief fight, he fell into the water and quickly was sinking with the armor he had on; but my father swiftly dived into the water and pulled him up to the boat where others could pull him back into it. Because of this personal debt to my father and the longtime friendship between them, Caesar was most eager to help advance my career. My total sense of loyalty, when deserved, and my excellent writing ability greatly impressed Caesar and he told me this; however, my superb training and superior ability in both Greek and Latin were what cemented our personal relationship to the point he chose me to work with him as a military secretary. Caesar was a brilliant literary man and wanted someone who was very well trained in Latin and Greek and very familiar with the classics of the day. Even though he was the great field commander, he relaxed by talking about literature whenever possible.

I also was an easygoing type of a person and had no desire to be a Caesar. He knew he could trust me and he did; I never betrayed that trust. After all these years, I still believe a man is only as good as his word and loyalty to persons he loves and respects. My great models were my father and Caesar himself; and you dear Guido are a worthy continuation of that great tradition which includes my beloved son and mentor, Horacio Leonardo.

Guido: A Roman all the way; you will never get an argument from me on that view. Is what we know of Caesar accurate? Is the man that is presented to us the man he actually was?

Mark: Taking into account that only words are left to describe the human dynamic concoction he encompassed, the accounts are relatively accurate. I say this because he was so sincere that his countenance, voice and eyes mirrored a great soul that you wanted to know and support; this presence cannot be even remotely presented in words. Plutarch was one of the men that knew of my not aging and I helped him with what he wrote of Julius Caesar and many of his contemporaries. He of course was not someone who supported Caesar's worldview and did not put in many of the anecdotes that would have explained how uniquely kind and generous this man was; in spite of that, Plutarch's picture is fairly accurate and our arguing over what would go into it many times led to many of the anecdotes being included in his paper on Caesar. Caesar was really quite different than men like Pompey[2], Cicero[3], Crassus[4], Sulla[5] and other contemporaries of his as well as those after him; he was obviously a far more caring man than were these. He was more like the Roman Emperor, Marcus Aurelius[6], who you know was born a few centuries later.

Guido: While I might dispute motive with you, his bravery, clemency, loyalty to friends and overall greatness are indisputable. I am so excited, I can hardly speak. Tell me more about Caesar to help me understand what he was like.

Mark: As I knew from when we first met, you are fascinated by him as I always have been. If I can help you understand him more than I know

---

[2] Pompey (B.C. 106-46). Known as Pompey the Great. Roman general and political leader. Was defeated by Caesar in the Roman Civil War and murdered in Egypt.
[3] Cicero (B.C. 101-43). Marcus Tullius Cicero. Roman politician, philosopher and writer. The greatest orator of Ancient Rome. [4] Crassus (B.C. ?115-53). Marcus Licinius Crassus. Roman general and politician who joined with Caesar and Pompey in the first triumvirate. [5] Sulla (138-78 B.C.). Luciuis Cornelius Sulla. A Roman general and dictator who seized power from his rival, Marius. [6] Marcus Aurelius (121-180). Marcus Aurelius Antoninus. Roman general, Emperor and stoic philosopher.

you already do, then I will be very satisfied. To help you love him would make me ecstatic. Caesar would like that and would have loved you as do I. He was a very caring man with a very strong voice. It was deep and resonated with tremendous sincerity and believability. He was very charismatic in a very fatherly way. He was impossible to not want to support completely and make totally successful in whatever he attempted. I believe his known health problems made him more philosophical and sensitive to what disease can do to the body and mind. Additionally, he was a brilliant speaker and writer. I never knew anyone who spoke a concise and perfect Latin the way he did—and this includes the ungrateful Cicero.

Guido: You knew Cicero too?

Mark: Oh yes, he was such a pompous fool; a false idealist on the wrong side of history. He was willing to servilely lick at the dung encrusted boots of the demagogue Pompey while he brutally attacked Caesar and everything he stood for. The irony is that Caesar forgave him for not supporting him in the great Civil War and then Cicero gleefully supported his enemies after he was killed. His being killed in the proscriptions of Mark Anthony[7] and the lack of support to spare him by Augustus Caesar[8] were most fitting; and I say this as one who has never really been happy to see anyone be killed; regardless of the merits of such an act. While it was ghastly, there was little pity in me when Anthony had his tongue and hand put on the walls of Rome.

Guido: But history has been much kinder to the image of Cicero than you are.

Mark: To begin with, I was a friend of Caesar and saw that the pathetic group of patricians that made up the oligarchy that ruled Republican Rome was decadent, out of contact with reality and incapable of ruling what in effect was our Roman Empire. Cicero pandered to the wealthy amongst them and somehow fell completely under the sway of Pompey the Great. However, he never realized the Republic had seen its day and there was a need for a new type of government to address the needs of a huge and unwieldy empire. The fact the Empire survived for five hundred years in Rome and another thousand years in Constantinopal certainly shows Caesar clearly knew what he was doing and Cicero had no idea or clue: What a horrid disloyal fool with a senselessly putrid thinking process; a reckless insipid clown in the garb of a philosopher.

---

[7] <u>Mark Anthony</u> (B.C. 83-30). Roman general and follower of Julius Caesar who lost at Actium to Octavius Caesar in 31 B.C. [8] <u>Augustus Caesar</u> (63 B.C.-A.D. 14). Grand nephew of Julius Caesar and first Roman Emperor.

Guido: But was he the great orator we think of when simply his name is mentioned?

Mark: The man was superbly eloquent and I will always feel his impeccable literary Latin is the standard upon which all must be compared. However, Caesar met the standard in that he spoke and wrote magnificently and in a far less ornate way. The thing that bothers me is that Cicero accepted the clemency of Caesar after the great Roman Civil War and then gleefully took part in the plot to kill him. And yes Guido, he did take part in the plot. I remember the event of which I now speak as clearly as if it just happened. Caesar had only recently been murdered and I was as down emotionally as I can be; the weather was stormy, cold and cloudy; Rome was in an unsettled mood and destiny seemed ready to bring havoc on her for taking part in the murder of its greatest and noblest product. I felt helpless to forces of destiny way beyond my power to resolve or understand. It was at that desolate moment, in my presence, just outside of the forum, that Cicero actually loudly bragged of his involvement in the murder of Caesar; and I remember him embracing Brutus after the cowardly murder and saying: "We have saved Rome and my dagger was there in his heart at a philosophical level. The cleansing of Rome was done by shedding his dictator blood as a sacrifice at the feet of the statue of our Pompey the Great. I actually felt I saw the stone eyes of our great commander mock the bloody and lifeless body of tyrant Caesar as he lay lifeless and powerless at his great stone feet. The blood seemed to be flowing in his veins as if the great statue took in the soul of our mighty Republican hero and commander. I waved and believe his eyes twinkled with a satisfied but somber look and his stone arm saluted me to acknowledge the return of Republican

173

Rome." Cicero saw I overheard him and at first looked embarrassed; and then defiantly looked me in the eye and said it again and louder in the stirring strong manner of the great orator he was. I told him what an insignificant tiny brained and ungrateful scoundrel he was with no vision of what Rome needed. I then pushed him hard and walked away. There was total silence and I expected to be killed as I walked away; but the knife never came into my back. I never knew what happened and why I was spared; but I knew some form of destiny was on my side and I would live a long time.

Guido: I really do not know what to say. Your words and presence give life back to people that long ago ceased breathing and are reduced to dust. I must know how you have done it. At a less emotional level, let me simply ask what you have been doing over all these centuries?

Mark: I have done so many things it is almost hard to believe; however, my primary role has been one of teacher. I have had a chance to teach Latin, Ancient Greek and history to thousands of students at hundreds of universities throughout the Middle East, North and South America, Africa and Europe. Even though I have primarily taught Latin and Ancient Greek, among others, I have spoken and taught Portuguese, Spanish, Catalan, French, German, English and all their variations from early Latin and Anglo-Saxon days. I have learned hundreds of languages and in many cases languages that flourished and now are extinct. To tell you a strange truth about me, as a man that has always loved languages, the extinction and radical changes in them in some ways have been more painful than most of the other experiences I have had to adapt to in my long life.

Guido: Have you ever been married? Have you been in love?

Mark: Oh yes, many times to both questions. I have married some of the most wondrous, and yes, even a few of the most impossible women over the centuries. Except for the extremes where I rarely venture, I believe I have experienced every expression and experience of love that man can contemplate. I have had many children and all have given me joy; and some of course have also been disappointing. Sadly, I have often had to leave when my children were young. I must add, I have had few children the past few centuries and have always tried to leave them secure in their futures as best I could. Only God can judge me as a parent and husband.

Guido: Knowing you as I do, I am sure you have tried to do your best.

Mark: I have, but I will need a kind God to judge me as I am not comfortable in this area at all. Loneliness and passion can overwhelm reason and lead one into acts and relationships that should not be entered. I have done that, but my intentions have generally been good. In many ways, I would have preferred my long life as a healthy seventy year old; the passions would be much more under the control of reason. To have an active sex drive and need for intimacy for so many centuries has been so much harder than you might imagine. I have tried everything from abstinence to out of control libertine activities over the centuries. I am now more moderate and reasonable and hope Byronic type passions do not return.

Guido: *(Said jovially.)* Give me two thousand years at seventy-five and the sparks would fly! I could still populate a colony for Rome!

Mark: Oh Guido!

Guido: But seriously Mark, I believe the personal dilemmas you have experienced as a long living thirty-five year old have given you meaning in life to meet your specific personal needs; and remember Mark, the rules of a normal progressive life space do not apply to you. How does one adjust to the loss of loved ones over so long a period? How does one deal with the normal sexual, emotional, family and professional needs of a never aging thirty-give year old? Seeing people you love die is a very difficult thing; but then if one has a set of religious beliefs or a view we are all tied together in one way or another, as I know you and I do, then we do not see death as terminal but simply something that renews and continues in the form of new persons. These are the kinds of issues and dilemmas you have been forced to resolve for yourself. I am sure you have done as well as anyone else could have under your strange life circumstances; and I sincerely mean that dear friend.

Mark: You would have loved Mario Leonardo; his questions and statements to me were very similar. Old dear friend, you sound like you have learned a lot over the years.

Guido: Cannot the same be said of you?

Mark: In reality, I really have learned how little I know; for the more one knows the more one really knows how little he or she knows. I so often feel my thinking and actions are more like a conditioned rat in the maze than a rational human being.

Guido: You are being too tough on yourself and seem weary.

Mark: Rightfully or wrongfully, I do not feel I am being too tough on myself. For sure, I am weary. While I was not fearful of you, it was stressful to me to know you knew and I must explain all to you.

Guido: I am overwhelmed and certainly not trying to hurt you.

Mark: I know that Guido, but the fears were in place anyway; for often feelings overwhelm reason in spite of affirmations to counter their great power over us.

Guido: Dear Mark, I understand your concerns and desire to end them in relation to me. My father always told me when all is said and done, only a man's word measures his integrity and place in both earth and heaven. I fully accept that and swear to you on his grave and memory to me: I shall never betray you.

Mark: *(Spoken very emotionally.)* I know that as sure as God created you and me in his image and placed us together; but still the doubts and fears can just plain overwhelm my rational thought.

Guido: May I change the subject to an area I have some questions and it will also give us a period to calm our passions?

Mark: For sure...and a good idea.

Guido: Can I assume you also knew Lord Byron?

Mark: Oh yes, in fact I more than knew Byron. He and I were intimate friends and lived in Italy through one of the most exciting times I have experienced in all my years. The times shortly after the French Revolution, the age of Napoleon, its aftermath, the attempts to unify Italy and the time that Europe was again remade were so exciting. Byron was a human colossus; his moods were incredible but his genius and friendship never failed him for those he saw his equal and for whom he cared. He was a throwback to ancient Rome and Greece; he would have been understood then. He really became the reincarnation of Rome in the then present. And like the Greek Prometheus[9], he really stole the celestial fire and brought it to earth so we could have a more just earth for all; the fire burned brightly and he passionately sought freedom for the individual versus the State. He would fit well into current times; he was really more than a century ahead of his time.

Guido: Did he know who you were?

---

[9] Prometheus. A Titan in Greek mythology who angered Zeus by taking fire from Olympus and giving it to human beings.

Mark: No, he never knew. It was his love of Latin and Greek language and classics that drew us together.

Guido: This of course explains your conversations with Mary and the English Lit folks.

Mark: Exactly. That whole group thinks it knows so much about Byron and others I knew personally and who often were even my friends. In fairness, it is really all in fun on my part and they actually learn from it.

Guido: *(With humor in his voice.)* I actually think they learn very little! *(They both laugh.)* But please finish on Byron as you even have me interested in him as a classicist.

Mark: I taught him much and he learned eagerly and brilliantly. He always said I taught him to love Greek and Latin while his teachers in England taught him to hate both. Because he was such an individualistic and really egocentric dynamo, he never really thought about how I knew what I knew. We embraced often, drank together, often too much, rode horses together, and shared many things that I really would be embarrassed to talk to you about; however, my friend Ovid[10] would have been proud of us. It was with Ovid and Byron that I happily and sometimes sadly tasted the far ends of human passion and emotion.

Guido: My God, you knew Ovid also?

Mark: Very well; I spent time with him during his exile at semicivilized Tomus[11]. The city of Rome was his lifeline. He really could not cope away from her; the poor man died so sadly and so totally alone. On his death bed he told me I was the one element in Tomus that was pure Roman; he felt we were a Roman island in a world of near savage chaos.

Guido: *(Oh my! Just incredible!)* For now, let us finish with Byron. It sounds like he really expanded your view of life.

Mark: Oh yes. While I am not always proud of the passions I unleashed with him and what he taught me about them, I did learn how powerful and beautiful human passions are and feel I am able to express passions in a much more outgoing, honest and expressive manner. I owe him for that very, very much. I was not ready for such feelings when I was with Ovid; and really the environment we lived in was not conducive for me to cultivate such passion; also Ovid was dead emotionally and Byron so

---

[10] Ovid. (B.C. 43-A.D. 17). Roman poet of love and mythology. [11] Tomus. Ovid was banished by Augustus Caesar to Tomus on the Black Sea.

brilliantly alive in Italy. Italy really intensified his passions and the match was perfect for both; and some of this rubbed off on me.

Guido: Was Byron as we think of him?

Mark: Oh yes...except his great loving soul could only be understood by knowing him as a friend. Since Rome fell, he above all others would have made a great Roman in the tumultuous last days of the Roman Republic.

Guido: You really get excited when you talk about him; and his negative reputation really seems to bother you.

Mark: Absolutely. He is often presented as a lecherous rake and that is really not at all the case. I believe if a man like William Hazlett, the great but moody English literary critic, had gotten to personally know him, then the impression and historical verdict we have of him at this time would be very different. The fact they never met and each criticized the other from a distance, led to much of the criticism Byron has more or less endured due to the false history we have of him at this time.

Guido: Oh Mark, I still am baffled by all of this and really overwhelmed. Here we are talking about people and events as if centuries ago are only weeks.

Mark: It is really not overwhelming if you have lived it. I have known many of the greatest persons of all time, as far as history is concerned, and have known equally great persons that no one knows of at this time. Just to address friends of mine of the Elizabethan period, we all know who Burbage[12], Ben Johnson[13] and William Shakespeare[14] were, but no one knows of Charles Mitchell, Harold Jones and Judy Smith.

Guido: Who in the world were these persons?

Mark: For one example, Judy Smith was a great thinker who helped both Ben and William with many of their plays and many of the great quotes that each is now given credit for having written. I also would be lying if I said I had not helped Ben with some of the Ancient Rome based plays. I might add that that rascal was one of the most exciting and thought provoking men I have ever met in my life. Shakespeare was genteel; but very dull and even forgettable when compared to old Ben. Ben also was one of the people who knew about me and kept it a secret. In fact, in the year 1618, he saw me off as I left from London and went to Paris. Shakespeare suspected, but really did not live long enough to know about my situ-

---

[12] Burbage (?1567-1619). Great British actor in the plays of Shakespeare, Johnson and Fletcher. [13] Ben Johnson (1572-1637). British poet and dramatist. [14] William Shakespeare (1564-1616). British poet and dramatist.

ation; and we really never developed the kind of relationship that Ben and I did. The closest thing to his figuring my situation out was the time he asked me why I did not seem to age and knew so much about the past. I laughed it off and said it was really he who was such a knowledgeable person and he kindly but inappropriately assumed I knew much more than I did. I then made my statement about above all else, to thine own self be true; he laughed, said he liked the statement and then used it in Hamlet. I might add, he was apparently convinced to the point he left it alone; but I know he had his doubts. The man really was a thief, but he robbed magnificently and made everything he did uniquely his own. Ben has the reputation from John Dryden[15] for robbing like a monarch; but to Shakespeare it was his great art; and it was he who always improved on the original.

Guido: God, you even knew Shakespeare!

Mark: *(Said humorously.)* Please just call me Mark.

Guido: *(With a chuckle.)* You devil you.

Mark: Now you are closer to the truth. *(Both laugh.)*

Guido: How do you know Shakespeare still had doubts in his mind about you?

Mark: Shakespeare was no fool. He studied people intently and could not figure me out. And remember, I also had already lived many centuries and could detect when people were tuned into me. William was tuned into me but I was able to keep him off balance as to who I was. He died shortly thereafter and death ends all questions that might be raised.

Guido: Even though English Lit is not my field, to hear about Shakespeare at a personal level is incredible.

Mark: *(Said jovially.)* And just another period in my life; but let me tell you a little more about Shakespeare. After he stopped writing plays, I saw him one additional time in a coffeehouse in London shortly before he died. He said he was thinking of writing a play about a man who did not age. As you might imagine, I was feeling very nervous when he asked me what I thought about the idea. I said I thought it would be a good idea. He smiled and said he probably would not write it because no one would believe it. Shakespeare then hugged me, gave me a knowing look, wished me good luck, said goodbye and told me never to forget him; and I have not.

Guido: Then he did know.

---

[15] John Dryden (1631-1700). British writer, literary critic, poet and dramatist.

Mark: I think so, but will never know for sure. If he did, he never said anything to Ben or other persons we knew in common.

Guido: Oh my!

Mark: But Guido, as I told you, he was really not anywhere near as exceptional an individual as Ben Johnson or many others of the same period. In reality, he really was kind of a pale and unassuming fellow. I say this even though he was an actor and certainly an interesting, sensitive and nice person. That he would have ended up one of the greatest literary giants of all time is very surprising to me. In fact, I thought he wrote too much and too quickly to have ever had a chance to be such a genius; and believe it or not, I said this to Ben, he agreed and stated such in his beautiful tribute to Shakespeare.

Guido: But Mark, you more than any one of us who has ever lived, must be aware geniuses are not always noted in their own time.

Mark: *(Said humorously.)* I certainly do and that is probably why I am still not noted as being a genius after more than two thousand years on earth! But I really am not yet ready to die to become one!

Guido: *(Said sincerely.)* Mark my dear friend, does it really seem possible you have lived over two thousand years?

Mark: Yes, in the sense I have seen so much; but no in that two thousand years is really a very minimal time on earth. There are times I remember Caesar and Charlemagne[16] as clearly as I do you or persons today; and at other times they seem as distant and far away as the many centuries that separate them from me. As far as time is concerned, I believe there is really no difference between two thousand years and seventy years from the middle point of eternity. Something that happened a week ago can seem a lot longer than a thousand years ago. It is really just hard to say or explain. The only thing I know for sure about life is that a normal lifespace is really a tiny little speck of time; to not use it in a way to give yourself pleasure and help others is very foolish indeed; and the standard for using my longer lifespace is the same and I believe I have generally met the standard.

Guido: Mark, from what I have known of you over the years, I can say you have.

Mark: Thank you Guido.

---

[16] <u>Charlemagne</u> (742-814). Founder of first empire in Western Europe after the fall of the Roman Empire.

Guido: *(Said humorously.)* For speaking the truth, a thank you is not necessary. *(Spoken more seriously.)* Of all the people you have known, who do you believe really lived a life to meet that standard?

Mark: Horace, without a doubt.

Guido: You answered that so quickly.

Mark: Horace knew how to relax, enjoy friendship and life. He also was a great poet who, maybe more than anyone else I have known, was able to present himself in writing as he was in person. To read Horace is to know him. He never was out of control emotionally and was a kind, congenial and wise man. He chose to be a friend of Augustus Caesar, Maecenas[17], Virgil[18] and all the other notables of his day; but he also enjoyed the humblest of persons as much. He felt every person had a story to tell and lessons from his or her life could teach us something about making our life more successful; but we had to be able to listen to find it out. Horace was not a would be Caesar but a trusted friend of a great Caesar; such persons are rare and to be cultivated and cherished.

Guido: Is that not how you are and see yourself?

Mark: Guido, you are a perceptive man; and yes, I do humbly and sincerely see myself that way; and my life, thoughts and behaviors are aimed at being such a person. The standard is not always met, but the attempt is never lacking.

Guido: That is why you are probably still alive and can be sane after so many centuries with persons that do not live that way at all. I might live two thousand years as a seventy-five year old, but would have passions too strong to accomplish the feat as a thirty-five year old; I would actually kill or be killed and the end result would be the end of me.

Mark: Probably very true my dear Guido; however, it was men and women like you that made Rome great and endure for a thousand years.

Guido: I must say thank you for that statement. I am still amazed at what I have already learned; and hope you do not mind my seeking you out again, and again and again to talk.

Mark: Absolutely not a thousand times. Guido, my friend, I am sure what you know about me is such that you will want to talk and pick up as much information as you can. I will be available as you desire.

---

[17] Maecenus (B.C. ?70-8). Gaius Cilnius Maecenas. Roman writer, politician, friend of Augustus Caesar and patron of literature. [18] Virgil (B.C. 70-19). Publius Vergilius Maro. Greatest poet of Ancient Rome who wrote its national epic: The Aeneid.

Guido: Are you worried I will disclose you and misuse what you are telling me?

Mark: No Guido, you are not that kind of a man *(with a chuckle)* and no one would really believe you anyway. The field I have stayed in and the areas in which I am an expert have led me over the centuries to be with people such as yourself who would not misuse me or the information I give them. Those are the coincidental reasons I have been able to move from job to job and century to century in a somewhat unimpeded fashion.

Guido: Have there ever been people who have betrayed it?

Mark: Oh yes, but fortunately for me and persons I have loved and cared for, the few who have were not believed when they told how long I had lived; and at times where such a situation was potentially a risk to my life, such as during the Inquisition in Spain[19], I was able to leave and move to a new environment. In fact, up until this century, it was really quite easy to move and not be known from one area to another.

Guido: If I seem to be in a swoon of excitement, it is because I am. Mark, in all you have seen over the past two thousand years, what is something you think about a lot in a special way?

Mark: Oh boy, not as easy a question to answer as it seems... *(Mark squints his eyes and silently thinks for a moment.)* Okay...In that they were the first forty-five years of my life, and I went through normal biological change the first thirty-five, I think a lot in a special way of those years and what they meant to me: parents, first family members, youth, first friends, the last days of the Roman Republic, knowing Caesar intimately, the great Roman Civil War and the beginning of the Roman Empire.

Guido: That makes sense; but can you think of something more specific?

Mark: Well, as the years have gone by, I often think in a special way of the calm nature of Horace and the way he showed it in interactions with me. Specifically, after we had been on a calm and very pleasant horse ride, I remember being with him at the base of the mountain Socrate when he wrote about it in his beloved ode. I can still see the brilliant sunlight spectacularly luminating his body and making him look like an oracle of poetic wisdom. He was as if in a trance as he observed, thought and then wrote immortal poetry.

---

[19] <u>Inquisition in Spain</u>. Period in Spain when the Roman Catholic Church persecuted non-Roman Catholics.

Guido: I love the description and the conveyed images. I believe you briefly talked about this at that recent get together at Professor Quigley's home.

Mark: That is true. In addition to his writing, we were there together for some hours on that perfect sun drenched day and calmly talked about how we were feeling. He was a temperate and reasoning man and I always enjoyed the tranquility of discussing things with him. Horace was a man who perfectly represented his famous statement: Auream quisquis mediocritatem Diligit[20]. Probably due to our earlier discussions, later in that day I was experiencing very sad feelings. He noticed I was down and asked what I was feeling. I told him I was very sad about all the people I knew and loved being dead over the past century. Horace kindly embraced me when I was in tears and advised me what was needed in my life was more fun and not so much seriousness. He intently looked me in the eyes and said in his most mellow and sensitive voice tone a statement I cannot forget and which has always been helpful to me when I am too serious and even melancholy: Misce stultitiam consiliis brevem[21].

Guido: He gave you great survival advice and it is not surprising you often think of him and his calm nature.

Mark: *(Said pensively.)* Yes, I do... I really do.

Guido: You seem upset. Have I offended you somehow?

Mark: Oh no, not at all. I am sorry and will try to explain. This type of conversation is sometimes hard for me in that I am digging deep into my memory and remembering happy days and a long dead friend I loved so much.

Guido: I understand and it really is similar to those feelings you had so long ago with Horace.

Mark: Very true and thank you again Guido for your understanding. Let me try to explain something else positive and special to me that always gives me great pleasure when I think about it; and I believe you will find it interesting to know. I also briefly talked about this at Mary's home. I am again thinking of Horace and me at the base of Socrate and the connection of the fact that 1800 years later I rode a horse on the same trail with Lord Byron to the same mountain, at the same spot and he also wrote poetry pertaining to it. Even though he did not know how long I

---

[20] Auream Quisquis Mediocritatem Diligit. A person should pursue the golden mean in life. [21] Misce stultitiam consiliis brevem. Put some silliness in serious things.

had lived, we discussed Horace and his odes and I believe I had some impact on what he wrote at that time in Childe Harold's Pilgrimage. In fact, he told me as much that day and many times again in the future.

Guido: I find it more than just interesting to know; it is a fascinating story to hear. Did you know Lord Byron well?

Mark: Yes, very well. He believed in individual freedom, hated blind societal cant and was really a throwback to the days of Ancient Rome. He knew the images and customs of Rome and really wanted Italy to reunite, as in the days of Ancient Rome; and again take its rightful place in the then modern history.

Guido: You seem to have liked him very much.

Mark: I did; but then that was an exciting time and he was probably the primary literary exponent of what was occurring politically. He was like lightning in the sense he gave breathtaking light and vision to a time of growing democracy and simultaneously shocked the privileged aristocracy and their long outdated views of their supremacy over the common person. The deformation of his foot seemed to be justification for nature to make other parts of his mind and body seem perfect. But at a personal level Guido, and as I said before, we actually did many things I really would be embarrassed to tell you about and would gladly do again if we could again get together. *(With a laugh.)* I might not survive much longer if I had another year with Byron. *(Said seriously.)* We are all made up of memory banks Guido, and it just so happens my memory banks are really long compared to the normal person; and amazingly, it does not seem really possible I have lived over two thousand years; it just does not seem that way at all...not at all.

Guido: Oh Mark. Oh Mark. We will talk much and I hope you will be ready to meet your granddaughter and my long time friend, Maria Leonardo.

Mark: Even though I know she knows about me and I will be very anxious, I look forward to meeting with her; in fact, I greatly look forward to meeting and getting to know her.

Guido: I am very happy about that. She really wants to get to know you.

Mark: Good. I know we will get on terrifically.

Guido: Without a doubt...and I must know why you do not age.

End of Scene

Scene 4

(The setting is the home office of Dr. Guido Bucciferri. At this moment, Guido and Maria are in the room and psychologist Dr. Judy McIntire is just coming in.)

Judy: Guido, it is good to see you, you big teddy bear. *(They give each other a hug.)* I have not seen you since the battle of Tuffy and the late and nearly great President Assassino[1] of our university. Why you want a psychologist here and did not tell me why, makes me think you again have something interesting to talk about.

Guido: Judy, we have something incredible and exciting to talk about today; even if that sounds a bit trite. Judy, I also would like you to meet a dear friend of mine of many years, Maria Leonardo. She is a professor emeritus from the University of Rome, with whom I have done much work pertaining to Ancient Roman studies and research for more years than seems possible. And to impress you, she did her doctorate at the same university as yourself.

Judy: *(Spoken with enthusiasm.)* Well, we have a Georgetown Hoya with us then!

Maria: Yes we do and those are certainly some of the happiest days of my life. Washington D.C. in the early thirties was an exciting place to be. I also did my last two years of high school in D.C. when my father was a special scholar at Georgetown in 1930-1932.

Judy: Then you really are a Hoya! You certainly must be older than you look or you started high school when you were five years old.

Maria: You are very kind and I can see why you are in your field. I am glad we are meeting today.

---

[1] I have not seen you since the battle of Tuffy and the late and nearly great President Assassino…. This statement relates to the events in the drama by John H. Braccio: "The Football Coach and the University President or Power Play at State University of America".

185

Judy: Well, I only try to speak the truth. Guido, tell me what is happening?

Guido: Let us all sit down here and talk. We have some time that we can talk prior to a visit of a rather remarkable fellow. Judy, I am not sure how to approach this, so I will simply give it to you straight out. If you do not believe it, then fine. We are not looking for approval or for you to analyze us. What we ask is that you be helpful with your insights in a rather extraordinary set of circumstances. In fact, the circumstances are so extraordinary that we are among a very favored few that have ever experienced it.

Judy: Because I know you are not senile and do not believe in magic, I doubt I will question what you are saying and certainly want to find out what is going on. If you think this is going to be more interesting than what happened to old Tuffy and Colosso, then shoot!

Guido: *(Looking at Maria with a puzzled look on his face.)* Maria, how do I say it?

Maria: As you said, straight out.

Guido: Said simply, you are going to talk to a man today who has been alive for over two thousand years.

Judy: *(A look of shock comes over her and she speaks very slowly.)* I guess maybe I spoke too soon and am beginning to wonder what is happening here Guido. Are you aware of what you are telling me?

Guido: I am completely aware of it; and it is also true he is Maria's grandfather. On top of that, he looks no more than thirty-five years old. He is a contemporary of Julius Caesar and was actually someone who took down his commentaries as he fought in the war against what is now France, Germany, Britain and then during the great Roman Civil War. Additionally, he has been a friend of such persons as Horace, Ovid, Boethius[2], Charlemagne, Lord Byron, William Shakespeare and Ben Johnson.

Judy: Did you forget that hippopotamuses can fly? Oh my! You look serious. Do you have any idea what you are expecting me to believe?

Maria: Judy, as incredible as what Guido says seems to be, it is true. I never would have imagined such a thing in my whole life. I have verified handwriting written by the same person over more than a two thousand year period. I have a picture of him from 1880 with my father and Guido

---

[2] Boethius (480-524). Anicius Manlius Boethius. Roman Christian philosopher and writer who was killed after being falsely accused of treason.

186

has one of him in an unaged state from the 1930's in a faculty picture at the University of Buenos Aires. But there is no point in going back over how we know this to be true. I really believe your being here can be helpful to us in that we do need a good reality check for what is occurring. I say this even though I know what I believe to be true is true: The door is closed to disbelief.

Judy: Oh my! I do not know what to say...*(with a chuckle)* and for me to be speechless is rare indeed.

Guido: Judy, please have patience in this situation; and understand this is a very emotional time for Maria from a personal and professional point of view; and it is absolutely overwhelming to me emotionally at a professional level. The two of us have lived one hundred and fifty-three years combined and this is the most staggering thing we have ever encountered.

Judy: Well Guido, you can certainly add my years to that and the years of everyone else that is living on earth today if they heard of such an amazing this. Has he stated this is in fact the truth?

Guido: Yes, he has, but my only desire is that you will listen and if you feel appropriate, have questions for him. He is a good man; and I request you never share this information with anyone.

Judy: I will surely listen and for sure will have questions; and dear Guido, I certainly will never say anything. *(With a tone of humor.)* You can be sure I will never say anything!

Guido: Even in the humorous tone you use, your word is good enough for me; and Judy, you do know him.

Judy: *(Looking somewhat startled.)* I know him?

Guido: You do, in fact you have been to his home and have talked to him various times.

Judy: Well, just let me out of suspense and tell me who he is.

Guido: He is Mark Fredericks.

Judy: *(With an amazed look on her face and tone in her voice.)* Mark! I certainly do know Mark and it is honestly impossible to believe; however, if I were to pick anyone to have done this, it would certainly be Mark.

Maria: What you do mean by that Judy?

Judy: Well, I have had many discussions with Mark at various get togethers and have always been amazed at how much he seems to know about so many things. As a psychologist, I have always had the nonscientific belief I could look into a person's eyes and really get some impression of their soul. It sounds trite, but I really believe it is true and is what separates the academic psychologist from the clinical psychologist. I have seen in Mark's eyes the obvious knowledge and understanding of someone who has seen and experienced much; more than seemed possible for the life he says he has lived. It is not that I thought he has lived two thousand years or longer than the fifty years he has said he has lived in the thirty-five years he looks like he has lived. *(With a laugh and jovial tone in her voice.)* Now does that not sound like some kind of doubletalk? But seriously, it was just something I saw in him; something that was just different; something that was kind of ethereal.

Guido: Maybe after one has the facts, one can look back and see what one missed; but I felt the very same way after I found out about Mark.

Judy: Maria, what do you think of Mark?

Maria: I really do not know; I do not know him; I will be meeting him at least officially for the first time as soon as he comes. I have no idea what to think or say. The one thing I do know is that I greatly desire to talk to him about my father and really see if he in reality is my grandfather.

Judy: Then you have some doubts?

Maria: Not really, but yes.

Judy: Do you think you will be able to determine if he is or is not your grandfather? *(Appearing self-conscious.)* I actually feel silly having this discussion.

Maria: *(Nodding her head up and down.)* I will know; I will know.

(At this moment there is a ring from Guido's doorbell and he leaves the room to open the front door.)

Judy: Maria, are you really up to this today?

Maria: If I am not, then everything I have studied and prepared for my whole life has been a waste. The fact I am seventy-eight and he is my grandfather that I have never met before is remarkable in itself; particularly when I see how he will appear. The fact he married my grandmother, raised my father and lived during the period of time I have studied and loved my whole life is overwhelming to me. Due to his impact on my father's choice of profession, he is inadvertently the

188

reason I am in this field. It is just all overwhelming and my feelings are torn a hundred ways; but my overall feeling is one of excitement and anticipation.

Judy: I am really excited for you, even though I find this whole thing hard to believe.

Maria: Trust me Judy. I think he is as you say in the United States, the real McCoy.

(Enter Guido and Mark. Everyone is standing, not moving and looking at Mark; and nothing is said for some seconds.)

Mark: Please do not behave as if I am something really strange. I am a human being just like all of you here and only have the advantage or disadvantage of having lived a very, very long time. *(Appearing nervous, he continues to speak.)* Maria, I have followed your career with great satisfaction and can only say I loved your father as much as I know he loved you.

Maria: Buongiorno, Marco. Io sono Maria Leonardo di Roma[3].

Mark: Molto piacere di consoscerla[4].

Maria: Even though I definitely recognized the voice in English after all these years, I had to hear it in Italian; and with that said, I ask you if you were the man who visited the home of my father so very long ago on that horrible stormy evening?

Mark: Oh yes Maria, that was me. I had just come in from Argentina and felt it was imperative to see your father; he felt the same way. We had met various times over the years and had communicated in writing for decades and I wanted to be there to make sure he did not die without seeing me and the two of us saying a final farewell; the tears we shed that evening made the night outside symbolic on a tiny scale of the emotions and feelings we let loose. Getting there that night in a carriage was almost impossible and the horse that brought us bolted a few times and gave every indication he would not take us to our family home. What I remember the most about that evening was the emotion between the two of us and what we meant to each other over the years and also the wondrous things he said about you.

Judy: I now see why you and Guido have been so sure about this.

---

[3] <u>Buongiorno, Marco. Io sono Maria Leonardo di Roma</u>. Good morning Marco, I am Maria Leonardo from Rome. [4] <u>Molto piacere di conoscerla</u>. I am very pleased to meet you.

Guido: We are not children. We have done our homework.

Maria: I am just so confused and have trouble understanding this. *(Her voice wavers and she appears very emotional.)* Why did you even have my father and why were you with him up until he was twenty-five? Then why did you leave and not have a relationship with him or me?

Mark: To answer you, and I will try, I must start with your grandmother. She was a wonderful and kind woman. She was very ill when I met her and I desperately fell in love with her so long ago. I really believed she had very little time left on earth and the idea of a pregnancy seemed really impossible. Enough to those that say miracles are not possible. In fact, not only did your grandmother conceive but your father was born very healthy. We loved him and each other deeply. We lived, danced, laughed, cried and loved in a wondrously happy period. Even now, the images of that time seem like a pastoral fantasy representing peace rather than the turmoil resulting from the urban confusion and constant dilemmas in decision making I have now lived with for over a century.

Maria: How close were my father and grandmother?

Mark: Like the trinity. He spoke so kindly and lovingly of her. They were so close that their relationship was like the smell of roses and the sight of the sun in a rainbow. That was why her death was so tragic. It was one of my saddest days and the saddest day of your father's life when she died on his thirteenth birthday. I promised her on her deathbed to look after your father the whole of my life and I never backed off from that responsibility. I said this even though your grandmother did not know of my history and really had no reason to not believe I would look after your father. Of course, you know we had contact throughout his life. In the files in your home, there is correspondence with me at different universities and with different names; I will tell you the names and a check of the handwriting will verify that.

Maria: Oh Mark, I have done my own research; *(with a chuckle)* remember, I am your granddaughter. The names are Pierre Rosseau, Howard Pierce, Louis Friedlis and Jose Regal.

Mark: *(Clapping his hands.)* Bravissimo!

Maria: Did my father resent the fact he did not live with you throughout his life?

Mark: To some degree I am sure, but we lived separate as adults as many children and parents do and I actually was closer to him than any family members I have ever had in my life; including my own brothers, sisters and parents. I actually learned a lot from your father. I was with him nearly every day for the first twenty-five years of his life and he had the same identical interests as mine. Also something occurred you might not have really thought about. He actually gave me insights and advice in that I am always thirty-five years old and he was a man that grew and gloriously matured over an eighty year period. Maturity and wisdom do not come only by living a long time; I strongly believe the aging of the body has an impact on one's maturity level. In many, many ways, your father was wiser and more mature than I as the years went on and we often even switched roles when we would meet at conferences or at places throughout the world. It was a unique experience for me and certainly one I will never forget. I have often been a guarded confidant to others, but he was the only true long term confidant of my life. *(With a cracking voice.)* He was my own blood and we were in contact all his life, even if not on a frequent personal basis after I left in 1880.

Maria: I actually never thought a relationship would develop that way.

Mark: Maria, you and I probably have more in common at this time in relation to memories of your father as a parent as opposed to the memories I have as his father. Even though I am your grandparent, I really see you as a person to be respected and honored due to your age, obvious sensitivity and academic and research achievement.

Maria: I thank you for that. Mark, I have a question I have to ask you.

Mark: Please ask it.

Maria: *(She is very emotional and has a hard time speaking.)* What did my father really think of me? What did he say to you that would be helpful to me?

Judy: Are you okay Maria?

Maria: Oh yes. I am just emotional. Please go ahead Mark.

Mark: He loved you deeply Maria, and was astonishingly proud of the fact you were following in his footsteps as he had mine. You also are a duplicate of Mark's mother and my wife; whom we both loved deeply. I remember seeing you various times through the years and even thought to myself how much you looked like her. I actually have wanted to speak to you many times very badly and say who I was; but I did not. *(With a pensive voice tone.)* How sad I am for that.

Maria: *(Tears come to her eyes and her voice is very emotional.)* Then you actually have seen me over the years at various times.

Mark: Many times. I also have written to you to give you advice and leads on things I knew would be helpful to your career. Do you remember the letter that was sent to you from Ankara with an old map showing possible ruins near Paris, France of the Roman period?

Maria: Yes, I do remember that. That actually led to a major discovery by my team of an old Roman Fortress.

Mark: You also are aware you were not able to make contact with the person who sent you the letter.

Maria: I do and that really was a surprise. Was that you Mark?

Mark: Yes it was; I sent that letter to you when I was on a trip to Turkey.

Maria: I am now putting all this together. There have been many things I have come across over the decades that many have said have made me exceptionally lucky; I am now thinking you have had something to do with all of that? Is that true?

Mark: Yes.

Maria: Like the ancient manuscript that showed the location of the library near the Tiber River?

Mark: Yes. You will remember our talk in Rome when we discussed it; I was the man dressed as a priest that suggested you check out a book in the Vatican. You commented on my strange accent; it was actually me disguising my voice because you had heard me talk to you that evening in our family home and I feared you would recognize it.

Maria: *(Showing great emotion.)* Oh my! Oh my! That man was you?

Mark: Yes, and we hugged as you thanked me. I was trembling with emotion that day as hugging you was so important to me.

Maria: Oh my! Oh my! I remember how emotional you were but did not think any more about it. Oh my! It is just incredible.

Judy: Maria! You are looking a little faint. How are you feeling?

Maria: Believe me Judy, I have never felt better in my life. An emotional but true loving and learning experience. It is times like this that give us a glimpse of what to expect in the eternal hereafter.

Guido: *(Said jovially.)* Mark, you certainly have an impact on everybody.

Mark: I really feel just like all of you. I have simply lived a long time. If you think of yourself in the middle of eternity, seventy-five years is little different from two thousand. I must say to you Maria, even though

I am really a calm man who is not prone to great passion, it is just a spine tingling delight getting to know you in person and letting you know who I am. Jupiter could never have felt more satisfied. I have wanted many times to say who I was, but truthfully really thought the shock would be too overwhelming; I also am very cautious by nature. I now think not telling you who I am was a character flawed mistake on my part.

Maria: Please do not feel bad. The present is what we have control of and we are together.

Mark: Thank you for your kindness. It is just so hard to change patterns of behavior that in my case have been ingrained for centuries and have led to my survival; and honestly, when I have talked too openly, there have been some problems in the past that have nearly led to my death as well as persons I have loved. *(Somewhat confused.)* But...but I know that fear had no merit with you Maria and...and.

Guido: *(Said with concern.)* Mark, are you okay?

Mark: Oh yes, do not worry. Conflicting thoughts, feelings and images of a long past sometimes confuse and throw me off balance, but I am fine.

Maria: How have you survived all these centuries?

Mark: By being very proficient in languages educated and sensitive people have always wanted to learn; and having the type of personality that has allowed me to move into new countries and civilizations without being a threat and actually being very valuable at least to a few influential persons all the time. With all the revolutions that have taken place over the centuries, I have always had a place to go and good jobs to obtain.

Guido: But have you been in situations without funds or problems in a way you could not survive?

Mark: For a bit of humor, my being here shows I could survive. *(All laugh.)* But seriously Guido, there have been problems to some degree, but not at all to the level you might believe. I have always been able to put treasure away in different parts of the world that I live or might live. In times of crisis, gold will always get you through. I remember a time back in 524 when my good friend and Roman Philosopher, Anicius Manlius Boethius, and most of our friends were either killed or in hiding. Due to my knowledge of the Gallic languages still in use then in France, I was able to find help to escape and make my way to Britain. There I was able to find treasure I had actually put there during the campaigns with Caesar. In those last days of the Republic, prudent persons often did such things. Caesar actually accompanied me on horseback to the isolated place near a forest with hills where I hid the gold. I was fearful to go alone and Caesar went with me. He saw my prudence and conservative lifestyle as humorous, but he never mocked me. The great Caesar himself actually helped me dig the hole to put in the gold. I remember crying when I dug up the gold and remembered putting it in there nearly six hundred years before with Caesar by my side. Ironically, I did not know when I hid the gold I would live as long as I have; but it was as I said before, simply a precaution in a very precarious world by a very prudent man.

Maria: Like my father, you have always been judicious in your actions; and even if you were very wrong to worry about me, I understand and again say we only have the present to build upon.

Mark: *(Said pensively.)* Wrong I was with you, but it is the only way I could have survived all these centuries.

Maria: I am just amazed by all of this; I am spending a time where words really show how feebly they express emotions. I find a grandfather who really seems more like a grandson and he tells me things about my grandmother I never knew and then about my father when he was very young; and this all comes from a person who says he feels more like a son to my father than his father. *(With a chuckle.)* This is really all amazing!

Judy: It may be amazing to you, but it is somewhat overwhelming to me.

Guido: *(Said with humor.)* You really get used to it after you spend some time with the information.

Maria: Mark, I have a strange question for you. Even though Guido said something about a potion, how did you ever get this ability to not age and were you the only one who got it?

Mark: I have been surprised how few people have asked me how this actually really happened. I have generally just simply stated my body system is a little different and the aging system is in a state of hibernation and I just have not grown older. Not very scientific, but it always seems to satisfy those that find out I do not age. While I put Guido off initially to some degree, it is still true in the case of Guido and now you Maria, that the questions have more related to what I have seen and done as opposed to who I am and how this has occurred. I probably put Guido off a bit in that the full story seems so impossible; and even to me who has lived it.

Judy: I certainly would have gotten into who you are; but basically am here to make sure that Guido and Maria are able to cope with everything.

Mark: *(With a chuckle.)* You are also here to see if I am a fake; is that not true?

Judy: I guess it does not take someone to have lived two thousand years to figure that out.

(A laugh from everyone.)

Mark: Let us all sit down and be comfortable. But first Maria, I would greatly desire a hug from my only close living blood and the daughter of my son, great friend and mentor.

Maria: *(With great emotion and tears.)* For sure. *(They both emotionally embrace for a few intense moments.)*

Mark: The story is so incredible and even unbelievable to me now. *(He looks at Guido and speaks.)* While I explained some of the key facts to you Guido, I will now explain everything in detail. I will include facts about Caesar and his famous crossing of the Rubicon.

Maria: Please go forward with the story; I cannot wait.

Guido and Judy: Amen.

Guido: *(With a chuckle.)* I knew you could speak Latin, Judy.

Judy: That is all of it, and please continue Mark.

Mark: It all happened at dusk the day before Caesar crossed the Rubicon and began the great Roman Civil War. Caesar had been dictating to me and said, "Marco, let us go out on our horses for me to do some thinking". He had been very reflective that day, as he had been recently, as he thought about the enormity of crossing the Rubicon and in effect bringing all out civil war to the whole Roman world; and which for all practical purposes would end hundreds of years of the Roman Republic. Caesar realized what would occur and the colossal proportions of such a result even bewildered the greatest field commander of all time. He called an able lieutenant named Junius to go with us and the three of us went for some hard riding over the hilly and wild terrain. Caesar rode in silence and with fierce speed and intensity. I have always believed that relentless ride mirrored the feelings going on inside of him right before he made the decision to begin a war that still impacts on us in terms of the languages, laws and customs used in the Western World today. As we rode, we came upon a fire with a group of persons, who were as now, called Basques. They were listening to a person who certainly would have the look of what we would call a witch. She had long strange black hair and was speaking in the language of Basque. The four people around the fire seemed very fearful when we approached on our horses. I advised Caesar this could be a very dangerous situation and we would do best to keep going in that we had no support troops with us if problems were to occur. Caesar said with great conviction, "Nonsense, I am not afraid and can promise you that death will not be allowed to come to me this evening". We abruptly stopped and Caesar went right to the group and began talking as Junius and I meekly walked behind him. They spoke Latin and we began talking about what they were doing. The woman who looked like a witch, whose name was Iribarren, told Caesar she believed destiny had brought him to her and she had a power that could give a great leader like him greater power than he or anyone else had ever had or could ever have on earth. He seemed very intrigued and we sat down with these strange persons. I was not at all comfortable and certainly kept my eyes looking around as Caesar talked to the woman. Junius, the other persons and myself were totally silent and listened as she talked to Caesar as if mesmerized by him and his presence. She told the most incredible story of a potion that had once been used by chieftains in her part of what we now call Spain long before the coming of the Romans. She said a magic man unknown years ago was able to master the body and came up with a potion that, if drunk by a person, would stop the aging process and the person could potentially live forever. It had been used by various persons over the centuries and except for them, all had died of one unnatural form or another. Caesar knew of such whispered stories when in Spain but never believed it possible; he later told me this. Iribarren claimed she had lived five hundred years and the four men with her anywhere from three to eight hundred years. She then said they were the last ones with the power and were weary and ready to die. She said life without power or purpose for potential leaders such as themselves in a Roman world was not what they wanted. I really thought this was too incredible to be true. Caesar had a great eye for determining what was accurate and not accurate. He had a religious belief about a supreme being that while not Christian, was very sincere and believed a God would make this potion available to him. He saw nothing unusual in a group of superior persons having this ability. He also spoke of his ability to govern for hundreds and even thousands of years to make Rome be as great as possible. The woman said the formula for the potion had been lost long ago and there was only a little left in a strange bottle she had with her. Their goal that evening had been to destroy it and to give up their lives for now long forgotten religious beliefs they felt would allow them to become royalty in an eternal afterlife kingdom. All of a sudden Iribarren began speaking

Basque and the four had an animated discussion about which we did not know. Finally, Iribarren said they agreed that Caesar could use the potion in that the dream had been that the potion would go to a great ruler.

The fact Caesar was with them was not so inspiring to them and seemed only the natural consequence of the creator of this formula many hundreds and maybe thousands of years before. Caesar promised Iribarren he would be a fair and benevolent ruler to the Basques. The always generous Caesar, then said he wanted us to share the potion. He then took the bottle with all the bravery for which he is noted and took the first drink from the bottle; he then offered it to Junius and me. Junius with great bravado immediately took a drink. I really had no desire but definitely felt it would be rude to the great Caesar to not drink; so I drank it. Iribarren then took the bottle and threw the rest into the fire and smashed the bottle on the rocks around the fire. Quite honestly, I never imagined this potion would have the power it did. Caesar believed it and so did Junius. As we stood up and were ready to do, the four of them began chanting and in a final violent chant, each rose up, got into a circle and killed one another with ceremonial swords. I still can feel the chill in the early evening air as we somberly saw what was occurring. As the last body movement and moan ended, a large group of birds flew over us and seemed to be lamenting for their deaths. I cannot explain in words how bizarre it was to take part in that experience so long ago. The night was coming on as we were briefly immobilized in thought by what had occurred. The fire was becoming weaker and Caesar abruptly said it was time to go and he knew destiny would guide him the next day; whatever he would do. Caesar upon our return, sent a detail to give them a proper burial. As we talked that night, Caesar told me he felt all that occurred was an omen for him to immediately begin the battle; to liberate Rome from Pompey, Cicero and the absurd tradition bound and out of tune leaders of the Republic. You now know how and when Caesar made the decision to absolutely cross the Rubicon without a doubt the next day. As he himself said and I related to Plutarch, the die was cast. I and then Junius were the first two to be aware of the decision, even though the general belief was that he was going to begin the war shortly. This experience with the Basques and the potion solidified his decision and fired him up for action. I can still see him with animation telling us the war must begin to save Rome from herself! The cool evening wind rustled into our tent through the night and I can see as clearly as I do this moment the hair of Caesar blowing in the wind with the light coming from the reddish glow of the torches we were using for light. His shadowed face showed the pain of such a decision; but his Jupiter eyes and presence said the right and need to do it were never in doubt. When Caesar made a decision, it was thought out and not done in anger; and the outcome was never in doubt.

Guido: This whole story is astonishing and certainly something no one is aware.

Maria: *(Said with humor, awe and respect.)* Well grandfather, what happened then?

Mark: The next day we crossed the Rubicon and began what we now call the Great Roman Civil War.

Junius was killed due to foolish impetuousness before we even got to Rome in a skirmish with pro-Pompey troops; and only Caesar and I were left with the belief we would live for centuries; and I only because Caesar believed it.

Guido: Did Caesar tell anyone about this?

Mark: Oh yes, and only one person; can you imagine who it was?

Guido: Brutus?

Mark: You are a Roman, I can tell that!

Guido: Did Brutus believe this?

Mark: Even if he did not, it was an additional incentive for him to kill Caesar. He and I discussed this matter shortly after the assassination of Caesar. I sought him out and really thought he would kill me as he knew I was certainly not his supporter. He told me he could stand me living a thousand years; but the idea of Caesar ruling Rome for a thousand years was too much. He said the power needs of Caesar were such that even fifty years of his total rule would lead to the complete decimation of Rome as we knew it at that time. Brutus said he loved Caesar not less but Rome more; and to the point he had to kill his beloved stepfather Caesar. At a party with Shakespeare and Ben Johnson shortly after I arrived in London, I told this story and William loved it.

He later even said it inspired his famous quote from Brutus about not loving Caesar less but loving Rome more; but that is a story for another time.

Maria: Do you really believe Brutus believed it?

Mark: It is really hard for me to believe he did and I certainly had my doubts. The thing the belief had in its favor was that Caesar himself believed it. I had seen his intuitive powers as had Brutus. The one thing that Brutus had noticed was that Caesar's health, after a consistent decline over the years, really stabilized and he seemed in a relatively unchanged state since he crossed the Rubicon. I also noticed this as did Caesar; he said as much to me various times when we were alone. While he believed he would not age from the beginning, I now began to believe also. It was not logical that his strength did not diminish and stayed the same during the physically and mentally taxing battle years of the Roman Civil War; one would expect years of arduous battle over the then known world would weaken a person; particularly someone with some definite physical problems of a chronic and progressive nature.

Maria: Did Brutus tell anyone else about Caesar's potential to live forever?

Mark: I believe not in that he felt this knowledge could have led to more people supporting Caesar than was already the case. It would indeed seem to make him a God. It also seemed so absurd that Brutus might be seen as crazy.

Maria: Then why did he not kill you?

Mark: I really do not know except he really had no reason to dislike me. We had actually gotten on quite well. He was an intellectual and saw me more as an intellectual and high level recording officer who took notes for Caesar rather then his supporter. I also think he might have felt after he was acknowledged as the savior of Republican Rome, I could have been of service to him when he wrote his memoirs. He would have wanted to write his interpretation on how the Republic was saved and could have used my first hand information on Caesar before and during the Civil War. I really do now know, but it is simply another situation in my life where I might have been murdered but was not.

Guido: Oh Mark. I continue to be amazed by what you say. I still cannot even imagine a living person having walked with Caesar, Brutus and my beloved Horace himself.

Mark: I can actually tell you again, again, again, again, and again—It is not that amazing if you have done it. But Guido, I do have a great story I would like to share with you, Maria and Judy; particularly because it is about Horace and even includes a few other very notable luminaries of the day.

Guido: Please tell.

Maria & Judy: By all means.

Mark: *(Said with a friendly voice.)* Then I will begin. The day was a hot and steamy summer day in August. I was walking through a seedy section of Rome with Horace, Virgil, Ovid and a few other intellectuals of the day that are unknown today. We were walking some distance from the Forum and came upon a slave auction. These were among the worst and brutal things I have ever seen in my life; but I will not talk about that at this time. My story relates to a situation that shows the uniqueness of Horace as a human being. There was a slave from Parthia that was tied to a chariot and being beaten by all the low level Romans that were walking by. The Parthians were horribly hated for the great defeat they had inflicted on Crassus as well as other Roman attempts to beat them in battle or by guile. This hatred led to them being killed in the most diabolical ways when they were captured and made slaves. It became sport for a person to buy a Parthian slave, tie him up in public and then leisurely watch with friends as the Roman rabble would kill him in gruesomely slow and creative ways that are impossible to describe without making one feel sick and nauseated. The more horrid and unique the method, the more applause from the owner, his or her friends and the rabble watching. Horace saw the spectacle, walked over and pushed the people away who were beating on this unfortunate man. The owner came up initially in a huff but immediately backed off when he saw a group of good friends of Augustus Caesar was intervening. Horace was well known and the corpulent, intoxicated, sweaty and well to do merchant humbly and servilely asked what he might do to please Horace and his illustrious friends. Horace told the owner he wanted to buy the slave. The crowd was angry and told the merchant to not sell him. The owner was in no position to turn down Horace. He told Horace the price and he calmly pain ten times what the owner asked in an attempt to show what value he placed on the person.

The gleeful owner missed the point; but like you dear Guido, we did not. Horace took the man with us to the home of one Marcelus Romanus, a sensitive and well to do citizen of that time. Horace had the man bathed, his wounds taken care of and dressed in a fine toga. He then had him brought to where we were relaxing and talking. As soon as he saw the nervous man, he called him forward and asked him what he had done to become sold as a slave. He indicated he had fought against the Romans and was captured. He figured it was his fate to be killed horribly and was going to accept it as the price of losing. He eloquently stated history is written by the victors and the defeated do their share by being forgotten forever after dutifully dying silently in a miserable manner. Horace found out he was a relatively well educated man and was impressed that he had learned quite passable Latin while in captivity. To the incredible surprise of the man and maybe also to us, he freed him and got him papers approved by Caesar himself so he could return to a part of the empire where he could eventually return to Parthia. The view of Horace was that the man did not deserve what had occurred to him and was willing to give him another opportunity. He hated brutality and even though he was a great believer in the manifest destiny of Rome, he was willing to take risks and help persons at individual levels when problems occurred. He also attempted to help whole nations by impacting on Augustus himself to be a man of peace for all people; particularly those who could not help themselves. I can guarantee you he had much more success than we know at this particular time.

Guido: Amazing! But not surprising from what we know of Horace.

Maria: To have lived as long as you must be wonderful; particularly with your intellectual curiosity.

Mark: Dear friends...You make a lot over the fact I have lived so many years. While it may be a feat, it is really not as impressive as you may think. If I could allow each of you to spend each of the next twenty-one years in different places in the world in this time period...or twenty-one years in different centuries back to the time I was born, you would realize how little of a difference there is in what you would learn. People have not changed at all. In that each generation dies off and a new one comes forward, each is not aware of the group that came before and sees its generation as totally unique and even separate from the past genera-tions; and most interestingly, most of us meet a very limited number of people in a lifetime and it really does not matter whether you have met them like I have over two-thousand one hundred years or in one average life span. Also understand that a very curious and outgoing person would meet far more people in fifty years than a quiet and shy person in two thousand.

Maria: But you have lived twenty-one hundred years and you can not try to compare that to twenty-one years.

Mark: Let me put it another way. If I could allow you to live twenty-one hundred years over the next fifteen years in different parts of the world, you would definitely realize you have seen as much as I over twenty-one hundred consecutive years. I know this may not make much sense, but I think if you really think about it, and you will, you will see the confusion I seem to be saying makes much sense. We really do not change as a race and new ideas are just a rewriting of old ones that are somehow packaged as a great new truth for the generation that embraces it.

Guido: Well I guess that may really be true; but I will need to think about it a bit.

Judy: Me too. *(With a chuckle.)* In fact a big bit.

Maria: *(Appearing flushed and anxious.)* Oh my goodness! Oh my! This whole discussion is just—just so incredible.

Guido: Maria, are you okay?

Maria: I think so; it is just hard to express these feelings I have that cannot be explained to you or really understood by me. My whole youth is back in breathtaking waves of constant images.

Mark: I hope I am not hurting you in any way; I could not deal with that. Please tell me what is happening.

Maria: *(With a very warm voice tone.)* Oh Mark, you are not hurting me at all. On the contrary, you are giving me great pleasure; it is just the amount and depth of it all that has me both astonished and bewildered.

Judy: Guido, I think it would be a good idea if you and I were to leave Maria and Mark alone. Even though I am desperate to talk more to Mark and am sure I will have another opportunity at another time, I believe they need time alone to talk about matters and work things out that are so complicated and hard for them or us to comprehend.

Guido: I really believe that is true.

Maria: Judy, I sincerely thank you for your sensitivity to the situation. I would greatly appreciate it if you two would leave at this time but would never offend you by asking it.

Mark: I feel the same way.

Maria: *(Said very sincerely.)* Guido, are you offended?

Guido: Not at all. I have known and loved each of you for many years and simply have no words to explain how much I want you two together alone to talk and get to know and care for each other.

Maria: Thank you Guido.

(All stand up and give embraces to each other in silence. Judy and Guido leave. Maria and Mark pull two chairs together, hold hands and look intently at each other.)

Mark: I feel so good to have this opportunity to get to know you. I not only see your father in you but also the eyes and face of your grand-mother and the woman I loved so deeply. I never knew her beyond forty years old. I can now see what she would have looked like later in life. I think in life there are magical moments when words cannot even remotely express one's feelings; I am in one of those moments when I have the type of ecstasy that allows me to have some conception of what heaven will be like while living here on earth. Maria, you have no idea how I feel at this moment.

Maria: Mark, I really believe I do in that I feel the same way. In my aged state in comparison to you, I also feel a depth of feeling that is really hard to explain to you. It was probably similar to how my father felt when he knew you back so many years ago. I am not sure whether I should be crying or laughing in joy. The result is more a feeling of satisfying peace and tranquility. I do believe that Guido's great hero and your friend Horace would fully understand the way we are feeling. It is controlled passion with great pleasure. It is the flawless beauty of the controlled Mozart versus the golden full voiced and limitless passion of a singing Mario Lanza.

Mark: On all points I believe what you say is true. My concern is what to do now. That is all I have been thinking about since I knew we would meet and talk today. I have no right to the feelings I have at this time in relation to you and me, but I really believe I would like to share your last years with you and get to know you as a granddaughter; and even though I again say I have no right to my feelings, also as a mother figure. I say this even though I deserve punishment from the Greek Goddess Nem-esis[5] for not knowing and caring for you decades ago. I really am alone

---

[5] Greek Goddess Nemesis. The goddess of vengeance or retribution in Greek mythology.

in so many ways and since your father died, I have not had anybody I can really feel comfortable with in the sense of true family. Guido has been very close, but it is not the same.

Maria: What you desire is really something I could only have dreamed. As you know, my mother died when I was a young girl and my father when I was twenty-one. I have never married and even at this late date in my life, would like a son. I have always had income, friends, status and activities to do; and for that I am greatful; but since Papa died, I have not had family like you represent. To be with you as my son, grandfather or just plain family would fulfill one of my greatest needs and wants in life and also make me feel so much closer to my beloved long dead Papa. *(With her voice cracking with emotion.)* Mark, you can be many wonderful things to me.

Mark: While I know the time is late and your years are not too many Maria, I really want to become close to you and get to know you very well. As one who has had innumerable disruptions in living arrangements and life conditions, I have had dreams for many years of returning to the old family estate that I initially bought in 1868 and got to love so deeply after your father and I lived there. I would love to be able to live there and share many things and experiences that your father and I had at that estate over a twelve year period. Those were among the happiest days of my long life and I would greatly enjoy returning there with you and sharing time with you; the pleasure of which cannot be measured. I remember planting so many of the now huge trees on the estate with your father when he was a teenager. In the last walk your father and I took when you first met me, we talked about them and the names we had given them back in the late 1860's and early 1870's. I will share all with you that you do not know. The tears of joy I will shed would shipwreck poor old Neptune for lack of water in his realm.

Maria: *(Said very warmly.)* Oh Mark, you are making me so happy. I am really glad you are able to talk to me comfortably in that you know my time on earth is short; and apparently you are willing to live with another person you could grow to care for that would also die; sadly just like all the others.

Mark: I would cherish the opportunity. I have learned effective living necessitates having people to interact with and mutually care for each other. Love and friendship certainly run together and both necessarily are in place at the same time. The special situation with us is the connection we have at a blood level as well as our loving the same person from

205

our own vantage points. As I told you, it is a bond I sadly have not developed and I really do hate myself for not having made contact before; and I might add, I rarely second guess myself under the rational that once a decision is made, I must live with it and its consequences. Getting the opportunity to know you at this late date in your life really excites me and makes me know I have been missing something for a long time that you apparently have also missed. I actually pray we can offer each other something that will make our lives more beneficial and rewarding.

Maria: I always pray and am now praying for the same thing you desire. As I said, I have been lonely in spite of constant interactions with people and you can help change that. I hope you can close out things here at the university and move back home immediately as I am impatient as the sand of my time on earth is short and running out. *(She begins weeping.)* The idea of having you return to your home, our home, his home, is such a wonderful thought. You certainly know how alone one can feel over so many years, in spite of many people near. We all need someone to love and care for. I so much want and even need family to love; and I hope it can be you.

Mark: How my emotions bubble with Jupiter level passion and power! I will certainly return as soon as I can and promise it will be very shortly. I also have so many things I would like us to do together. There are excavations to do, lost documents to find and just so many discoveries and things we can do that will be exciting for both of us. If you would like, we can even include good old reliable and caring Guido. I really love him deeply as a friend.

Maria: It just sounds so wonderful; and yes, let old Guido be with us as he can, because I love him also. With you, I can now have family to love like most people have; and I have not had since my father died. In a true sense, his death left a deep gap in both of our lives at an emotional level.

Mark: So let it be Maria and let us come together as loving family. We will enjoy each other and cement our relationship with the love we both share for your father and my son.

(They strongly embrace and walk off together.)

End of Scene

Scene 5

(The setting is at the Leonardo family home. The eighty-seven year old Guido is on his way into the study to talk to Mark and the very ill ninety year old Maria. Maria is not in the study and Guido is walking very slowly. While he is in good health, he is certainly showing the signs of his age. The servant has let Guido in and he is now coming into the room with Mark. With excitement they both see each other, come to each other and embrace.)

Mark: Guido dear friend, it is so good to see you again. I am so happy and pleased you are able to come today. It is so important to Maria that you come; and I know your health is not good. I saw that when you were last here three months ago.

Guido: I would have come today for any one of a million reasons.

Mark: *(With a warm smile and voice.)* The always noble and caring Guido.

Guido: How is Maria doing?

Mark: Very poorly. She has dramatically failed physically in the past few months. Her great heart is still willing but the body is just worn out.

Guido: I believe her being with you and taking part in the great discoveries and research she has done while with you is why she has the serene attitude she has in these last rapidly passing moments of her life. I actually know this because she has often said this to me.

Mark: You are kind Guido and I pray you are right for that would make me very satisfied indeed; however, I am again coming to one of those great dilemma watershed periods in my life. I am about to lose a granddaughter and a mother figure; I also sadly know the years are becoming very hard for you to complete Guido and volcanic feelings of despair are overcoming me.

Guido: *(Said with bravado.)* You are right, but Maria still lives and there is a little fire left in this chariot I borrowed from Mars; and I am still fully able to raise hell!

Mark: *(Said warmly.)* Of course you are.

Guido: Where is Maria?

Mark: One of the staff is taking her for a stroll in her wheelchair in the garden. She is silently but obviously reminiscing over her whole life. She has recently been doing this everyday for a few hours and I have been generally doing it with her; however, she knew you were coming and wanted me here to meet you and then call her.

Guido: In that she asked me to come in such an urgent tone, I am assuming the worst.

Mark: You can certainly assume the worst. Physicians have said it is somewhat of a miracle she is still alive at this time and believe she has not been ready to die yet. I firmly believe she really wanted for the three of us to be together again one last time before she died. She is as magnificently stubborn as was her father *(he is in tears)* and my son. *(He gains composure as Guido hugs him.)* She said her greatest life experiences since her father died began when the three of us first got together back at State University of America and she does not want to enter the next state until the three of us are together. (Mark begins crying hard and Guido holds him in his arms.)

Guido: Mark, you have made her life so full as you have mine. As you once said, the difference between seventy-five years and two thousand years is nothing when one is in the middle of eternity; sooner or later we all will be together. While we know for sure our bodies will age and wear out, your death will be due to an unforeseen accident or act. Death and eternity are guaranteed and what we all share once life begins.

Mark: *(Said with resignation.)* I think I am ready for eternity dear friend and it will not be an accident; I may do it at any time. (In the background Maria has quietly come into the room and has overheard the discussion.)

Maria: *(Said with fire in her voice.)* That is about the stupidest thing I have ever heard!

There is so much for you to do that the three of us began together twelve years ago. This is not the time to give up but rather the time to move forward with greater than ever vigor. You are the continuation of me, my father and Guido. As Guido said and you know, you are not immortal and will certainly join us one day; but to kill yourself would be without exception, the greatest tragedy in my life: The Greatest! We all have the same spiritual beliefs, and as a result, we will certainly meet in the afterlife and have a grand old time. Also believe there is a plan in life for what is happening to you, to me and to Guido. As Lucan[1] said: Nil fucimus non sponte Dei[2]. And remember Mark, our group will include Caesar, Horace, Seneca[3], Boethius, Mario Leonardo...and if there is a God who can find good in bad behaviors in basically good persons, also your friends Ovid and Byron.

---

[1] Lucan (39-65). Marcus Annaeus Lucanus. Roman poet. [2] Nil fucimus non sponte dei. Nothing can be done without the approval of God. [3] Seneca (B.C. 4-65 A.D.). Lucius Annaeus Seneca. Roman writer, philosopher and politician.

Mark: Maria, put that way, I am ready for such company now; however, I understand what you are saying and am sure I will be able to carry on. However, I am so sad about the prospects of living a life without you and Guido. The years are emotionally weighing on me heavily. The intensity of my feelings for your father was so great that his loss still hurts me so after seventy years. I have the same type of an attachment to you and really am feeling very alone. The prospects of going on without you as family is just horribly depressing.

Guido: It is depressing but it is up to you to carry on with what has been done to this point. Maria is ninety and I am eighty-seven. I am sure you will find a way to do work in the future that will be done as a continuation of what we have done with you. Time moves on and there will be new and exciting people for you to meet and love just as we have done together. Life continues and there is a continuity to the whole system. You simply have the fortune or misfortune to live generation after generation while the rest of us grow old, weary, die and pass over to our spiritual eternity.

Mark: I actually think I am to the point I could accept my death; in fact, it seems almost like it would be warm and inviting.

Maria: *(Said sharply.)* Please stop that silly talk! That is the insipid talk that often comes before suicide and my only family blood relative will not be allowed to do such a thing while I am able to live. My father and your son lived as long as he could with gusto and never gave up. You will note your granddaughter is doing the same thing.

Guido: It is really not for a group of oldsters like ourselves to try to be steeling you up for the future; however, the future is bright and your tomorrows are going to be greater than your yesterdays. It is your responsibility to move forward and enjoy the future and we will hopefully be very warm and important memories to you. I also plan to see you in the eternal after- life. I again ask if it were not you that said that seventy-five years and two thousand years are insignificantly different when in the middle of eternity? Do not lose heart and move forward. Mark, you have also become the son I never had and I want you to go on and enjoy yourself. Maybe even have a son and name him Guido!

Mark: *(In tears.)* I just do not know what to do. I am at such a loss.

Maria: *(Said warmly and very compassionately.)* Mark, I am not dead today and tough old Guido seems to have a lot of life left in him. Why not just enjoy us for whatever time we have left together and worry about our being gone when it occurs.

Mark: *(Wiping back his tears.)* I will try, but my feelings are so strong it is just hard to be in control of myself at this time. I have worked so hard for many years to be like the tranquil Horace, and today I am awash with enough passion to move the universe.

Guido: Try to have faith in the future and know there is much to be done. We all love Roman history and its legacy to the modern world. Go into every discovery you make and give better insight to the living to help us in the difficult years to come. I envy you and your opportunities at this time Mark. Try not to see what is occurring in a negative sense but as a time for you to be a new and even more effective person for yourself and those you are going to touch in the years that are still allocated for you. For whatever the reason, you were given the gift of a long life and I want you to enjoy it and use it in a positive way. The old biblical statement about great expectations for those to whom much has been given[4] seems to fit you very much.

Maria: Mark, it is a fact I will die shortly; but do not feel sad. I will be happy to get rid of this aging body and take the last step to a pleasable eternity without pain and illness. *(Mark begins crying.)* I really want you to realize the love I give you, more as a mother than anything else, includes the desire you continue and move forward and do your best for us and yourself. What you do in the future will be for the memory of Guido and me. We each have the same message for you. For whatever roles we have had over our lifetimes, you clearly have become more of a son to us than anything else. I certainly love Guido in the sense of a great friend.

Guido: I will now say something that cannot be taken back. As Horace said: Nescit vox missa reverti[5]. I guess it is okay for us to say at this late twilight time of our lives that many years ago we certainly consummated our friendship with passions and feelings that have been rewarding and necessary in the space of our long lifetimes.

Mark: It seems like a lot of words to say you two slept together. *(Everyone laughs.)*

Maria: That is true and I am not ashamed to say it to you at all. It simply shows again we have ended up as a real family and there is great love among the three of us for each other. Please use the time you have left

---

[4] The old biblical statement about great expectations of those to whom much has been given. Luke 12:48. "For unto whomsoever much is given, of him shall be much required." [5] Nescit vox missa reverti. Once something is said, it cannot be taken back.

in a way to make each of us proud of you and you proud of whatever we gave you.

Mark: I promise I will do the very best I can; and even though I will weep and be very depressed when each of you is not with me, I will never forget the memories and will always think of you *(with his voice cracking)* as beloved parents, friends and colleagues. *(Gaining his composure.)* This may seem strange, but let us have a toast for the lives we have had, whatever time we have left, and the eternity we will share in the afterlife. Lucan, another friend of mine of long ago, discussed with me many times what Maria said earlier. I often think about it and it has so much meaning for us today: Nil facimus non spotne Dei.

Guido & Maria: So true.

(Mark goes to a cabinet and pulls out three ornate ancient glasses and a bottle of wine. He pours the wine and hands one to each of them.)

Mark: I want to toast to all you two have meant to me, do mean to me and will mean to me in all the lifetime I have left. Love and affection are the feelings that come to my mind as the only way to express the relationship we have had. I also would like to toast my son and your father Maria, *(he fights back the tears)* the great and wonderful man he was to you and me; and also for his influence on Guido in that in many ways his influence on both of us has made us the persons *(looking at Guido)* you love.

Guido: Before we take a drink, I would like to wish the best to all of us and say this is one of those moments in my life that will never be forgotten; and as long as Mark walks the earth, this will be a moment for him to remember and recall about us. We will of course remember this moment in the afterlife, but this is a magical moment to remember on our little spinning globe when three committed to each other loving spirits totally communicated and shared unabashed human and family love.

Maria: It is now my turn to give a toast to my dear and beloved Mark and Guido! In my aged and dying body, my soul and passion still burn greatly and my toast is for the memories we have had together and to say they represent the happiest years of my life since the death of my beloved Papa. Mark, I thank you for being all the things you have been to me and give the same salute to my cherished Guido. On that note I would like us all to toast and may God look after all of us in this life and in the next.

(All break into a combination of tears and laughter as they hug each other in a three way embrace. They then stand back, fight back the tears, hit the glasses and all say salute and take a drink.)

All: Salute!

End of Scene

Scene 6

(The year is 2100 and the setting is the Great Academic Hall at State University of America. There is going to be an acceptance of a world level significant multiple million dollar contribution given to historical studies of Ancient Rome in the name of a long ago eminent professor of Ancient Roman history at State University of America: Guido Bucciferri. The grant has been given by the World Historical Association of the United Nations and will include a perpetually funded professorship that will be called The Guido Bucciferri Professorship of Ancient Roman History. Additionally, there will be a perpetually funded Department of Ancient Roman History that will be called The Guido Bucciferri Department of Ancient Roman History. The grant was given after a review by prominent Ancient Roman historical scholars and the final determination was made by a brilliant Latin language and Ancient Roman history expert at the University of Paris, Professor Pierre DeGaulle. After reviewing the work of a large number of persons that have made great Roman history contributions over the centuries at different universities, it was determined by him and the worldwide group of experts that Guido Bucciferri deserved the award due to the enormous contributions he made to Ancient Roman history in his nearly seventy year career. Probably the turning point in the decision to give it to him was that while his discoveries and contributions to Roman historical scholarship were always impressive, they were most significantly made between his seventy-fifth and ninetieth birthday. Such indomitable spirit was felt to warrant the huge contribution in his name to the university and the prestige that certainly comes with such an award from a worldwide organization such as the United Nations. President Klemczak is getting ready to speak and introduce Dr. Haddad from the United Nations who will then introduce Dr. DeGaulle to give the major presentation. There is an invited group of prominent university staff and supporters who have come for this historic meeting.)

President Klemczak: On behalf of State University of America, the citizens of this great state, of this nation and of the world who desire to know the history that helps give perspective on who we are and how we got ultimately to where we are now, it is with great pleasure I accept this major contribution to honor a professor who gave his whole life to his beloved university and who made contributions to Ancient Roman history at a level that this grant is being made in his name: Professor Guido Bucciferri. Not only will there be an endowed professorship in his name, but there will be a department named after him. I also think for those who have a sense of history and want to achieve later in their lives, it is important to know his contributions, while always significant, hit there crowning point after his seventy-fifth birthday. They also occurred at a time when the university was still reeling from the disgrace of the infamous President Assassino, who was out to destroy the university and eventually died himself as the price of his evil deeds. His name is only mentioned here due to the infamy he brought upon this university in contrast to the golden glory brought by Professor Bucciferri at approximately the same time in history. In those dark days when things looked so bad for this university, Guido Bucciferri made tremendous contributions to the field of Ancient Roman history due to discoveries of previously unknown documents written by Horace and other Romans over an extended period of time. This put State University of America in the world limelight and helped deflect the horrid reports that still came out at that time as Dr. Assassino tried to destroy the university for his own egocentric glory. Professor Bucciferri often stated he hoped his work would help deflect some of the horrible news reports that kept coming out about State University of America back in those horrid days of the early 1990's. Let me guarantee you it did just that and continued for some years. With that said, I now defer to the United Nations and ask Secretary Haddad to come forward.

(Secretary Haddad comes forward to the podium and shakes the hand of President Klemczak.)

Secretary Haddad: It is a great pleasure to be here today and offer this grant and the resulting prestige to State University of America in the memory of Professor Guido Bucciferri. There were literally hundreds of persons that were considered for this award for their work over the centuries; but it was just that Dr. Bucciferri's particular contributions were so unique and extensive that he convincingly seemed to be the natural person to receive it. As Professor DeGaulle has gathered the most information about Dr. Bucciferri, it will be his formal presentation that will actually spell out how this award ended up coming to State University of America in his name. I simply state it is an honor to be here and certainly wish State University of America the greatest success in the application of this grant over the coming years and hopefully centuries.

(Dr. Pierre DeGaulle comes forward to the podium and shakes the hand of Secretary Haddad.)

Dr. DeGaulle: Thank you Secretary Haddad, thank you President Klemczak and thank you United Nations for making this award to this fine university that will be so essential to all of us in the world now and in the future to help develop the definitive comprehensive world center for Roman History.

The Roman Republic and then Empire clearly represent a period of time that planted in fertile ground so many of the roots that still live and are blooming at a minimum in the Americas and all the physical area that once was the Roman World. This is not to diminish other histories and cultures of our time or in the past, but simply to indicate this is an effort by a world wide body of great prestige to make funds available to systematically study Ancient Rome in one approved world class center; and I can promise you there are yet so many discoveries to be made in our lifetimes and the lifetimes of those who come after us. I would like now to say some words about Professor Bucciferri. When a person is dead nearly a century, we accept the memories of the person do not live in the memory banks of anyone alive, but in the records that are left behind by those who knew, judged and loved that person. Using that information, one can clearly see Professor Bucciferri was a highly respected, kind and caring man. While he never married, he passionately loved life, children, family, friends and people in general. The image that comes to my mind is of a man who was beloved by all people who met and knew him. He was a passionate and gentle man and always loved the equally gentle Horace. The centuries have passed and the year count is well over two thousand years since Horace died; but the image of him is still vitally alive and was best represented in the personality and achievements of Guido Bucciferri. I actually feel as I pull on my beard that I can actually hear his hearty and manly voice, see his sensitive almond shaped gray eyes, his somewhat squat frame, his receding hairline and experience the presence of his enormous physical and mental energy levels. I can see the artists, historians and intellectuals of Ancient Rome smiling and nodding in agreement and telling us he indeed was a Roman and one of them; that he was a man to be loved and remembered in the same vein as his beloved Horace. With Virgil, Ovid, Terence[1], Lucan, Juvenal, Caesar and Boethius watching, I can see Horace himself broadly smiling and embracing Guido warmly, calling him brother and a fellow Roman. He is giving him symbolic honorary Roman clothing and medals and inviting him to talk, eat and drink with literary giants of Ancient Rome as all stand and applaud him.

I can actually feel myself touching his large warm hand and feeling the excitement and mutuality that comes from meeting someone who loves the same things you love. I can also visualize him way back in the 1990's with his great friend from the University of Rome, Professor Leonardo, and can even see them together making discoveries about Ancient Rome when she was in her eighties and he in his seventies and eighties. They

[1] Terence (B.C. 185-159). Publius Terentius Afer. Roman dramatist who was very sophisicated and appealed to the more refined and cultivated patrician class.

were a magnificent duo and each made the other greater through the sense of commitment, loyalty and professionalism they shared between them. You are aware there is the Ancient Roman Archaeological Center and endowed professorship named after her at the University of Rome that has been in existence for ten years. I also had the pleasure to give the talk as the award was accepted. The center at State University of America in the name of Professor Guido Bucciferri will make a comparable setting for historical research at this university as the University of Rome grant did for archaeological research; and each will be the world leader in its respective field. Because Dr. Bucciferri and I would share so many common interests, I actually see him as a friend; someone I feel I can visualize walking the planet with me and sharing the excitement with him as his eyes show him discoveries from Ancient Rome. He stated these discoveries went into his soul and made him a greater and more sensitive human being. He was able to be a good friend to many and a dear friend to those who knew him on an individual and intimate level. The image of him in his rolly polly state; with his dapper English hat and cane; and shaking your hand with the old traditional heavy hand of the Italian peasant stock from which he came; along with that exciting twinkle in his expressive eyes are certainly things those who knew and loved him could never forget. The strong manly voice that came forward from him with kind and sensitive statements was always in the memories of those who knew him and certainly never forgotten until they died. I think it is safe to say the man whom he idolized and looked up to most from Ancient Rome, Horace, would certainly have loved him as a friend and have been honored to have been with him and known him at a personal level. In my belief structure, Guido and Horace are together in an eternal state of peace and satisfaction. We hope the memory of what Guido has done in the field of Ancient Roman historical discoveries will have us remember him as a modern historical Horace and one who continued the tradition of top level scholarship for his generation to be passed on to all of us that love Roman history and its legacy to us through the centuries. It is on this note I would like to turn over the letter of commitment for the center and the endowed professorship in the name of Professor Bucciferri to President Klemczak. *(Looking toward the sky, Dr. DeGaulle speaks.)* Guido, old friend, wherever you are, your memory lives this day and shall as long as human beings care and love Ancient Rome and bigger than life human beings such as yourself. *(President Klemczak shakes Dr. DeGaulle's hand and accepts the grant. Everyone stands and strongly gives applause. There is then a pause and the people begin to leave. Two persons are left and begin talking to each other.)*

219

Charles Smith: Harry, there is something about this Professor DeGaulle that perplexes me.

Harry Root: Well, what do you mean? What is it? He certainly appeared quite inspirational and committed today.

Charles Smith: I know that is true and I cannot figure it out. Something is different about him; I really feel I know something about him but I cannot put my finger on it.

Harry Root: Are you thinking he spoke like he knew Professor Bucciferri? If so, I am sure that was done for impact in trying to show a relationship at a continuity level among him, other Ancient Roman scholars and Bucciferri himself.

Charles Smith: There is something different here; let me look at my notes and my historical information. It might have to do with the book I read about Guido Bucciferri and people who worked with him. I do not know what it is, but there is something here and I am going to try to find out what it is.

Harry Root: You English Lit folks never seem to give up on things like this. This is a man whose expertise is Ancient Roman history and the person about whom he speaks was an expert in Ancient Roman history; and somehow you find something different or perplexing when there is an obvious connection.

Charles Smith: It is strange and I will admit that; however, there is something here and I plan to figure it out.

(They both walk away.)

The End

Marital Betrayal
or
The Effects of a Husband Philandering on the Professional Woman from a Traditional Home Background

A modern/traditional tragedy

Written By:
John H. Braccio, Ph.D.

Table of Contents

A Preface To
"Marital Betrayal
or
The Mental Health Effects of a Husband Philandering on the Professional Woman from a Traditional Home Background"

This one act drama is a dialogue between a psychologist and patient. It is like one of literally hundreds of sessions I have had in my private practice as a psychologist. The patient is a woman from a traditional home background who is also a professional; she is in her low forties and typically comes from a background where her parents or grandparents came from a country where the traditional roles of male and female were clear. The man works and the woman stays home. Even though the patient has left this traditional home and role, she still carries many of the old values as she adjusts to the situation of finding her husband has been maintaining an affair with another woman for a five month period. I have arbitrarily made her an Italian-American due to my own ethnic background, but she could have come from one of innumerable different groups. While she has felt she is modern and has moved up in the professional ranks, she finds herself in a very isolated situation after she discovers the infidelity of her husband. She cannot tell her father because he will defend her initially but then will question what she did that led the husband to the point he had an affair. Her mother will be angry, but believes marriage is forever and will suggest she pray to the Madonna to have the strength to forgive her husband as well as praying for the husband so that he will be forgiven and able to go to heaven. This places her in the situation of being isolated from her family and being crushed emotionally by what has occurred. As modern as she is, she carries many residual values from her upbringing and they will just not allow her to emotionally or physically break away from her husband and this is a terribly destructive situation from a mental health point of view. The two children, ages 18 and 20, initially side with her but eventually tire of her moodiness, tears, yelling and inability to get over the effects of the affair. Having been raised in a modern home environment and not aware of the cultural upbringing of their mother, their feelings are that Dad feels bad for what he has done and as the months pass, it is time for her to forgive, forget and get on with her life. The depths of her despair and feelings are hard to understand by persons who are not familiar with the traditional woman and I can simply verify that the agony she is experiencing is horrible and frequently can lead to the destruction of the rest of her life. I have had this one act drama read over by a number of clients and friends, many of whom have had similar experiences, to give it a good reality check. The final copy reflects some insights given by the reviewers. I believe it is safe to say this drama reflects the feelings of a traditional and professional woman who has found her husband of more than twenty-two years has had a long term affair.

List of Characters in Order of Appearance

Psychologist

Patient

One Act Drama

(Drama setting - A modern and comfortable office of a psychologist in the 1990s. The patient has entered the office and the two are meeting each other for the first time. The patient seems very anxious and uncomfortable. The psychologist senses this and tries to make the patient feel comfortable through an open and accepting type of verbal and non-verbal communication.)

Psychologist: Please sit down. I hope you feel comfortable with me today. *(The patient sits down.)*

Patient: I don't really, but I have to talk to someone.

Psychologist: *(The psychologist also sits down and speaks.)* That sounds fair and straight forward. I want you to know you can tell me what you desire and it will go no further.

Patient: I've never done this before. There's so much in me.

Psychologist: Today, we'll have a general and open discussion of what your feelings are and about what problems you believe need to be resolved. We also will try to determine if I can be helpful to you. In your own way, please tell me what is on your mind.

Patient: When my friend Judy knew I was hurting about something, she told me you were her therapist and suggested I should see you; but at that time, I was not ready to see anyone. I gradually told her everything and she has been wonderful; but I'm not being fair to her as I keep telling her the same thing and make her feel as powerless as me. I'm now ready to talk to someone like you; oh, am I ever.

Psychologist: Please help me. What happened and tell me your feelings?

Patient: I'm not sure how coherent I am and if you can follow it.

Psychologist: Just relax, do not worry and do your best. Please feel comfortable here. No one will know what we talk about. Please feel safe. If you'd like, tell me something about yourself.

Patient: Okay. Here it goes. First of all, I come from a traditional first generation home. English was my second language. My father ran the house. He and my two brothers were the best and my mother and I were second best and only worthy when obedient. I always tried to please my parents by being perfect. I was an excellent student; a good daughter; active in school events; why, I even graduated with honors as a teacher and have been teaching school for twenty-two years. We even planned our two children around my summers off.

Psychologist: Was it hard trying to be perfect?

Patient: Oh God yes. You never make it and so you're never happy. It's hell.

Psychologist: Have you ever tried to change?

Patient: No. It's too hard.

Psychologist: We can address this being perfect issue at another time. For now, tell me what has convinced you there's a need to meet with me?

Patient: *(With great emotion.)* I'm here because I'm in total emotional agony. I always have a burning headache and feel like a horrible pair of pliers are constantly squeezing my guts and tearing me up. The problem and reason I'm here is that my husband had an intense affair for five months. It ended seven months ago today. They screwed, they talked intimately, they traveled together and he lied to me as he led a double life. What do you think of that?

Psychologist: Sounds like you are angry and very hurt.

Patient: You're sure right about that. How could he go to bed with me, say he loved me and screw that bitch? I feel so dirty and used.

Psychologist: Sounds very painful. How did you find out about it?

Patient: I found out and caught him by checking up on inconsistencies in what he was doing and what he said he was doing. I was stupid for a long time, but I woke up eventually. A smart wife gets to know her husband; and when there are inconsistencies in him and his behavior, she checks them out. After probably not wanting to believe what thoughts were coming into my mind, I began checking out what he was doing with what he said he was doing and caught him in his lies. I began finding he was charging gas in places we don't go. On a day he said he was going to the office all day when I was out of town, I checked the speedometer before I left and when I came home. He had put 200 miles on the car and would not talk about it when confronted. Then I hired a private detective and had him followed. A video was taken of him and the bitch in a restaurant together. When confronted, he admitted what he had been doing. Oh, how loving and attentive the asshole looks in the film. He's hugging her, looking into her eyes from a few inches away, making small talk, and taking pecks and kisses with warm authority. My having caught him still makes me very angry; my catching him is much worse than his freely admitting what he did. He did not tell me and only did after he had no choice. I'm so crushed. Do you understand?

Psychologist: I have not lived it but I can try to understand you as you explain your feelings; and they are very intense.

Patient: I feel like a volcano that will not explode; the pressure is always at a peak but will not erupt. It's hell and I'm always emotionally strung out and my body feels like it'll wear out.

Psychologist: Has it been like this all the time since you found out?

Patient: Yes, and that's why I'm here. *(In tears.)* It must end. Please help me. I just can't go on like this anymore.

Psychologist: I will try to help you take control of this situation by yourself; that's the goal. I must admit, it's real tough and the road to recovery appears very difficult.

Patient: Thank you for being honest with me and seeming to care.

Psychologist: I will be honest with you and I do care. At a more basic level, what are the feelings you have on a daily basis?

Patient: I don't know. I sometimes laugh but feel depressed at all times. I feel that Fred, the husband I trusted and loved, let me down and I'm now alone in the world. Fear, anxiety, pain, hopelessness, anger and loneliness are all working as a whole to make me feel lost and out of emotional control all the time. Tell me something: Is it something in my background or something else that just will not let me either deal with this in the right way or let it go?

Psychologist: It's hard to just give you a yes or no answer on that; however, I believe it would be hard for anybody to just let it go without feeling a lot of pain and rejection. Particularly when it was not just a one night thing. It was an extended situation and you caught him. Is that not true?

Patient: Yes.

Psychologist: That makes it even harder because you don't know when it would have ended. Now lets look at your background. In my experiences, most women who have been raised as first generation Italian-Americans have generally been trained that marriage is forever; you stick with it, even if the husband does things like have an affair. Tragically, the woman often believes she must be inadequate or doing something inappropriate if the husband is running around.

Patient: God, it seems like you know me!

Psychologist: I think part of the Italian culture is still there even though you are really far removed from Italy physically and from a home with the traditional male/female roles. You work and live a more modern life role, but your values in this crisis seem to go back to the early training in your home.

Patient: Oh God, I feel so empty inside. *(With a resigned tone.)* I don't like to admit it, but I really think what you have been saying is true, even if I hate it and feel powerless to change it. I also knew from talking to Judy that you could identify with my cultural background; but, can you help me?

Psychologist: I promise to try to do my best. What are your feelings inside of you right now?

Patient: As always, the same. I know I'm saying the same thing over and over again. Are you tiring of me and my stupid story?

Psychologist: Not at all. Please explain what the feelings inside you are like right now.

Patient: I go from anger to depression to a total despair; and then back again; and to make things worse, they all seem to merge at times into a feeling that has no name and is so horrible that it would defy description unless you have experienced it yourself. It just never seems to end; it's with me all the time and it's consuming me. I was trying to sort this out at first. I was so distraught and I just couldn't believe it. I was trying to keep my balance but I had feelings that overwhelmed me; they still do. Now, I guess I'm trying to deal with who he is and what this situation has done to me.

Psychologist: What has it done to you?

Patient: It's changed me. I don't enjoy anything. I don't want to say I'm feeling sorry for myself, but I really am. I'm not at all relaxed around people. In fact, I like to get away from people. I'm only relaxed when I'm on automatic behavioral pilot with my parents, my family and the families of my brothers. It's all a front and my husband and children don't want to hear about how I feel and I cannot tell my parents or the rest of my family. Somehow, all of us, while at my father's home, live in an outdated world where my father rules with help from the other men. They sit at the table after we all eat; they talk about whatever they want while we clean things up and talk to each other about cooking and any other stereotypical female topics. I'm used to it and can accept it in spite of its absurdity.

Psychologist: It doesn't sound healthy.

Patient: It's not, but it's safe.

Psychologist: How about interaction with other people?

Patient: I'm staying away from friends, because I can't stay away from my thoughts on the affair and don't want to talk about it to other people. Except for my friend and your patient, Judy, I haven't poured my guts out to anyone. I sporadically talk about what happened to one old friend, but she ends up hurting more than I do after we talk. That's not my way to hurt her so much with my pain and I really talk to no one else. It also is true I've always been the support for others and not the reverse. At work, I only go to the lounge to get some coffee and go back to my desk. I don't do the social things with co-teachers I used to. Carefree joy is as foreign to me now as the love I thought Fred and I once had for each other.

Psychologist: You really feel you are estranged from people.

Patient: It's like I'm in a hellish limbo where no person or thing makes me happy; and even worse, no one cares. You know what I mean?

Psychologist: Tell me more please.

Patient: I don't like anything. I hate chocolate chip cookies and pizza. I hate vacations. I don't even like summer. I wish I could relax and just let it go. It's too hard for me. I get up in the morning and that is the first thing that comes to my mind. My gut is in knots and my inner being in agony. It just stays with me all day. Happy memories burn painfully when compared to how I feel now. I just don't want to see people while I feel this way; stupid, but that's the way I feel and behave.

Psychologist: What is the feeling like everyday?

Patient: Everyday?

Psychologist: Yes, how intense is it?

Patient: Intense beyond my dreams before this happened. I try to shake it. I gear myself up to the point I'll be able to not think about it; but as the day progresses, I cannot relax at all and the thoughts overwhelm me and turn into feelings that are as horrible as debilitating. And at all times, day and night, the thoughts and feelings are always very painfully near. It's like walking in a chilling fog that one cannot escape and which seems to penetrate the body; and it's always there and controls what you can see and how you feel.

Psychologist: How about when you are around your son and daughter?

Patient: The same. I feel horrible around them. I function somewhat, but they make me zombielike with their lives in such order as they ignore my reality. They try to kid me out of it or just plain get angry and frustrated with me. Our home is not like mine was and the kids are really typically American. They don't have my background; and as a result, they don't understand the feelings I have at this time. But as with my parents and brothers, it's not healthy but it's safe to be with them and say little. To be totally honest with you, often I just want to run away from everyone and everything.

Psychologist: Where would you go?

Patient: I don't know, wherever I could. I see myself leaving and just going and going; to no place in particular; just going.

Psychologist: Let me back up. You start the day with horrible feelings and they never end. Is that not true?

Patient: Yes. I get up and try to get ready to go to work. From that moment on, my tortured feelings get progressively worse. The thoughts just keep hitting me again and again as they pull me down further and further as the day progresses; my resistance wears down.

Psychologist: Are you wearing down more as each day passes?

Patient: Absolutely. I get worse day by day and my husband and kids demand I get better; what a catch 22.

Psychologist: So during the day you are always thinking of this.

Patient: Yeah, always. The thoughts and feelings are overwhelming in their pain, intensity and relentlessness. *(With a resigned tone.)* I know I keep saying the same thing over and over again.

Psychologist: Don't worry. I want you to say whatever is on your mind.

Patient: I never imagined there could be such a hell on earth; that was just some crazy thought the nuns threw at us when I was in school. But even with them, hell on earth was to be for the person whose conscience tortured him or her for doing wrong things. I'm tortured and have done nothing but try to be a good and loyal wife.

Psychologist: And as you said before, things get worse as the day progresses. Does this mean that when you come home at night, you're still thinking about all of this?

Patient: Oh yes. It's more of the same. The hurt only increases until I go to bed. After having a hard time going to sleep, I then wake up various times during the night and the cycle begins again; and to make things worse, the louse is always calmly sleeping next to me. Am I being redundant?

Psychologist: Yes, but such is the very painful condition you're in with such neverending compulsive thoughts. Do you wonder what he's doing when he's not with you?

Patient: Not really, because I generally know where he is. We now keep in fairly close contact.

Psychologist: So the feelings are not about him and what he's doing now as much as the effects of what he did and how you are dealing day to day with your feelings.

Patient: Yes. I sometimes think I can hold everything together. Then I go through this horrible anger thing; it takes me over. I cannot get rid of this anger. It's overwhelming; as I said, I feel like a volcano in the constant process of exploding; but the explosion is never complete and the intense pressure never leaves.

Psychologist: What brings on the anger?

Patient: It can be anything; but it's really about the implications of what occurred.

Psychologist: In what sense?

Patient: Of what happened? *(With an irritating tone.)* Don't you get it? *(A contrite tone.)* I'm sorry. Do you understand?

Psychologist: I'm trying. Don't worry about me; I'm here to help you clarify your feelings. Tell me more about the implications.

Patient: That he had this affair. The seriousness of it all; particularly when you consider what he always said about his wonderful self.

Psychologist: What does this mean?

Patient: Fred always thought he was the best. He would be fat as hell and see himself as Arnold Schwarznegger in the mirror. He would sing in the bathroom in a baritone monotone and believe he was Mario Lanza. Always he said he was better than the average Joe or he was so ready to criticize anybody else if they did something wrong. Fred often said how lucky I was to have a man like him as a husband and friend. It's that shit that pisses me off. He lied about who he was and I believed him for twenty two years. The whole foundation of our marriage was phoney.

Psychologist: Please tell me more.

Patient: When I think about all his sanctimonious bullshit; how much better he said he was than other men; that he was morally above anyone else; that everybody was down there and he was way, way up there; oh my, just unadulterated malarkey and hypocrisy. I believed it all and felt I was up there too because I was with him. He has now tumbled to the ground and I'm with him and under his God damn sexually soiled body. Oh, how I hate him for what he has done to me; and Fred goes through life with his designer clothes and sports convertible like he and life are perfect.

Psychologist: Have you told Fred how you feel?

Patient: Yeah, but you know whenever I try to discuss how I really feel, he gets angry and doesn't want to talk about it or says we have talked about it enough. In effect he says I've had enough time to get over it. He even is finishing my thoughts for me as he always did before. Whenever I say I need to express my feelings and for him to quit finishing my thoughts, he gets angry and walks away in indignation. I always react to that with anger and terrible hurt. He then plays the victim and gives me the silent treatment. Sadly, I eventually give in and talk to him; he then may forgive me, be angry or softly and firmly tell me to try harder. Isn't that pathetic?

Psychologist: So what do you do?

Patient: I feel horrible, do not give in to him as quickly as before, end up losing, hate myself for my weakness and wind up with no husband to talk to about anything. He's just there to give me a pat on the back when I'm sad but not complaining. He'll go by, touch my shoulder, say things are going to work out, say he loves me and not to worry. I know him well enough to know what he's trying to do: Look like the contrite and looking for forgiveness husband who must live with a vengeful and unforgiving bitch. Oh, how I hate him! Oh, how I hate men like that bastard. He is my brother, my father and my son. They have a penis and think they can mind fuck their mothers, sisters, wives as they fuck any whore they want.

Psychologist: It really hurts; I can see that very clearly. What you're saying is that he will not talk to you about your feelings. Isn't that true?

Patient: He wants to forget it and will not deal with the issues or implications that the affair has raised. He's done with it and the hell with my feelings. Fred now tells me I have the problem because I'm sad and can't get over his treason to our marriage vows. What do you think of that?

Psychologist: I think your interpretation is sadly correct. Often the victimizer declares a time limit for the victim to live by. If the person is not over the hurt and pain in that time limit, then the person is bad and the other person becomes the victim. In other words, the victim becomes the culprit. Has he told you how guilty or how bad he feels for what he has done to you? Has he said he will try to do better?

Patient: At first, he was an angel and promised me anything as long as I didn't leave him. He cried openly and literally begged me on his knees to stay and forgive him. He took a lot of verbal and even a little physical abuse from me stoically. He seemed to show true emotion and guilt. He showed a level of feeling like he hadn't since our wonderful courtship. As I said, he cried, begged me to stay and said he was sorry beyond words; that he didn't mean for it to happen. He said he was trying to do better and wouldn't fuck other women and would treat me like the queen he said I was. He actually has been better in terms of being with me and letting me know where he is at all times; but that doesn't ease the pain of the betrayal.

Psychologist: Do you feel better about knowing where he is at all times?

Patient: I do, but it doesn't take away the constant throbbing agony I feel at all times. I just need to let him know what he's done to me and us. He says there was no emotion or love in what happened; that he still loves me and it's time to quit feeling sorry for myself and get on with my life by looking to the future with him. His handsome dark looks, fine clothes, manicured nails, gold jewelry, fine colognes and deep masculine voice make him so God damn convincing; but I know what a lying asshole he is and can no longer be charmed by the snake he is.

Psychologist: Do you think he's accepting guilt?

Patient: He was but no more. I'm the one who has been motivated by guilt my whole life. I know I didn't cause this situation but I feel debilitated by it and somehow guilty for what he did. Isn't that crazy?

Psychologist: Who taught you that?

Patient: My parents and family.

Psychologist: Do you believe you've always been motivated by guilt?

Patient: Yes. I wouldn't do anything to upset my mom and dad when growing up because I didn't want to hurt them or have them think poorly of me. Now I do nothing to bother them because I don't want to deal with their disapproval. I keep everything inside me and I drown in the anger and frustration for not letting my feelings out. I'm a coward; and a very unhappy one.

Psychologist: That is most unfortunate and something we can address at a later time. What do you think Fred felt for her?

Patient: I don't know; he says he felt nothing for her and to quit asking.

Psychologist: Was there a lot of sexual intimacy between the two of them?

Patient: *(With anger.)* You mean fucking? *(With a contrite tone.)* I'm sorry.

Psychologist: Please, say anything you want. I want you to feel safe here.

Patient: I believe yes. He will not tell me. He says it's not important or he cannot remember.

Psychologist: Were they together a lot?

Patient: They were always together. Every night I worked adult education and on his weekly business overnight trips. They talked every day on the phone; sometimes for hours. Oh what a bastard he was and what a fool I was for so long. The image of him primping in the mirror and making himself look so good for her still really pisses me off. Fred would ask me how he looked, kiss me and then go to fuck the bitch.

Psychologist: How long did the relationship go on?

Patient: Five months.

Psychologist: Five months.

Patient: He was living a lie. He said he loved me and we had sex; but it wasn't good sex and not frequent. How could it be good or frequent; he was always with her. What scum he is; and I caught him.

Psychologist: Were there others?

Patient: He says no. *(Crying.)* I never doubted him and look what he did to me; he ruined my life and my dreams.

Psychologist: I can see how hurt you are over what happened. He really lived a double life.

Patient: *(Sobbing.)* Oh he faked it real well! I had no idea what was going on. I trusted him; I loved him; he was my man; he was my dream come true; I would've done anything for him.

Psychologist: What was going on in his mind at that time?

Patient: I don't know. I have asked him that many times. Fred says she meant nothing to him other than being a good friend. The asshole says this even though she lives an hour from our house and they have no professional or family connection whatsoever. He also says I must believe the affair is over, forget it and make the best of what I now have at home. I don't want that doctor; I want something better than living a lie where all my dreams and feelings have died simultaneously and I have nothing to live for.

Psychologist: Has he given you a reason why he had the affair?

Patient: Yes.

Psychologist: What is it?

Patient: He had quite a list and I have them memorized. He said he did it because I had no interest in him; I wasn't warm; I always wanted him to be different; I wasn't caring; I was more interested in things; he didn't think I gave a shit about him or the marriage anymore; he was very unhappy and getting older; he was feeling lonely; and all together these made him vulnerable to a warm and caring person. He also said it was an escape from the reality of our dull and boring day to day living.

Psychologist: A lot of reasons and some real negative ones about you. In what sense was the affair an escape?

Patient: From me? From responsibilities? Who knows. I don't know and he won't talk about it anymore.

Psychologist: What are your feelings about his reasons for having the affair?

Patient: I'm crushed and angry as hell at him, at her and at me for being so stupid. He would never talk to me and regularly rejected me sexually and always emotionally; but he was my prince. I somehow accepted this and thought I was being looked after; and I also thought I looked after him; and pretty damn well under the conditions he allowed. If I'd known how he felt, I gladly would have sought out counseling for us; but he never would have gone. He feels psychologists are crazy and people that go to see them are weak people who won't be responsible for their lives.

Psychologist: A negative view for someone who seems to have desperately needed counseling before, during and now after the affair. How does he explain his feelings about having sexuality with both of you at the same time?

Patient: He says it was nothing. He says in spite of all his complaints, he always loved me and the sex with her meant nothing. If you can imagine, he compares a fuck with her to a good meal or a good shit.

Psychologist: In my work, I find men often make little or no connection between love and intimacy like women generally do. A woman says you love or you don't love; and when you do love, sexuality is the wonderful result. I am certainly not justifying it, but I do find men can generally separate love and sex if they so desire.

Patient: I know you're not justifying it, but I want to say something. Now here's a man that was with this woman for five months at least three or four times a week. They had sex routinely and regularly took vacations together when he said he was working, hunting or fishing with friends. Now what does that mean? How do you live with that? Do I believe he didn't really care for her? He tells me she was just a fuck, a good friend and now forget it. What was it doctor? Is it fair for me to know his feelings?

Psychologist: I think what you ask of him is fair. You want to know more about his feelings and their relationship. Was it a sexual thing; a communication relationship; was she a soulmate; was she a friend; did he love her for awhile; does he still love her or was it something different yet?

Patient: I don't know, but I deserve to know what he felt for her and what the relationship was. For sure, it seems to have been much more than them just being friends and/or soulmates.

Psychologist: I agree, but it would make you feel better if he saw her as just a friend or excuse my language - a good fuck.

Patient: Yes, but I don't want him to lie about it. I really know he cared for her more than that; and he may still care for her. This was a full blown affair for five months that only ended because I caught them.

Psychologist: Agreed, but I think if you had a good answer from him on how he felt for her and does now, then you could more easily move forward. I think he'll have to come up with the answer.

Patient: If I had a true answer from him, it would make me feel somewhat better. They talked daily and saw each other all the time. Whatever it was, it was and will always be utterly unacceptable to me. But remember, he will not tell me anything more anyway; he has declared I've had enough time to be over my pain and I need know nothing more. That asshole! I hate him so for what he's done to me and continues to do with his damn attitude.

Psychologist: So, what type of affair they had is not the major issue now.

Patient: No. He lied to me and I don't think I can ever trust him again. Honesty and fidelity are not desired but required personal characteristics in a relationship; if they're not there, there's no trust and a true love relationship cannot exist.

Psychologist: Okay, that's really the issue then. You don't trust him at all. Let's add some possible facts. Let's say he told you yes, he was in love and he thought he wanted her; but when everything came into the open, he saw what he was doing was stupid and he wanted you and you alone. Would you feel better if he said that?

Patient: I don't know but that hasn't happened and won't.

Psychologist: You were asking me earlier what I think. Well, let me tell you what I think and please know I could be wrong. I simply want to give you a reasonable interpretation of what occurred for you to think about, react to and compare with other possible interpretations. I believe you think he's minimizing what the relationship was. It's also possible that because it's over, he's minimizing what it was. To him, it's irrelevant what it was and if he were to tell you he really was in love, then I think he believes you would feel much, much worse; and, he is probably right. The fact it's at least more than just a friendship is reasonable to assume based on the level of activity, intimacy and communication over a five month period. The fact she lives an hour from your house and has no professional or family connection whatsoever also leads to the conclusion the relationship was more than just a friendship. So I can understand your questions. However, I guess the question I'd ask you, after giving you an interpretation of your husband's affair, would be this: Does it really matter what happened at this time?

Patient: It doesn't matter. In that he's lying under all circumstances, he's an untrustworthy asshole any way you look at it.

Psychologist: I think it does matter to you. You want to know what relationship they had and whether he loved her and even loves her now.

Patient: Yes! You're right to some degree; however, the trust is gone and probably the relationship in the long run. Things will never be the same when you live with a God damn liar who philandered on you. The image of him regularly and piously reading the gospel in church during his affair pisses me off; such hypocrisy.

Psychologist: What would it take for you to believe he's being honest?

Patient: As I said, it doesn't really matter and I really don't care other than curiosity. He's a liar, has proved and continues to prove he could care less about me, my feelings and about us as a couple. I just want to feel good again. I just want to enjoy myself. I used to love to take long walks in the country just to smell the fresh air and see nature at work; and now I would hate it. I just want to be able to look out and see the sunshine and say it's a good day and I'll enjoy it. I've even thought I just want to be with someone I feel at ease with; and I don't feel at all at ease with him. It's often painful just to be around him. Sometimes I'll be working around the house and look up and he'll be looking at me; I think to myself that I don't know him and maybe never did. I don't like that feeling after twenty-two years of marriage; it wasn't my dream. I feel cheated and raped to the core.

Psychologist: In effect, you can't get beyond this can you?

Patient: No. The pain rips me apart and into painful reflection. The thoughts of the affair come in front of me in graphic detail again and again to bring me lower and lower. I see them laughing, talking, screwing, eating and sleeping together. I just plain hate it and it tears me into emotional bits and pieces.

Psychologist: Do you cry a lot?

Patient: Alone and yes a lot. I really wonder at times how I keep any liquid in me. It's hell. I really wish I were a man. Their emotions are so cold and simple. They just cause hurt and don't care.

Psychologist: It is tough....so tough for you. What type of crying is it?

Patient: It's very sad. I whimper and cry with dull painful feelings of hopelessness. Oh God, how I suffer! *(She begins crying and tries to gain her composure.)* Am I boring you with the same story over and over?

Psychologist: Not at all and as I said, please feel you can share your feelings in an emotionally safe environment. Now back to the crying; what brings it on and when does it happen?

Patient: The thoughts that bring on the crying are always with me. But the tears come especially at night. I'll be laying in bed and thinking; then I get that awful feeling in the pit of my stomach; then the despair; then the memories and images; then the image of him screwing her and her swooning in ecstasy; then seeing me alone at night school working for the two of us; then the feelings of total betrayal literally overwhelm my whole being; then the tears come and can last for hours. As I said, the thoughts come in relentless waves and I can't stop crying. It's like a sad musical score. I'm the orchestra crying out the thoughts that come to my mind. I worked so hard for our future and here I am feeling raped of my dignity, destroyed emotionally, having horrible self-esteem and no-where to go but further into the depths of hurt and despair.

Psychologist: And there are no answers to your important questions about the affair.

Patient: No, and I really think I've dealt with that. Fred's no good and I know it; and being with someone I cannot trust is just not acceptable. I'm forty-two years old and should be entering a stage in life where with my daughter away at school and my son going away to college next year, my husband and I should be entering the most peaceful times in our lives together. Instead of that, I have only great hate, rage and resentment for him; that no good bastard. (Crying.) He took everything from me... everything...just everything.

Psychologist: You see the situation as tragic and you feel horrible. Do you ever have any hope at all for the future?

Patient: Never. There was always hope whenever I had problems before; but now there's none. To live without hope is just plain shitty.

Psychologist: Is this the worst thing that has ever happened to you?

Patient: Oh God yes! Absolutely. My greatest dream in life was to have a loving husband; but that dream is dead with him and probably forever. I remember one night, shortly after having caught him, I was crying in his arms real hard; he held me but would not say anything other than things would work out. He was more like my emotionally distant dad rather than my loving husband. It was that night that I knew my dream with Fred never in reality came true and I was alone in the world, living a horrible lie.

Psychologist: It sounds like a horrible realization.

Patient: You don't know how bad; it has turned my life around in a horrible way. When dreams die, we die also.

Psychologist: Do you love your dad?

Patient: At some level. At other levels, I resent and think I hate him for his control over me without giving me understanding. I also resent my brothers being so close to him and getting all his attention, teaching and caring. His business success only reinforces his rock hard view of the world. You ought to see him at the head of the table; he's like a king.

Psychologist: What would he say if you told him about your feelings that he favored your brothers?

Patient: He'd deny it and get angry. Then I'd feel horrible.

Psychologist: What if you told your father about the affair?

Patient: He'd be nice at first, very nice actually; but then he'd wonder what I did to cause Fred to run around. He'd become angry with Fred, but he'd punish me with his doubts about me.

Psychologist: Have you told your mother?

Patient: Oh, God no!

Psychologist: Why not?

Patient: She'd utterly fall apart emotionally; she'd tell me to pray to God and the Madonna to have the strength to forgive and stay in the marriage. If you can imagine, she'd also want me to pray for my husband so he'd change and could go to heaven. She'd worry about that! I would feel much worse.

Psychologist: Then she's very traditional and you would feel worse if you told her.

Patient: Very much so to both statements. If I told her, she'd go to church everyday; lose weight and appear to the family even more out of control emotionally than her normal self; she'd cry hours each day; say rosaries and somehow take all the blame for what's occurred. However, with the crying and what I call her tyranny of weakness, my problems would grow enormously as she put her problems on me. *(Emphatically.)* I will never tell her.

Psychologist: I see why you haven't told them. It also shows why you're feeling so isolated. In times of crisis, it's hoped family will be supportive and offer a safe emotional harbor for the person in emotional need.

Patient: I agree, but there's no safe harbor in my family. To smile when I'm dying inside is my role with my parents and brothers; to see my husband behave like everything is fine enrages me; to see the kids behave like nothing happened hurts me; and my being too proud to talk to most of my friends who care about me and who would be concerned about what has happened to me makes me hate myself. I guess I just have to say I'm forty-two years old and ought to be able to figure things out without my parents or husband telling me what's the right thing to do; but they've done this for such a long time in my life; sometimes without my even knowing about it.

Psychologist: Isn't that maybe part of what's happening now? What you do and how you feel needs to be your choice and not that of anyone else. You need to live your own life. As far as your marriage in concerned, under the current circumstances, maybe you want to leave your husband or maybe you don't. However, you can't discuss this situation or your feelings with anyone rationally. Based upon your support system, unresponsive as it is to your needs, the answers to any questions you have about this whole matter are in place and they are against you. If you tell your father, he'll wonder where you failed because your husband was running around on you; if you tell your mother, she'll go into depression and tell you to pray to find forgiveness for your husband as well as her wanting you to join her in praying for his forgiveness so he can go to heaven. Not much for you and your feelings it seems. In effect, you've been raised in a certain way and in this crisis, you feel stuck with the kind of solutions you were trained to use in a far less effective period of your life. You felt you were beyond this training but you now feel you're stuck with your feelings in the current situation because your support system consists of those who trained you. In effect, even though you're the victim, you'll feel like a failure and heartless if you do not forgive him. It saddens me how even the best of Christians can misuse the concept of forgiveness to make persons who are badly hurting inside feel guilty for not being able to forgive persons who are not worthy of it because they have not fully admitted guilt for the harm they've caused. We know what Christ did to the bad thief on the cross.

Patient: Oh yes! Absolutely. You have it 100 percent. I have an unhealthy support system and have always felt I picked up some perverted concept that makes me feel very guilty and bad even when I've clearly been the victim.

Psychologist: That is what I see as the primary conflict in your not being able to move forward right now.

Patient: I'm sure it's because of the way I was raised. At least I think so. Why else would I feel so used by my family that I haven't even talked to about Fred's affair?

Psychologist: Do you believe you could really leave Fred?

Patient: I want to be with someone who will listen to me; care for my feelings; share things of the heart with me; love me; fuck only me and do these things forever. My mouth has become shitty; I hope I do not offend you.

Psychologist: Not at all; I understand. Is Fred listening now? Can he be what you want or need?

Patient: He'll never listen and is never going to be what I want or need. He'll be to me what he decides to be and that's it; I have no input. I must put up, shut up or leave.

Psychologist: Is he emotionally cold?

Patient: Yes and no. His public self is very warm and Italian. He's warm to me as long as I do what he wants, behave like he wants, think what he wants and never question his views about me or anything else.

Psychologist: It's hard to believe he could have almost nonchalantly done all of this to you. I mean to have maintained the affair not just for a weekend or a day, but for months. He really lived a dual life; and from a man who has claimed a certain level of moral perfection. That really doesn't fit, does it?

Patient: You really do get it. What a strange nightmare it is; he claimed to be perfect and I enjoyed the glow of his now known hypocrisy. I feel so powerless, ashamed and in a dream world of false righteousness. It's hard to believe it happened....worse, that I've gone along with it so long.

Psychologist: It is very hard for you to believe it happened.

Patient: As silly as it sounds, I don't believe it happened; but then I know it did. I guess I've learned from my mother to just ignore or deny a problem if it were too unpleasant or I couldn't change it. I can't do that in this situation, even though I'm trying; maybe I'd be better off if I could.

Psychologist: I believe there are many negative and painful things you can't just pretend didn't occur; they will either happen again, or as in your case, the shame and internal anger will destroy you if you don't get your feelings out in a wholesome way. You also must arrive at some legitimate resolution as to what has occurred and what you'll do about it.

Patient: Oh yes again! I think you're right.

Psychologist: Did you really previously see Fred as a superior type of person morally?

Patient: Oh God, no, but I trusted him completely. I say this even though he was a great hypocrite to the face of people he didn't like. He would always find fault with people but be so friendly to them in person. I remember some years ago he hated a priest and his plans for a church renovation; but that didn't stop him from heading up the committee to get donations for it and to publicly praise the priest for his greatness and desire to help our parish with the addition. But overall, he's been a good man. The children love him as does his family and my family. He's worked hard and has been a good co-provider. But of superior moral character; absolutely not, even without his philandering and trampling of marriage vows.

Psychologist: Is he humble now?

Patient: *(With a chuckle.)* Better, but humble never. God will kneel to the power of the devil before Fred is humble.

Psychologist: Unfortunately, you may be right. Now, back to more of my opinions. The positive thing is that when given a choice, Fred definitely wanted you. He cried and begged you not to leave him. That's what makes me think it was probably a combination of lust, limited common interest and infatuation. These limited things in common initially probably kept them together. I would make a prediction though: I predict that along the way, he figured out they didn't have nearly as much in common as the two of you and really wanted out. I find that in many affairs or relationships, people start out having something in common and they communicate in that common area. This is true whether it is computers, psychology, education, or whatever. They get together more and more, they communicate more and more in their common area and then they have sexual intimacy. Gradually, there's nothing more to talk about because they have either few or no other things in common as they often start or continue spending a lot of time together. They begin seeing the hard edges of the person's personality and then things start separating. If what I'm saying did occur, then Fred was really glad he got caught. He just dropped the whole affair immediately and now wants to get on with his life with you and just forget the affair.

Patient: I think you may be right; but what about me and my shattered feelings?

Psychologist: That of course is the problem if I'm right. Fred is not thinking of your feelings now or he won't admit it. As I said, he now gladly has you back and is trying to have things back to normal. He's actually free again.

Patient: That makes some sense. She'd just gotten a divorce before they met. She wanted Fred but he left her to keep his family; at least he screwed her over too. What an irony; we both loved him and he crushed

244

each of us emotionally. She wants him and I really think I don't. I'm so confused and hurt. I hate her, but I even feel a little sorry for her; that bitch.

Psychologist: But you're still feeling lost, alienated and not sure what to do with your life or your great hurt and anger.

Patient: I feel like all of that all the time. I don't know if I'm ever going to get over what I feel and I don't like it. It's not just a case of feeling sorry for myself. I know it's changed me; the way I look at things; the way I feel generally about people; about life, and particularly about Fred. They're times when I think I could enjoy killing him very, very slowly; but then I realize how enjoying such thoughts is really destroying the caring person I think I am. But these nightmarish thoughts and feelings keep coming to me in relentless attacks.

Psychologist: It sounds terrible to hear how these feelings continue to torture you. I really see this as very destructive for you from a mental health and probably also from a physical point of view.

Patient: Absolutely. As I keep saying, I feel drained emotionally and physically all the time. I go to bed all tensed up; wake up all tensed up and stay all tensed up until I go to bed. It's really hell; *(with a touch of humor)* and the Catholic Church no longer has a purgatory to give me some reason to endure it all.

Psychologist: A little humor in difficult periods goes a long way in making one feel better. Do you ever get feelings you want to end it all?

Patient: Yes, but my old Catholic upbringing will not allow suicide. It's beyond reasonable thinking to me and I really wouldn't risk eternal hell, silly as that sounds.

Psychologist: That is a very reasonable thought to many persons I know. Do you think you could ever really hurt him physically?

Patient: Not really. My thoughts are just fantasies to relieve the horrible hurt and hate. There's not a violent bone in me. For sure, what I fantasize about doing and what I really would do are two completely different things. I hit him a few times after I found out, but it hurt me more than him physically; I even now feel horribly guilty about it and and hate to admit I ever did it.

Psychologist: Then you're not violent. You're feeling alienated, angry, frustrated, hurt and feeling all alone in your suffering.

Patient: Absolutely. Yes one million times. But you can't really understand how it feels if you haven't been there.

Psychologist: Very true. I can only try to understand as you guide me through your feelings. With that help from you; and I know how hard it is for you to express these feelings, I can attempt to help you by being a neutral but concerned person trying to clarify feelings and directions you might take in your life.

Patient: Anything you can do to help me will be appreciated.

Psychologist: Please tell me what you really want in your life in the foreseeable future.

Patient: I want to be happy again and have purpose for living. I know life is short and my life now is one of continual suffering.

Psychologist: You must do the hard work, but I will try to help.

Patient: That's fair and all I can ask. I feel better knowing I can talk to someone like you; but I'm afraid these feelings may never leave me, and if they do, I may not like the person I'll become. As I said, my dreams are dead and so is much of me.

Psychologist: While I'm an optimist, I admit your road is very hard and the direction you will take is unknown to either of us. However, I predict you can become an even more effective person through these experiences; the level of growth will be determined by what you learn and what you do as a result of it.

Patient: I'll try as hard as I can. For now, I just want to learn how to relieve some of this horrible pain that's always with me. I feel we can talk and I'll try to be open with you and clarify issues and try strategies to help me take control of my life.

Psychologist: That's all I can ask. For now, we can say we have begun.

The End